The Critical
Performance

STANLEY EDGAR HYMAN

The Critical
Performance

✳

*An Anthology of American and British
Literary Criticism of Our Century*

✳

VINTAGE BOOKS : NEW YORK

1 9 5 6

ACKNOWLEDGMENT is hereby made for permission to reprint the following: "Montcorbier, alias Villon" by Ezra Pound from *The Spirit of Romance*, all rights reserved, used by permission of the publisher, New Directions. "Hamlet and Orestes" by Gilbert Murray from *The Classical Tradition in Poetry*, Harvard University Press, 1927, used by permission of the publisher. "Andrew Marvell" by T. S. Eliot from *Selected Essays of T. S. Eliot*, copyright 1932, 1936, 1950 by Harcourt, Brace and Company, Inc., used by permission of the publisher. "Charlotte and Emily Brontë" by Sir Herbert Read from *Collected Essays in Literary Criticism*, Faber and Faber Ltd., used by permission of the author and the publisher. "Tragedy and Comedy" by Scott Buchanan from *Poetry and Mathematics*, The John Day Company, Inc., copyright 1929 by Scott Buchanan, used by permission of the author. "Fifteen Lines From Landor" reprinted from *Speculative Instruments* by I. A. Richards by permission of The University of Chicago Press. "Alice in Wonderland" by William Empson from *Some Versions of Pastoral*, all rights reserved, used by permission of the publisher, New Directions. "D. H. Lawrence: A Study of the Bourgeois Artist" by Christopher Caudwell from *Studies in a Dying Culture*, John Lane The Bodley Head Limited, used by permission of the publisher. "Narcissus as Narcissus" by Allen Tate from *On the Limits of Poetry*, copyright 1948 by Allen Tate, used by permission of the publisher, Alan Swallow. "Yeats and His Symbols" by John Crowe Ransom from *The Kenyon Review*, used by permission. "On Rereading Balzac" by William Troy from *The Kenyon Review*, used by permission. "The Rise of Theatricals" by Constance Rourke from *The Roots of American Culture* by Constance Rourke, copyright 1942 by Harcourt, Brace and Company, Inc., used by permission of the publisher. "A Rage of Goodness" by R. P. Blackmur from *Accent*, Autumn 1942, used by permission of the author and *Accent*. "Symbolic Action in a Poem by Keats" by Kenneth Burke from *A Grammar of Motives*, copyright 1945 by Prentice-Hall, Inc., used by permission of the publisher and *Accent*. "George Herbert" by L. C. Knights from *Explorations*, George W. Stewart, Publisher, Inc., used by permission of the author and the publisher. "The Guilty Vicarage" by W. H. Auden from *Harper's Magazine*, used by permission of the author. "Oedipus Rex" by Francis Fergusson from *The Idea of a Theater*, Princeton University Press, used by permission of the publisher and *Accent*.

© STANLEY EDGAR HYMAN, 1956
PUBLISHED BY VINTAGE BOOKS, INC.

FIRST EDITION

PREFACE

The INTRODUCTION to this collection of critical essays was written separately and published as *The Armed Vision: A Study in the Methods of Modern Literary Criticism* in 1948. It is available in the original Knopf edition and in a 1955 revised Vintage edition, abridged by two chapters, the bibliography, and a small amount of other matter. It is assumed that the two books will be read in conjunction, *The Armed Vision* as a means to place and characterize the essays in *The Critical Performance; The Critical Performance* as a means to document, extend, and perhaps refute the contentions in *The Armed Vision*. What I have to say about the contemporary flowering of literary criticism the earlier book says at some length; what can be shown of its brilliance and variety of emphasis and mood in one small volume is put out for display here.

More specifically, this anthology represents a number of criteria of selection perhaps less common in the making of collections of literary criticism than they might be. The first is to show our critics only in practice, performing their lively labors on a writer, a form, a work, or a body of work, not theorizing or contending except as theory or contention might arise out of the critical performance. Where several of these essays seem rather remote from a literary text, they are either, like Miss Rourke's, sketching in a background of "practical letters" from which a literary form draws sustenance or, like Caudwell's, criticizing the philosophy of a writer as it emerges from his books.

A second aim is to give some sense of the rich harvests of method and idea, even intellectual fashion, on which modern criticism has drawn, so that some of the essays have an historical significance for their dates (if never, I hope, solely that). "We should use," Burke's essay says, "whatever knowledge is available." Thus, Pound's 1910 chapter introduces a range of comparison that includes the plastic arts and poets from Dante to Whitman. We see the endless fertility of Aristotle in the Auden and Fergusson essays, and get some sense of the territories uncharted by Aristotle (we might name them "Plato") in Buchanan and Richards. Eliot and Richards repeatedly invoke the incantatory name of Coleridge, and even Read's disenchanted essay manages "to revert to the old antithesis" between fancy and imagination. Unfortunately, Darwin is here hardly more than a mention by Empson, and Marx, apart from Caudwell's dialectics, is less visible in these essays (in Burke and Empson most, perhaps) than he was in our criticism for more than a decade. Frazer, however, is omnipresent, underlying Murray, Buchanan, Troy, Auden, and Fergusson, and Freudian psychoanalysis is turned on the writer by Read, on the imagery by Empson, and on the symbolic action in a poem by Burke. Buchanan draws on physics and mathematics, Blackmur on the ominous behavior of the Pine Processionary caterpillar, Caudwell on brain physiology, Blackmur and Tate on varieties of the Christian religion and Ransom and Knights on secular equivalents for it, and Auden finds himself suggesting a plot to Raymond Chandler.

At the same time, a tone of close preoccupation with the text is generally evident, whether in Blackmur's variants of plot and character in Dostoevsky, Fergusson's tragic rhythm of action, or Tate's metrics. The ultimate concern is always with the work, and here the critics sing in splendid concert: "To bring the poet back to life—the great, the perennial, task of criticism," says Eliot; "remove the slime with which they have been encrusted," says Empson. We see it not only in Eliot's and Empson's practice, but everywhere, from Richards's hesitant introduction of his own fine reading of the passage from Landor, to Troy's counterstatement in which Balzac becomes not a messy naturalist but a tragic poet.

A final aim of this anthology is simply to make available a number of important and useful critical essays not otherwise handy. Wherever possible I have avoided the anthologized chestnut, or even the essay regularly reprinted by its author (Tate's "Narcissus as Narcissus," in print in at least two of his books, is an inevitable exception, as an irreplace-

able example of a scarce genre, the poet's self-analysis).
Many of these selections have never been reprinted since
their first publication, or have never appeared in book form
(Richards anticipated one of my happiest resurrections, his
"Fifteen Lines from Landor," long buried in the files of
The Criterion, by reprinting it himself a few months ago).
A few essays have been revised for this appearance.

The inclusions are easy enough to justify, representing
as they do simply my own taste and opinion of the good
(in some cases, surely, of the best). The omissions, however, can be justified on no principle other than the necessity for keeping a volume of this sort down to publishable
size. It would not be hard to compile a comparable volume
including entirely different contributors, or several such
volumes, so rich are we in critical performers in our time.
It would be pointless to name the fine critics and essays
that had to be omitted, and any reader can readily make
his own list. Let it suffice to note that roughly half of the
critics who were the subjects of separate chapters in *The
Armed Vision* have been crowded out or omitted for a
variety of reasons, ranging from the absence of a suitable
short selection by some, to the all-too-ready availability
of the total work of others. It is my hope that these omissions are made less blatant by the fact that each of the
critics included carries with him a context of other criticism. Just as they cross-fertilize each other within the volume (Empson gives us the word "pastoral" for Miss
Rourke's "Noble Savage" material, Fergusson relates his
approach to Troy and Burke), so each points beyond these
confines, and we see Tate using Yvor Winters, Ransom
drawing on Cleanth Brooks, Burke taking off from G.
Wilson Knight, Knights exemplifying the theories of
F. R. Leavis.

Certain generalizations about the contributors suggest
themselves from the biographical notes. They are all established writers who have produced a body of critical work,
although some of them are not specialists in literary criticism but philosophers, classicists, historians, and critics of
art and the theater. All but four have published poetry,
and among them are several of the best poets we have.

The youngest, W. H. Auden, is pushing fifty, and the old-est, Gilbert Murray, has just celebrated his ninetieth birth-day. The ten born in America come from ten different states, including such unlikely cultural founts as Idaho and New Mexico, Missouri and Kentucky, but there may be significance in the fact that they all went to school in the East, and at least four attended Oxford, three as Rhodes scholars. Half the British-born critics come from York-shire (this is mysterious, and may be coincidence), they went to Oxford and Cambridge in about equal proportion, and they tend to teach at redbrick universities.

Finally, I should like to acknowledge various debts. Most of the contributors, or their publishers and repre-sentatives, have been remarkably kind. Harry Ford, Herbert Weinstock, and others have been boundlessly helpful. I am, as usual, particularly indebted to Mrs. Gladys Y. Leslie and the staff of the Bennington College Library. Miss Gertrude Syverstad kindly typed sections of the manu-script, and many friends assisted and advised. My wife, Shirley Jackson, has again helped beyond the possibilities of acknowledgment.

North Bennington, Vermont   *S.E.H.*
January 1956

CONTENTS

The Critical
Performance

Editor's Note

M*ontcorbier,* ALIAS *Villon* first appeared as a chapter in *The Spirit of Romance* (1910, revised edition 1952) by Ezra Pound. All rights reserved. Reprinted by permission of the publisher, New Directions.

Ezra Pound was born in Hailey, Idaho, in 1885, and educated at the University of Pennsylvania and Hamilton College. He lived abroad, mostly at Rapallo, Italy, from 1908 to 1945, and was active in the editorship of a number of literary magazines, as well as writing and broadcasting on political and economic subjects. Pound is the author of many volumes of poetry, most of them reprinted in *Personae: Collected Poems* (1926) and *The Cantos* (1948); he has published translations from a number of languages, available in *Selected Translations* (1953); and much of his literary criticism has been collected in *Make It New* (1934) and *Literary Essays* (1954).

ONE

Ezra Pound

Montcorbier, ALIAS *Villon*

The century between Dante and Villon brought into the
poetry of northern Europe no element which was distinctly new. The plant of the Renaissance was growing,
a plant which some say begins in Dante; but Dante, I
think, anticipates the Renaissance only as one year's
harvest foreshadows the next year's Spring. He is the
culmination of one age rather than the beginning of
the next; he is like certain buildings in Verona, which
display the splendor of the Middle Ages, untouched by
any influence of the classic revival.

In architecture, mediæval work means line; line, composition and design: Renaissance work means mass. The
Gothic architect envied the spider his cobweb. The Renaissance architect sought to rival the mountain. They raised
successively the temple of the spirit and the temple of the
body. The analogy in literature is naturally inexact; Dante,
however, sought to hang his song from the absolute, the
center and source of light; art since Dante has for the most
part built from the ground.

General formulas of art criticism serve at best to suggest a train of thought, or a manner of examining the individual works of a period. Such formulas are not figures
circumscribing the works of art, but points from which to
compute their dimensions.

The Renaissance is not a time, but a temperament.
Petrarch and Boccaccio have it. To the art of poetry they
bring nothing distinctive: Petrarch refines but deenergizes.[1]

[1] 1929: No, he doesn't even refine, he oils and smooths over the
idiom. As far as any question of actual fineness of emotion or cadence

In England, Gower had written pleasantly, and "Romance," the romance of the longer narratives, had come to full fruit in Chaucer. Where Dante is a crystallization of many mediæval elements, his own intensity the cause of their cohesion, Chaucer comes as through a more gradual, gentler process, like some ultimate richer blossom on that bough which brought forth Beroul, Thomas, Marie, Crestien, Wace, and Gower. He is part, some will say, of the humanistic revolt. There was no abrupt humanistic revolt. Boccaccio and the rest but carry on a paganism which had never expired.

After all these fine gentlemen, guardians of the Arthurian Graal, prophets of Rome's rejuvenation, and the rest, had been laid in their graves, there walked the gutters of Paris one François Montcorbier, poet and gaol-bird, with no care whatever for the flowery traditions of mediæval art, and no anxiety to revive the massive rhetoric of the Romans. Yet whatever seeds of the Renaissance there may have been in Dante, there were seeds or signs of a far more modern outbreak in the rhymes of this Montcorbier, *alias* Villon.

The minstrelsy of Provence is as the heart of Sir Blancatz, and the later lords of song, in England and in Tuscany, have eaten well of it. From Provence the Tuscans have learned pattern; the Elizabethans a certain lyric quality; Villon carries on another Provençal tradition, that of unvarnished, intimate speech. I do not imply that Villon is directly influenced by Provence, but that some of his notes and fashions had been already sounded in Provence. Thus the tone of a tenzone of Arnaut Daniel's, not quoted in Chapter II, suggests the tone of some of Villon's verses; even as the form of the Provençal canzon had suggested the form of the north French ballade.

Villon's abuse finds precedent in the lower type of sirvente, with this distinction, that Villon at times says of himself what the Provençals said only of one another. For precedent of Villon's outspokenness one need not seek

---

or perception he is miles behind Ventadorn or Arnaut Daniel. Petrarch systematizes a certain ease of verbal expression in Italian. An excellent author for an Italian law student seeking to improve his "delivery."

so far as Provence. The French mystery plays are not written in veiled words. To witness, this passage from a
Crucifixion play, when an angel says to God the Father:

> *Père éternal, vous avez tort*
> *E ben devetz avoir vergogne.*
> *Vostre fils bien amis est mort*
> *E vous dormez comme un ivrogne.*
>
> *Father eternal, you are wrong*
> *And well should be shamed,*
> *Your well beloved son is dead*
> *And you sleep like a drunk.*

Villon's art exists because of Villon. There is in him no
pretence of the man sacrificed to his labor. One may define
him unsatisfactorily by a negative comparison with certain
other poets, thus: where Dante has boldness of imagination, Villon has the stubborn persistency of one whose gaze
cannot be deflected from the actual fact before him: what
he sees, he writes. Dante is in some ways one of the most
personal of poets; he holds up the mirror to nature, but he
is himself that mirror.

Villon never forgets his fascinating, revolting self. If,
however, he sings the song of himself he is, thank God,
free from that horrible air of rectitude with which Whitman rejoices in being Whitman. Villon's song is selfish
through self-absorption; he does not, as Whitman, pretend
to be conferring a philanthropic benefit on the race by
recording his own self-complacency. Human misery is
more stable than human dignity; there is more intensity in
the passion of cold, remorse, hunger, and the fetid damp
of the mediæval dungeon than in eating water melons.
Villon is a voice of suffering, of mockery, of irrevocable
fact; Whitman is the voice of one who saith:

> *Lo, behold, I eat water-melons   When I eat water-*
>   *melons the world eats water-melons through me.*
> *When the world eats water-melons, I partake of the*
>   *world's water-melons.*
> *The bugs,*
> *The worms,*

The negroes, etc.,
Eat water-melons; All nature eats water-melons.
Those eidolons and particles of the Cosmos
Which do not now partake of water-melons
Will at some future time partake of water-melons.
Praised be Allah or Ramanathanath Khrishna!

They call it optimism, and breadth of vision. There is, in the poetry of François Villon, neither optimism nor breadth of vision.

Villon is shameless. Whitman, having decided that it is disgraceful to be ashamed, rejoices in having attained nudity.

Goethe, when the joys of taxidermy sufficed not to maintain his self-respect, was wont to rejoice that there was something noble and divine in being *Künstler*. The artist is an artist and therefore admirable, or noble, or something of that sort. If Villon ever discovered this pleasant mode of self-deception, he had sense enough not to say so in rhyme. In fact, Villon himself may be considered sufficient evidence seriously to damage this artist-consoling theory.

Villon holds his unique place in literature because he is the only poet without illusions. There are *désillusionnés*, but they are different; Villon set forth without the fragile cargo. Villon never lies to himself; he does not know much, but what he knows he knows: man is an animal, certain things he can feel; there is much misery, man has a soul about which he knows little or nothing. Helen, Heloise and Joan are dead, and you will gather last year's snows before you find them.

Thus the *Ballade of Dead Ladies*:

Tell me now in what hidden way is
    Lady Flora, the lovely Roman,
Where is Hipparchia and where is Thaïs,
    Neither of them the fairer woman,
Where is Echo, beheld of no man,
    Only heard on river and mere,
She whose beauty was more than human?
    But where are the snows of yester-year!

And where are Beatris, Alys, Hermengarde, and

> *That good Joan whom Englishmen*
> *At Rouen doomed, and burned her there!*
> *Mother of God, where are they, where?*
> *But where are the snows of yester-year!* [2]

Of his further knowledge,

> *I know a horse from a mule,*
> *And Beatrix from Bellet,*
> *I know the heresy of the Bohemians,*
> *I know son, valet and man.*
> *I know all things save myself alone.*

Or in the *Grand Testament,*

> *Je suis pecheur, je le scay bien*
> *Pourtant Dieu ne veut pas ma mort.*
>
> *I am a sinner, I know it well,*
> *However, God does not wish my death.*

Or in the ballade quoted:

> *Je cognois mort qui nous consomme,*
> *Je cognois tout fors que moi mesme.*
>
> *And I know Death that downs us all,*
> *I know all things save myself alone.*

It is not Villon's art, but his substance, that pertains. Where Dante is the supreme artist, Villon is incurious; he accepts the forms of verse as unquestioningly as he accepts the dogma and opinion of his time. If Dante reaches out of his time, and by rising above it escapes many of its limitations, Villon in some way speaks below the voice of his age's convention, and thereby outlasts it. He is utterly mediæval, yet his poems mark the end of mediæval literature. Dante strives constantly for a nobler state on earth. His aspiration separates him from his time, and the ordinary reader from his work. The might of his imagination baffles the many. Villon is destitute of imagination; he is

[2] Compare "Les Coplas" of Villon's Spanish contemporary Gomez Manrique.

almost destitute of art; he has no literary ambition, no consciousness of the fame hovering over him; he has some slight vanity in impressing his immediate audience, more in reaching the ear of Louis XI by a ballade—this last under pressure of grave necessity.

Much of both the *Lesser* and the *Greater Testaments* is in no sense poetry; the wit is of the crudest; thief, murderer,[3] pander, bully to a whore, he is honored for a few score pages of unimaginative sincerity; he sings of things as they are. He dares to show himself. His depravity is not a pose cultivated for literary effect. He never makes the fatal mistake of glorifying his sin, of rejoicing in it, or of pretending to despise its opposite. His "Ne voient pan qu'aux fenestres," is no weak moralizing on the spiritual benefits of fasting.

The poignant stanzas in which this line occurs, are comparable only to Lamb's graver and more plaintive, "I have had playmates, I have had companions."

Grand Testament

XXIX

Where are the gracious gallants
That I beheld in times gone by.
Singing so well, so well speaking,
So pleasant in act and in word.
Some are dead and stiffened,
Of them there is nothing more now.
May they have rest, but in Paradise,
And God save the rest of them.

XXX

And some are become
God's mercy! great lords and masters,
And others beg all naked
And see no bread, save in the windows;
Others have gone into the cloisters
Of Celestin and of Chartreuse,

[3] This may be a little severe. Murder was not his habit; we may, however, believe that he had killed his man.

> *Shod and hosed like fishers of oysters.*
> *Behold the divers state among them all.*

Villon paints himself, as Rembrandt painted his own
hideous face; his few poems drive themselves into one in
a way unapproached by the delicate art of a Daniel or a
Baudelaire. Villon makes excuses neither for God nor for
himself; he does not rail at providence because its laws are
not adjusted to punish all weaknesses except his own.
There is, perhaps, no more poignant regret than that stanza
in *Le Grand Testament,*

> *Je plaings le temps de ma jeunesse.*

> *I mourn the time of my youth,*
> *When I made merry more than another,*
> *Until the coming in of old age,*
> *Which has sealed me its departure.*
> *It is not gone on foot,*
> *Nor on horseback; alas! and how then?*
> *Suddenly it has flown away,*
> *And has left me nothing worth.*[4]

XXIII

> *Gone it is, and I remain*
> *Poor of sense and of savoir,*
> *Sad, shattered, and more black than ripe*
> *Sans coin or rent or anything mine own.*

He recognizes the irrevocable, he blames no one but
himself, he never wastes time in self-reproaches, recognizing himself as the result of irrevocable causes.

> *Necessitè faict gens mesprendre*
> *E faim saillir le loup des boys.*

> *Necessity makes men run wry,*
> *And hunger drives the wolf from wood.*

He has the learning of the schools, or at least such smat-
tering of it as would be expected from a brilliant, desultory
auditor, but his wisdom is the wisdom of the gutter. The

---

[4] *Et ne m'a laissé quelque don.*

dramatic imagination is beyond him, yet having lived himself, he has no need to imagine what life is. His poems are
gaunt as the *Poema del Cid* is gaunt; they treat of actuali-
ties, they are untainted with fancy; in the *Cid* death is
death, war is war. In Villon filth is filth, crime is crime;
neither crime nor filth is gilded. They are not considered as
strange delights and forbidden luxuries, accessible only to
adventurous spirits. Passion he knows, and satiety he
knows, and never does he forget their relation.

He scarcely ever takes the trouble to write anything he
does not actually feel. When he does, as in the prayer
made for his mother, the lament for Master Ythier's lost
mistress, or the ballade for a young bridegroom, it is at
the request of a particular person; and the gaunt method
in which he expresses his own feelings does not desert him.
Even here the expression is that of such simple, general
emotion that the verses can hardly be regarded as dramatic;
one almost imagines Villon asking Ythier or the bridegroom what they want written, and then rhyming it for
them.

Thus this lay, or rather rondeau, which he bequeaths to
Master Ythier who has lost his mistress:

> *Death, 'gainst thine harshness I appeal*
> *That hath torn my leman from me,*
> *Thou goest not yet contentedly*
> *Though of sorrow of thee none doth me heal.*
> *No power or might did she e'er wield,*
> *In life what harm e'er did she thee*
> > *Ah, Death!*
> *Two we! that with one heart did feel,*
> *If she is dead, how then, dividedly*
> *Shall I live on, sans life in me.*
> *Save as do statues 'neath thy seal*
> > *Thou Death!*

("Par coeur" in the last line of the original, has no equivalent in modern French or in English; to dine "par coeur,"
by heart, is to dine on nothing.)

The same tendencies are apparent in the following ballade, that which Villon made at the request of his mother,

"to be prayed to our lady." I give here stanzas I and III
from Rossetti's translation.

I

Lady of Heaven and Earth, and therewithal
Crowned empress of the nether clefts of Hell,—
I, thy poor Christian, on thy name do call,
Commending me to thee, with thee to dwell,
Albeit in nought I be commendable.
But all mine undeserving may not mar
Such mercies as thy sovereign mercies are;
Without the which (as true words testify)
No soul can reach thy Heaven so fair and far,
Even in this faith I choose to live and die.

III

A pitiful poor woman, shrunk and old,
I am, and nothing learned in letter-lore,
Within my parish-cloister I behold
A painted Heaven where harps and lutes adore,
And eke an Hell whose damned folk seethe full sore:
One bringeth fear, the other joy to me.
That joy, great goddess, make thou mine to be,—
Thou of whom all must ask it even as I;
And that which faith desires, that let it see,
For in this faith I choose to live and die.

Another interesting translation of this poem is to be
found among the poems of the late J. M. Synge. For the
ballade for the bridegroom I refer to Payne or Swinburne.

Villon is, if you will, dramatic in his *Regrets of the
Belle Heaulmière*, but his own life was so nearly that of
his wasted armouress, that his voice is at one with hers.
Indeed his own "Je plains le temps de ma jeunesse" might
almost be part of this ballade. Here are stanzas 1, 5 and
10 of Swinburne's translation.

I

Meseemeth I heard cry and groan
That sweet who was the armourer's maid;

For her young years she made sore moan,
And right upon this wise she said;
'Ah fierce old age with foul bald head
To spoil fair things thou art over fain;
Who holdeth me? Who? Would God I were dead!
Would God I were well dead and slain!

V

And he died thirty years agone.
I am old now, no sweet thing to see;
By God, though when I think thereon,
And of that good glad time, woe's me,
And stare upon my changèd body
Stark naked, that has been so sweet,
Lean, wizen, like a small dry tree,
I am nigh mad with the pain of it.

X

So we make moan for the old sweet days,
Poor old light women, two or three
Squatting above the straw-fire's blaze,
The bosom crushed against the knee,
Like fagots on a heap we be,
Round fires soon lit, soon quenched and done,
And we were once so sweet, even we!
Thus fareth many and many an one.'

This ballade is followed in the *Testament* by the ballade of "La Belle Heaulmière aux filles de joie."

Car vieilles n'ont ne cours ne estre
Ne que monnoye qu'on descrie,

For old they have not course nor status
More than hath money that's turned in,

is the tune of it.

In *La Grosse Margot* from "ce bourdel ou tenons nostre estat," Villon casts out the dregs of his shame.

Many have attempted to follow Villon, mistaking a pose for his reality. These experimenters, searchers for sensation, have, I think, proved that the "taverns and the whores" are no more capable of producing poetry than are philosophy, culture, art, philology, noble character, conscientious effort, or any other panacea. If persistent effort and a desire to leave the world a beautiful heritage, were greatly availing, Ronsard, who is still under-rated, and Petrarch, who is not, would be among the highest masters. Villon's greatness is that he unconsciously proclaims man's divine right to be himself, the only one of the so-called "rights of man" which is not an artificial product. Villon is no theorist, he is an objective fact. He makes no apology— herein lies his strength; Burns is weaker, because he is in harmony with doctrines that have been preached, and his ideas of equality are derivative. Villon never wrote anything so didactic in spirit as the "man's a man for a' that." He is scarcely affected by the thought of his time, because he scarcely thinks; speculation, at any rate, is far from him. But I may be wrong here. If Villon speculates, the end of his speculation is Omar's age-old ending: "Came out by the same door wherein I went." At any rate, Villon's actions are the result of his passions and his weaknesses. Nothing is "sicklied o'er with the pale cast of thought."

As a type of debauchee he is eternal. He has sunk to the gutter, knowing life a little above it; thus he is able to realize his condition, to see it objectively, instead of insensibly taking it for granted.

Dante lives in his mind; to him two blending thoughts give a music perceptible as two blending notes of a lute. He is in the real sense an idealist. He sings of true pleasures; he sings as exactly as Villon; they are admirably in agreement: Dante to the effect that there are supernormal pleasures, enjoyable by man through the mind; Villon to the effect that the lower pleasures lead to no satisfaction, "e ne m' a laissé quelque don." "Thenceforward was my vision mightier than the discourse," writes the Italian; and Dante had gone living through Hell, in no visionary sense. Villon lacked energy to clamber out. Dante had gone on, fainting, aided, erect in his own strength; had gone on to sing of things more difficult. Villon's poetry seems, when one comes directly from the *Paradiso,* more vital, more vivid; but if Dante restrains himself, putting the laments

in the mouths of tortured spirits, they are not the less poignant. He stands behind his characters, of whom Villon
might have made one.

Before we are swept away by the intensity of this gamin
of Paris, let us turn back to the words set in the mouth of
Bertrans of Altafort, "Thus is the counterpass observed in
me," or to the lament of Francesca. Whoever cares at all
for the art will remember that the words of this lament
sob as branches beaten by the wind:

> *nessun maggior dolore,*
> *che ricordarsi del tempo felice*
> *nella miseria; e ciò sa' l tuo dottore.*

The whole sound of the passage catches in the throat, and
sobs. Dante is many men, and suffers as many. Villon cries
out as one. He is a lurid canto of the *Inferno*, written too
late to be included in the original text. Yet had Dante been
awaiting the execution of that death sentence which was
passed against him, although we might have had one of
the most scornful denunciations of tyranny the world has
ever known, we should have had no ballade of stark
power to match that which Villon wrote, expecting presently to be hanged with five companions:

> *Frères humains qui apres nous vivez.*

> *Men, brother men, that after us yet live,*
> *Let not your hearts too hard against us be;*
> *For if some pity of us poor men ye give,*
> *The sooner God shall take of you pity.*
> *Here we are, five or six strung up, you see,*
> *And here the flesh that all too well we fed*
> *Bit by bit eaten and rotten, rent and shred,*
> *And we the bones grow dust and ash withal;*
> *Let no man laugh at us discomforted,*
> *But pray to God that he forgive us all.*

II

> *If we call upon you, brothers, to forgive,*
> *You should not hold our prayer in scorn, though we*

> *Were slain by law; ye know that all alive*
> *Have not wit alway to walk righteously.*[5]

Dante's vision is real, because he saw it. Villon's verse is real, because he lived it; as Bertran de Born, as Arnaut Marvoil, as that mad poseur Vidal, he lived it. For these men life is in the press. No brew of books, no distillation of sources will match the tang of them.

[5] Swinburne's translation.

Editor's Note

Hamlet and Orestes was the Annual Shakespeare Lecture for 1914, published in pamphlet form by the British Academy. This is a slightly revised version, reprinted by permission of the publishers from *The Classical Tradition in Poetry* by Gilbert Murray (Cambridge, Mass.: Harvard University Press; 1927).

Gilbert Murray, O.M., was born in Sydney, New South Wales, in 1866, and educated at St. John's College, Oxford. He taught Greek at the University of Glasgow, and from 1908 until his retirement in 1936 was Regius Professor of Greek at Oxford. He has been active in the amateur theater movement, the League of Nations Union, and various organizations for peace and world order, and has written and lectured extensively on public affairs, religion, and philosophy. Murray has published poetry, drama, and many verse translations of Greek drama. In the field of classical studies, his books include *The Rise of the Greek Epic* (1907), *Euripides and His Age* (1913), *Aristophanes* (1933), *Aeschylus* (1940), *Greek Studies* (1946), and *Hellenism and the Modern World* (1953).

TWO

Gilbert Murray

Hamlet and Orestes

In the first of these studies we considered the conscious study and imitation of classical literature revealed in Milton's poetry. In the second we considered the origin of that classical literature itself—not indeed the models which it consciously imitated, but the quarry out of which its marbles were hewn, or the spring whose waters ran in its great rivers. In the last chapter we saw how this original raw material of poetry, the primitive religious Molpê, for the most part was not wrought to its highest forms except by passing through fire and torment, and that for this reason poetry still, in a sense, finds its models in the Heroic Age. But the unconscious tradition in poetry is not only greater in extent, it also reaches much further back into the past, than any deliberate human imitation.

I propose now to consider the influence of this unconscious tradition in a region where its presence has not been suspected.

My subject is the study of two great tragic characters, Hamlet and Orestes, regarded as traditional types. I do not compare play with play, but simply character with character, though in the course of the comparison I shall naturally consider the situations in which my heroes are placed and the other persons with whom they are associated.

Orestes in Greek is very clearly a traditional character. He occurs in poem after poem, in tragedy after tragedy, varying slightly in each one but always true to type. He is, I think, the most central and typical tragic hero on the Greek stage; and he occurs in no less than seven of our

extant tragedies—eight if we count the *Iphigenia in Aulis,*
where he is an infant—whereas Oedipus, for instance, only
comes in three and Agamemnon in four. I shall use all
these seven plays as material: namely, Aeschylus, *Choephoroe* and *Eumenides;* Sophocles, *Electra;* and Euripides,
Electra, Orestes, Iphigenia in Tauris and *Andromache.* And
we must realize that before any of these plays was written
Orestes was a well-established character both in religious
worship and in epic and lyric tradition.

As for *Hamlet,* I note, in passing, the well-known fragments of evidence which indicate the existence of a Hamlet
tragedy before the publication of Shakespeare's Second
Quarto in 1604. These are:

1602. A phrase in Dekker's *Satiromastix,* "My name's
Hamlet: Revenge!"

1598. Gabriel Harvey's remarks about Shakespeare's
Hamlet. The true date of this entry is disputed.

1596. Lodge, *Wit's Miserie and the World's Madness:*
"He looks as pale as the ghost which cried so miserally at
the theater like an oysterwife, Hamlet, revenge."

1594. Henslowe's Diary records a play called *Hamlet*
as acted at Newington Butts Theatre on June 9.

The earliest reference seems to be in Nash's *Epistle*
prefixed to Greene's *Menaphon:* it is dated 1589, but was
perhaps printed in 1587. "Yet English Seneca read by
candle light yeeldes many good sentences, as Bloud is a
beggar, and so foorth: and if you intreate him faire in a
frosty morning, he will affoord you whole Hamlets, I
should say handfulls of tragicall speeches."

The play of *Hamlet* is extant in three main forms:

The First Quarto, dated 1603, but perhaps printed in
1602. It is entitled "The Tragicall Historie of Hamlet
Prince of Denmark by William Shake-speare, As it hath
been at divers times acted by his Highnesse servants in
the Cittie of London: as also in the two Vniversities of
Cambridge and Oxford and else-where." It is much shorter
than the *Hamlet* which we commonly read, having only
2,143 lines, many of them incomplete, as against the 3,891
of the Globe edition. It differs from our version also in
the order of the scenes and to some extent in plot. For in-

stance, the Queen's innocence of her husband's murder is made quite explicit: when she hears how it was wrought she exclaims:

> *But, as I have a soule, I sweare by Heaven*
> *I never knew of this most horride murder;*

and thereafter she acts confidentially with Hamlet and Horatio. Also some of the names are different: for Polonius we have Corambis, and for Reynaldo, Montano.

The Second Quarto, dated 1604, describes itself as "enlarged to almoste as much againe as it was, according to the true and perfecte coppie."

Thirdly, there is the Folio of 1623. This omits a good deal that was in the Second Quarto, and contains some passages which are not in that edition but have their parallels in the First Quarto.

Thus *Hamlet,* like most of the great Elizabethan plays, presents itself to us as a whole that has been gradually built up, not as a single definitive creation made by one man in one effort. There was an old play called *Hamlet* extant about 1587, perhaps written by Kyd. It was worked over and improved by Shakespeare; improved doubtless again and again in the course of its different productions. We can trace additions; we can even trace changes of mind or repentances, as when the Folio of 1623 goes back to a discarded passage in the First Quarto. It is a live and growing play, apt no doubt to be slightly different at each performance, and growing steadily more profound, more rich, and more varied in its appeal.

And before it was an English play, it was a Scandinavian story: a very ancient Northern tale, not invented by any person, but just living, and doubtless from time to time growing and decaying, in oral tradition. It is recorded at length, of course with some remodelling, both conscious and unconscious, by Saxo Grammaticus in his great *History of the Danes* (*Gesta Danorum*), Books III and IV. Saxo wrote about the year 1185; he calls his hero Amlethus, or Amloði, Prince of Jutland, and has worked in material that seems to come from the classical story of Brutus—Brutus the Fool, who cast out the Tarquins—and

the deeds of Anlaf Curan, King of Ireland. But the story
of Hamlet existed long before Saxo; for the prose *Edda*
happens to quote a song by the poet Snaebjørn, composed
about 980, with a passing reference to "Amloði." And it
must mean our Amloði; for our Amloði in his pretended
madness was a great riddle-maker, and the song refers to
one of his best riddles. He speaks in Saxo of the sand
as meal ground by the sea; and Snaebjørn's song calls the
sea "Amloði's meal-bin."

Besides Saxo we have a later form of the same legend
in the Icelandic *Ambales Saga.* The earliest extant manuscripts of this belong to the seventeenth century.

Thus our sources for *Hamlet* will be (1) the various
versions of the play known to us, (2) the story in Saxo
Grammaticus and the *Ambales Saga,* and (3) some occasional variants of these sagas.[1]

II

Now to our comparison.

1. The general situation. In all the versions, both Northern and Greek, the hero is the son of a king who has been
murdered and succeeded on the throne by a younger
kinsman—a cousin, Aegisthus, in the Greek; a younger
brother, Feng or Claudius, in the Northern. The dead
king's wife has married his murderer. The hero, driven by
supernatural commands, undertakes and carries through
the duty of vengeance.

In Shakespeare the hero dies as his vengeance is accomplished; but this seems to be an innovation. In Saxo, *Ambales,* and the Greek he duly succeeds to the kingdom. In
Saxo there is no mention of a ghost; the duty of vengeance is perhaps accepted as natural. In *Ambales,* however, there are angels; in the English, a ghost; in the
Greek, dreams and visions of the dead father, and an
oracle.

---

[1] There are, of course, numerous variants and offshoots of the
Hamlet story. See *Corpus Hamleticum* by Professor Josef Schick of
Munich.

2. In all versions of the story there is some shyness about the mother-murder. In Saxo the mother is not slain; in Shakespeare she is slain by accident, not deliberately murdered; in *Ambales* she is warned and leaves the burning hall just in time. In one of the variants the mother refuses to leave the hall and is burnt with her husband.[2] In the Greek versions she is deliberately slain, but the horror of the deed unseats the hero's reason. We shall consider this mother more at length later on.

3. In all the versions the hero is in some way under the shadow of madness. This is immensely important, indeed essential, in his whole dramatic character. It is present in all the versions, but is somewhat different in each.

In *Hamlet* the madness is assumed, but I trust I am safe in saying that there is something in the hero's character which at least makes one wonder if it is entirely assumed. I think the same may be said of Amloði and Ambales.

In the Greek the complete madness comes only as a result of the mother-murder; yet here too there is that in the hero's character which makes it easy for him to go mad. In the *Choephoroe,* where we see him before the deed, he is not normal. His language is strange and broken amid its amazing eloquence; he is a haunted man. In other plays, after the deed, he is seldom actually raving. But, like Hamlet in his mother's chamber, he sees visions which others cannot:

You cannot see them: only I can see.[3]

He indulges freely in soliloquies;[4] especially, like Hamlet, he is subject to paralyzing doubts and hesitations, alternating with hot fits. For instance, once in the *Iphigenia* he

---

[2] Halfdan is killed by his brother Frodi, who also takes his wife. Halfdan's sons, Helgi and Hroar, eventually burn Frodi at a feast. See Professor Elton's appendix to his translation of Saxo, edited by York Powell.

[3] *Choephoroe,* 1061; cf. *Orestes,* 255–279.

[4] *Iphigenia in Tauris,* 77–94, *Electra,* 367–390; cf. *Iphigenia in Tauris,* 940–978; *Choephoroe,* 268–305, and last scene.

suddenly wishes to fly and give up his whole enterprise, and has to be checked by Pylades:

> *O God, where hast thou brought me? what new snare*
> *Is this?—I slew my mother, I avenged*
> *My father at thy bidding. I have ranged*
> *A homeless world, hunted by shapes of pain. . . .*
> *. . . We still have time to fly for home,*
> *Back to the galley quick, ere worse things come.*
>
> PYLADES
> *To fly we dare not, brother: 't is a thing*
> *Not of our custom.*[5]

Again, in the *Electra* he suspects that the god who commands him to take vengeance may be an evil spirit in disguise:

> *How if some fiend of Hell*
> *Hid in God's likeness spake that oracle?*

One is reminded of Hamlet's words:

> *The spirit that I have seen*
> *May be the devil.*[6]

At the moment before the actual crisis he is seized with horror and tries to hold back. In the *Choephoroe* this is given in a line or two:

> *Pylades,*
> *What can I? Dare I let my mother live?* [7]

or with a different punctuation: "Let me spare my mother!" In the *Electra* it is a whole scene, where he actually for the moment forgets what it is that he has to do; he only remembers that it has something to do with his mother. Again he vows, too late, after the mother-murder, that, if his dead father had known all, he would never have urged him to such a deed; he would rather

---

[5] *Iphigenia in Tauris*, 93–103.
[6] *Electra*, 979; *Hamlet*, II, 2.
[7] *Choephoroe*, 899.

> *have knelt down*
> *And hung his wreath of prayers about my beard,*
> *To leave him unavenged.*[8]

In Shakespeare this belief is made a fact: the Ghost specially charges Hamlet not to kill Gertrude:

> *Taint not thy mind, nor let thy soul contrive*
> *Against thy Mother aught.*[9]

Is it too much to say that, in all these strangely characteristic speeches of Orestes, every line might have been spoken by Hamlet, and hardly a line by any other tragic character except those directly influenced by Orestes or Hamlet?

Now what do we find in the sagas? Both in Saxo and in *Ambales* the madness is assumed, entirely or mainly, but in its quality also it is utterly different from that of Shakespeare's hero. The saga Hamlet is not a highly wrought and sensitive man with his mind shaken by a terrible experience, he is a Fool, a gross Jester, covered with dirt and ashes, grinning and mowing and eating like a hog, spared by the murderer simply because he is considered too witless to be dangerous. The name "Amloði" itself means a fool. This side is emphasised most in *Ambales*, but it is clear enough in Saxo also and explains why he has combined his hero with the Fool, Brutus. Hamlet is a Fool, though his folly is partly assumed and hides unsuspected cunning.

4. The Fool.—It is very remarkable that Shakespeare, who did such wonders in his idealized and half-mystic treatment of the real Fool, should also have made his greatest tragic hero out of a Fool transfigured. Let us spend a few moments on noticing the remnants of the old Fool that subsist in the transfigured hero of the tragedies. For one thing, as has often been remarked, Hamlet's actual language is at times exactly that of the regular Shakespearean Fool: for example, with Polonius

---

[8] *Orestes,* 288–293.
[9] *Hamlet,* I, 5; cf. also the tone in III, 4.

in Act II, scene 2; just before the play in Act III, scene 2, and after. But apart from that, there are other significant elements.

(*a*) The Fool's disguise.—Amloði and Brutus and Shakespeare's Hamlet feign madness; Orestes does not. Yet the element of disguise is very strong in Orestes. He is always disguising his feelings: he does so in the *Choephoroe,* Sophocles' *Electra,* Euripides' *Electra* and *Iphigenia in Tauris.* In two passages further, he narrates how, in other circumstances, he had to disguise them:

> *I suffered in silence and made pretence not to see.*[1]
> *I suffered, Oh, I suffered; but as things drove me I endured.*[2]

This is like Shakespeare's Hamlet. It is also very like the saga Hamlet, who deliberately laughs in pretended idiocy to see his brother hanged.

Again, it is a marked feature of Orestes to be present in disguise, especially when he is supposed to be dead, and then at some crisis to reveal himself with startling effect. He is apt to be greeted by such words as "Undreamed-of phantom!" or "Who is this risen from the dead?[3] He is present disguised and unknown in the *Choephoroe,* Sophocles' *Electra,* Euripides' *Electra* and *Iphigenia in Tauris;* he is in nearly every case supposed to be dead. In the *Choephoroe* and Sophocles' *Electra* he brings the funeral urn that is supposed to contain his own ashes; in the *Iphigenia* he interrupts his own funeral rites.

No other character in Greek tragedy behaves in this extraordinary way. But Saxo's Amloði does. When Amloði goes to England, he is supposed to be dead, and his funeral feast is in progress, when he walks in, "striking all men utterly aghast."[4]

In *Hamlet* there is surely a remnant of this motive, considerably softened. In Act V, 2, the Gravedigger

---

[1] *Iphigenia in Tauris,* 956.
[2] *Andromache,* 980.
[3] *Orestes,* 385, 879, 478 f.; *Iphigenia,* 1361 (cf. 1321).
[4] *Gesta Danorum,* IV, 95.

scene, Hamlet has been present in disguise while the Gravedigger and the public thought he was in England, and the King and his confidants must have believed him dead, as they do in Saxo. Then comes the funeral—not his own, but Ophelia's; he stays hidden for a time, and then springs out, revealing himself: "This is I, Hamlet the Dane!" The words seem like an echo of that cry that is so typical in the Greek tragedies: "'Tis I, Orestes, Agamemnon's son!" [5] One is reminded, too, of the quotation from the pre-Shakespearean *Hamlet* in Dekker's *Satiromastix* of 1602: "My name's Hamlet! Revenge!" It may well be that these melodramatic appearances were more prominent in the tradition before Shakespeare.

(*b*) The disorder of the Fool.—This disguise motive has led us away from the Fool, though it is closely connected with him. Another curious element of the Fool that lingers on is his dirtiness and disorder in dress. Saxo says that Amloði "remained always in his mother's house, utterly listless and unclean, flinging himself on the ground and bespattering his person with foul dirt." [6] Ambales was worse; enough to say that he slept in his mother's room and "ashes and filth reeked off him." [7] We remember Ophelia's description of Hamlet's coming to her chamber:

> *his doublet all unbraced;*
> *No hat upon his head; his stockings fouled,*
> *Ungartered and down-gyvèd to the ankle,*
> *Pale as his shirt . . .* [8]

Similarly, Orestes, at the beginning of the play that bears his name, is found with his sister, ghastly pale, with foam on his mouth, gouts of rheum in his eyes, his long hair matted with dirt and "made wild with long unwashenness." "Poor curls, poor filthy face," his sister says to him.[9] In the *Electra*, too, he is taken for a brigand,[1] which

---

[5] *Andromache*, 884; *Iphigenia*, 1361; cf. his sudden apparitions in *Choephoroe*, 212 ff., *Electra*, 220, also the recognition scenes.
[6] Saxo, 88.
[7] *Hamlet*, II, i.
[8] *Electra*, 219.
[9] *Ambales*, pp. 73–75, 77.
[1] *Orestes*, 219–226; cf. 880 ff.

suggests some lack of neatness in dress; in the *Iphigenia*
we hear of his foaming at the mouth and rolling on the
ground.[2] In both plays, it is true, Orestes carries with him
an air of princely birth, but so, no doubt, did Hamlet,
whatever state his stockings were in.

(c) The Fool's rudeness of speech.—Besides being
dirty and talking in riddles, the Fool was abusive and
gross in his language. This is the case to some degree in
Saxo, though no doubt the monk has softened Amloði's
words. It is much emphasized in Ambales. That hero's
language is habitually outrageous, especially to women.
This outrageousness of speech has clearly descended to
Hamlet, in whom it seems to be definitely intended as a
morbid trait. He is obsessed by revolting images. He does

> *like a whore unpack his heart in words*
> *And fall a-cursing like a very drab,*

and he rages at himself because of it.

(d) The Fool on women.—Now the general style of
Greek tragedy will not admit any gross language. So
Orestes has lost this trait. But a trace of it perhaps remains. Both Orestes and Hamlet are given to expressing
violently cynical opinions about women.[3] The *Orestes*
bristles with parallels to the ravings of Hamlet's "Get-thee-
to-a-nunnery" scene.[4] The hero is haunted by his "most
pernicious woman." All women want to murder their
husbands; it is only a question of time. Then they will fly
in tears to their children, show their breasts, and cry for
sympathy. We may, perhaps, couple with these passages
the famous speech where he denies any blood relationship
with his mother,[5] and the horrible mad line where he says
he could never weary of killing evil women.[6]

Both heroes also tend—if I may use such an expression
—to bully any woman they are left alone with. Amloði in
Saxo mishandles his foster-sister—though the passage is

[2] *Iphigenia in Tauris*, 307 f.
[3] *Orestes*, 246–251, 566–572, 935–942.
[4] *Hamlet*, III, 1.
[5] *Orestes*, 552 ff., based on the quibble in Aeschylus' *Eumenides*,
657–661.
[6] *Orestes*, 1590.

obscure—and utters violent reproaches to the Queen. (The scene is taken over by Shakespeare.) Ambales is habitually misbehaving in this way. Hamlet bullies Ophelia cruelly and "speaks daggers" to the Queen. He never meets any other woman. Orestes is very surly to Iphigenia;[7] draws his sword on Electra in one play, and takes her for a devil in another;[8] holds his dagger at the throat of Hermione till she faints;[9] denounces, threatens, and kills Clytemnestra, and tries to kill Helen. There are not many tragic heroes with such an extreme anti-feminist record.

The above, I think, are, all of them, elements that go deep into the character of the hero as a stage figure. I will now add some slighter and more external points of resemblance.

1. In both traditions the hero has been away from home when the main drama begins, Orestes in Phocis, Hamlet in Wittenberg. This point, as we shall see later, has some significance.

2. The hero in both traditions—and in both rather strangely—goes on a ship, is captured by enemies who want to kill him, but escapes. And as Hamlet has a sort of double escape, first from the King's treacherous letter, and next from the pirates, so Orestes, in the *Iphigenia,* escapes once from the Taurians who catch him on the shore, and again from the pursuers in the ship. Ambales has similar adventures at sea; and the original Amloði seems to have had nautical connexions, since the sea was his meal-bin, and the ship's rudder his knife.[1]

3. Much more curious, and indeed extraordinary, is the following point, which occurs in Saxo, *Ambales,* and the Greek, but not in Shakespeare. We have seen that the hero is always a good deal connected with the dead, with graves and ghosts and funerals. In the sagas on one occasion he wins a great battle after a preliminary defeat, by a somewhat ghastly strategem. He picks up his dead—or his dead

---

[7] *Iphigenia,* 482 ff.
[8] *Electra,* 220 ff.; *Orestes,* 264.
[9] *Orestes,* 1575 ff.
[1] See also a pamphlet, *Grotta Söngr and the Orkney and Shetland Quern,* by A. W. Johnston, 1912.

and wounded—and ties them upright to stakes and rocks, so that, when his pursuers renew their attack, they find themselves affronted by an army of dead men standing upright, and fly in dismay. Now in the *Electra*, Orestes prays to his father:

> *Girt with thine own dead armies wake, Oh wake,*[2]

or, quite literally, "Come bringing every dead man as a fellow-fighter." One would almost think here that there was some direct influence—of course with a misunderstanding. But the parallel may be a mere chance.

4. I would not lay much stress on the coincidence about the serpent. Clytemnestra dreams that she gives birth to a serpent, which bites her breast. Orestes, hearing of it, accepts the omen: he will be the serpent. And at the last moment, Clytemnestra so recognizes him:

> *Oh, God;*
> *This is the serpent that I bore and suckled.*

We are reminded of the Ghost's words:

> *The serpent that did sting thy father's life*
> *Now wears his crown.*[3]

However, Shakespeare abounds in serpents, and I have found no trace of this serpent motive in the sagas.

5. Nor yet would I make anything of the point that both Hamlet and Orestes on one occasion have the enemy in their power and put off killing him in order to provide a worse death afterwards. This is important in *Hamlet*—

> *Now might I do it pat, now he is praying;*[4]

but only occurs as a slight incident in Sophocles' *Electra*,[5] and may be due merely to the Greek rule of having no violent deaths on the stage. Nor is there much significance in the fact that in both traditions the hero has a scene in

---

[2] *Electra*, 680.
[3] *Choephoroe*, 527–550, 928; *Orestes*, 479; *Hamlet*, I, 5.
[4] *Hamlet*, III, 3.
[5] Sophocles, *Electra*, 1491 ff.

which he hears the details of his father's death and bursts
into uncontrollable grief.[6] Such a scene is in both cases
almost unavoidable.

Let us now follow this father for a little while. He was,
perhaps naturally, a great warrior. He "slew Troy's thousands"; he "smote the sledded Polacks on the ice." It is a
particular reproach that the son of such a man should be
so slow-tempered, "peaking like John-a-dreams," and so
chary of shedding blood.[7] The father was also generally
idealized and made magnificent. He had some manly
faults, yet "He was a man, taking him all in all." He was
"a king of kings." [8] A special contrast is drawn between
him and his successor:

> *It was so easy to be true. A King*
> *Was thine, not feebler, not in any thing*
> *Below Aegisthus; one whom Hellas chose*
> *Above all kings.*[9]

One might continue: "Look on this picture and on this."

We may also notice that the successor, besides the vices
which are necessary, or at least desirable, in his position, is
in both cases accused of drunkenness,[1] which seems
irrelevant and unusual.

Lastly, and more important, one of the greatest horrors
about the father's death in both traditions is that he died
without the due religious observances. In the Greek
tragedies, this lack of religious burial is almost the central
horror of the whole story. Wherever it is mentioned it
comes as something intolerable, maddening; it breaks
Orestes down. A good instance is the scene in the *Choephoroe*, where Orestes and Electra are kneeling at their
father's grave, awakening the dead and working their own
passion to the murder point.

---

[6] *Choephoroe*, 430 ff.; Euripides, *Electra*, 290; *Hamlet*, I, 5, "Oh, all
you host of heaven," etc.
[7] *Electra*, 275 ff., 336 ff.; cf. 130, 245.
[8] *Ibid.*, 1066 ff.
[9] *Ibid.*, 320 ff., 917, 1080.
[1] *Hamlet*, I, 4; *Electra*, 326.

ELECTRA

Ah, pitiless one, my mother, mine enemy! With an enemy's burial didst thou bury him: thy King without his people, without dying rites; thine husband without a tear!

ORESTES

All, all, in dishonour thou tellest it, woe is me! And for that dishonouring she shall pay her punishment: by the will of the Gods, by the will of my hands: Oh, let me but slay, and then perish!

He is now ripe for the hearing of the last horror:

LEADER OF THE CHORUS

His body was mangled to lay his ghost! There, learn it all . . .

and the scene becomes hysterical.[2]

The atmosphere is quite different in the English. But the lack of dying rites remains, and retains a strange dreadfulness:

> *Cut off even in the blossom of my sin,*
> *Unhousel'd, disappointed, unanel'd.*

To turn to the other characters: in both the dramatic traditions the hero has a faithful friend and confidant, who also arrives from Phocis–Wittenberg, and advises him about his revenge. This friend, when the hero is threatened with death, wishes to die too, but is prevented by the hero and told to "absent him from felicity awhile."[3] This motive is worked out more at length in the Greek than in the English.

Also the friendship between Orestes and Pylades is more intense than—between Hamlet and Horatio; naturally, since devoted friendship always plays a greater part in antiquity. But Hamlet's words are strong:

[2] *Choephoroe*, 435 ff.; cf. Sophocles, *Electra*, 443 ff.; Euripides, *Electra*, 289, 323 ff.
[3] *Orestes*, 1069 ff.; *Iphigenia*, 675 ff.; *Hamlet*, V, 2.

> *Give me that man*
> *That is not passion's slave, and I will wear him*
> *In my heart's core, ay, in my heart of heart,*
> *As I do thee.*[4]

I find no Pylades–Horatio in the sagas; though there
is a brother to Hamlet, sometimes older and sometimes
a twin. In some of the variants also, such as the stories
of Helgi and Hroar, there are pairs of avengers, one of
whom is mad, or behaves like a madman.

Next comes a curious point. At first sight it seems as
if all the Electra motive were lacking in the modern play,
all the Ophelia–Polonius motive in the ancient. Yet I am
not sure.

In all the ancient plays Orestes is closely connected with
a strange couple—a young woman and a very old man.
They are his sister Electra and her only true friend, an old
and trusted servant of the dead King, who saved Orestes'
life in childhood. In Euripides this old man habitually
addresses Electra as "my daughter"—not merely as "child"
(παῖς), but really "daughter" (θυγάτηρ),[5] while she in
return carefully avoids calling him "Father," because that
is to her a sacred name and she will never use it lightly.
But in Sophocles she says emphatically:

> *"Hail, Father. For it is as if in thee*
> *I saw my father!"* [6]

In the Elizabethan play this couple—if we may so beg
the question—has been transformed. The sister is now the
mistress, Ophelia; the old servant of the King—for so we
must surely describe Polonius or Corambis—remains, but
has become Ophelia's real father. And the relations of both
to the hero are quite different.

The change is made more intelligible when we look at
the sagas. There the young woman is not a sister but a
foster-sister; like Electra she helps Amloði, like Ophelia
she is his beloved. The old servant of the King is not her

---

[4] *Hamlet*, III, 2.
[5] Euripides, *Electra*, 493, 563.
[6] Sophocles, *Electra*, 1361.

father—so far like the Greek; but there the likeness stops. He spies on Amloði in his mother's chamber and is killed for his pains, as in the English.

We may notice, further, that in all the Electra plays alike a peculiar effect is got from Orestes' first sight of his sister, either walking in a funeral procession or alone in mourning garb.[7] He takes her for a slave, and cries, "Can that be the unhappy Electra?" A similar but stronger effect is reached in *Hamlet*,[8] when Hamlet, seeing an unknown funeral procession approach, gradually discovers whose it is and cries in horror: "What, the fair Ophelia?"

Lastly, there is something peculiar, at any rate in the Northern tradition,—I will take the Greek later,—about the hero's mother. Essentially it is this: she has married the murderer of her first husband and is in part implicated in the murder, and yet the tradition instinctively keeps her sympathetic. In our *Hamlet* she is startled to hear that her first husband was murdered, yet one does not feel clear that she is perfectly honest with herself. She did not know Claudius had poisoned him, but probably that was because she obstinately refused to put together things which she did know and which pointed towards that conclusion. At any rate, though she does not betray Hamlet, she sticks to Claudius and shares his doom. In the First Quarto she is more definitely innocent of the murder; when she learns of it she changes sides, protects Hamlet, and acts in confidence with Horatio. In Saxo her attitude is as ambiguous as in the later *Hamlet;* she is friendly to Amloði and does not betray him, yet does not turn against Feng either.

A wife who loves her husband and bears him children, and then is wedded to his slayer and equally loves him, and does it all in a natural and unemotional manner: it seems somewhat unusual.

And one's surprise is a little increased to find that in Saxo Amloði's wife, Hermutrude, behaves in the same way as his mother has done. On Amloði's death she marries his slayer, Wiglek. Again, there is an Irish king, historical to a great degree, who has got deeply entangled

---

[7] *Choephoroe*, 16; Sophocles, *Electra*, 80; Euripides, *Electra*, 107 ff.
[8] Act V, scene 1.

with the Hamlet story. His name is Anlaf Curan. Now his wife, Gormflaith, carried this practice so far that the chronicler comments on it. After Anlaf's defeat at Tara she married his conqueror Malachy, and on Malachy's defeat she married Malachy's conqueror Brian. We will consider later the Greek parallels to this enigmatic lady. For the present we must admit that she is very unlike the Clytemnestra of Greek tragedy, whose motives are studied in every detail, who boldly hates her husband and murders him. But there are traces in Homer of a far less passionate Clytemnestra.

III

Now I hope I have not tried artificially to make a case or to press my facts too hard. I think it will be conceded that the points of similarity, some fundamental and some perhaps superficial, between these two tragic heroes are rather extraordinary, and are made the more striking by the fact that Hamlet and Orestes are respectively the very greatest or most famous heroes of the world's two great ages of tragedy.

The points of similarity, we must notice, fall into two parts. There are, first, the broad similarities of situation between what we may call the original sagas on both sides; that is, the general story of Orestes and of Hamlet respectively. But, secondly, there is something much more remarkable: when these sagas were worked up into tragedies, quite independently and on very different lines, by the great dramatists of Greece and England, not only do most of the old similarities remain, but a number of new similarities are developed. That is, Aeschylus, Euripides, and Shakespeare are strikingly similar in certain points which do not occur at all in Saxo or *Ambales* or the Greek epic. For instance, the hero's madness is the same in Shakespeare and Euripides, but is totally different from the madness in Saxo or *Ambales*.

What is the connexion? All critics seem to be agreed that Shakespeare did not study these Greek tragedians directly. And, if any one should suggest that he did, there are many considerations which would, I think, make that hypothesis unserviceable. Of course, it is likely enough that some of Shakespeare's university friends, who knew Greek, may have told him in conversation of various stories or scenes or effects in Greek plays. Miss Spens suggests the name of Marston. She shows that he consciously imitated the Greek—for instance, in getting a special effect out of the absence of funeral rites—and probably had considerable influence on Shakespeare. This is a highly important line of inquiry, but such an explanation would not carry us very far with Shakespeare, and would be no help with Saxo.

Neither can it be indirect imitation through Seneca. Orestes only appears once in the whole of Seneca, and then he is a baby unable to speak.[9] And in any case Saxo does not seem to have studied Seneca.

Will Scandinavian mercenaries at the Court of Byzantium help us? Or, simpler perhaps, will the Roman conquest of Britain? Both these channels were doubtless important in opening up a connexion between the North and the Mediterranean, and revealing to the Northmen the rich world of classical story. But neither explanation is at all adequate. It might possibly provide a bridge between the traditional Orestes and Saxo's Amloði; but they are not in any pressing need of a bridge. It does not provide any bridge where it is chiefly wanted, between the Orestes of tragedy and Shakespeare's Hamlet.

There seems to have been, so far as our recorded history goes, no chance of imitation, either direct or indirect. Are we thrown back, then, on a much broader and simpler though rather terrifying hypothesis, that the field of tragedy is by nature so limited that these similarities are inevitable? Certain situations and stories and characters— certain subjects, we may say, for shortness—are naturally tragic; these subjects are quite few in number, and, consequently, two poets or sets of poets trying to find or invent tragic subjects are pretty sure to fall into the same paths. I think there is some truth in this suggestion; and I shall make use of something like it later. But I do not think

9 Seneca, *Agamemnon*, 910–943.

that in itself it is enough, or nearly enough, to explain such close similarities, both detailed and fundamental, as those we are considering. I feel as I look at these two traditions that there must be a connexion somewhere.

There is none within the limits of our historical record; but can there be any outside? There is none between the dramas, nor even directly between the sagas; but can there be some original connexion between the myths, or the primitive religious rituals, on which the dramas are ultimately based? And can it be that in the last analysis the similarities between Euripides and Shakespeare are simply due to the natural working out, by playwrights of special genius, of the dramatic possibilities latent in that original seed? If this is so, it will lead us to some interesting conclusions.

To begin with, then, can we discover the original myth out of which the Greek Orestes-saga has grown? (I do not deny the possible presence of an historical element also; but if history is there, there is certainly myth mixed up with it.) The saga contains two parts:

(1) Agamemnon, "king of men," is dethroned and slain by a younger kinsman, the banished Aegisthus, who is helped by the Queen. (2) His successor, in turn, dreads and tries to destroy the next heir to the throne, Orestes, who, however, comes home secretly and, helped by a Young Queen, Electra, slays him and the Queen with him.

The story falls into its place in a clearly marked group of Greek or pre-Greek legends. Let us recall the primeval kings of the world in Hesiod.

First there was Ouranos and his wife Gaia. Ouranos lived in dread of his children, and "hid them away" till his son Kronos rose and cast him out, helped by the Queen-Mother Gaia.

Then came King Kronos with his wife Rhea. He, too, feared his children and "swallowed them," till his son Zeus rose and cast him out, helped by the Queen-Mother Rhea.

Then, thirdly—but the story cannot continue. For Zeus is still ruling and cannot have been cast out. But he was saved by a narrow margin. He was about to marry the

sea-maiden Thetis, when Prometheus warned him that, if
he did so, the son of Thetis would be greater than he and
cast him out from heaven. And, great as is my love for
Thetis, I have little doubt that she would have been found
helping her son in his criminal behaviour.

In the above cases the new usurper is represented as the
son of the old King and Queen. Consequently the Queen-
Mother, though she helps him, does not marry him, as she
does when he is merely a younger kinsman. But there is
one great saga in which the marriage of mother and son
has remained, quite unsoftened and unexpurgated. In
Thebes King Laïus and his wife Jocasta knew that their
son would slay and dethrone his father. Laïus orders the
son's death, but he is saved by the Queen-Mother, and,
after slaying and dethroning his father, marries her. She
is afterwards slain or dethroned with him, as Clytemnestra
is with Aegisthus, and Gertrude with Claudius.

There is clearly a common element in all these stories,
and the reader will doubtless have recognised it. It is the
world-wide ritual story of what we may call the Golden-
Bough Kings. That ritual story is, as I have tried to show
elsewhere, the fundamental conception that forms the basis
of Greek tragedy, and not Greek tragedy only. It forms
the basis of the traditional Mummers' Play, which, though
deeply degraded and vulgarized, is not quite dead yet in
the countries of Northern Europe and lies at the root of
so large a part of all the religions of mankind.

It is unnecessary, I hope, to make any long explanation
of the Vegetation-kings or Year-daemons. But there are
perhaps two points that we should remember, to save us
from confusion later on. First, there are two early modes
of reckoning: you can reckon by seasons or half-years, by
summers and winters; or you can reckon with the whole
year as your unit. On the first system a Summer-king or
Vegetation-spirit is slain by Winter and rises from the
dead in the spring. On the second each Year-king comes
first as a wintry slayer, weds the queen, grows proud and
royal, and then is slain by the Avenger of his predecessor.
These two conceptions cause some confusion in the myths,
as they do in most forms of the Mummers' Play.

The second point to remember is that this death and vengeance was really enacted among our remote ancestors in terms of human bloodshed. The sacred king really had "slain the slayer" and was doomed himself to be slain. The queen might either be taken on by her husband's slayer, or else slain with her husband. It is no pale myth or allegory that has so deeply dyed the first pages of human history. It is man's passionate desire for the food that will save him from starvation, his passionate memory of the streams of blood, willing and unwilling, that have been shed to keep him alive. But for all this subject I must refer the reader to the classic expositions of the *Golden Bough,* and their brilliant development in Dr. Jane Harrison's *Themis.*

Thus Orestes, the madman and king-slayer, takes his place beside Brutus the Fool, who expelled the Tarquins, and Amloði the Fool, who burnt King Feng at his winter feast. The great Greek scholar, Hermann Usener, some years since, on quite other grounds, identified Orestes as a Winter-god, a slayer of the Summer.[1] He is the man of the cold mountains who slays annually the Red Neoptolemus at Delphi; he is the ally of death and the dead; he comes suddenly in the dark; he is mad and raging, like the Winter-god Maimaktes and the November storms. In Athenian ritual, it seems, a cloak was actually woven for him in late autumn, lest he should be too cold.[2] Thus he is quite unlike the various bright heroes who slay dragons of darkness; he finds his comrade in the Bitter Fool— may we say the bitter Amloði?—of many Mummers' Plays, who is the Slayer of the Joyous King.

This is all very well for Orestes; but can we talk thus of Hamlet-Amloði? Is it possible to bring him into the region of myth, and myth of the same kind that we find in Greece? Here I am quite off my accustomed beat, and must speak with diffidence and under correction from my betters. But it seems beyond doubt, even to my most imperfect scrutiny of the material, that the same forms of myth and the same range of primitive religious concep-

[1] *Heilige Handlung,* in the *Archiv für Religionswissenschaft,* 1904.
[2] Aristophanes, *Birds,* 712.

tions are to be found in Scandinavia as in other Aryan
countries.

There are several wives in the Ynglinga saga who seem
to belong to the Gaia–Rhea–Clytemnestra–Jocasta type.
For instance, King Vanlandi was married to Drifa of Fin-
land, and was killed by her in conjunction with their son
Visburr, who succeeded to the kingdom. (The slaying was
done by witchcraft; but no jury could, I think, exculpate
Visburr.)

Visburr in turn married the daughter of Aude the
Wealthy. Like Agamemnon, he was unfaithful to his wife,
so she left him and sent her two sons to talk to him, and
duly, in the proper ritual manner, to burn him in his house
—just as the Hamlet of saga burned King Feng, just as the
actual Northern villagers at their festival burned the Old
Year.

Again, there are clear traces of kings who are sacrificed
and are succeeded by their slayers. Most of the Yngling
kings die in sacrificial ways. One is confessedly sacrificed
to avert famine, one killed by a sacrificial bull, one falls
off his horse in a temple and dies, one burns himself on a
pyre at a festival. Another—like Ouranos and Kronos and
the other child-swallowers—sacrifices one of his sons peri-
odically in order to prolong his own life. I cite these cases
merely to show that such ideas were apparently current in
primitive Norse society as well as elsewhere. But the matter is really clinched by Saxo himself. He not only gives
us the tale of Ole, King of the Beggars, who came in disguise, with one servant dressed as a woman, to King
Thore's house, got himself hailed as king in mockery, and
then slew Thore and took the crown. He definitely tells us,
in a story about the Sclavs, that "by public law of the
ancients the succession to the throne belonged to him who
should slay the king." [3]

So that when we find that the Hamlet of saga resembles
Orestes so closely; when we find that he is the Bitter Fool
and king-slayer; when especially we find that this strange
part of wedding—if not helping—their husband's slayer
and successor is played alike by Hamlet's mother, what-

[3] *Gesta Danorum*, 254, 277.

ever her name, Gerutha, Gertrude, or Amba; and by
Amloði's mother and by Ambales' mother, and by the
mother of divers variants of Hamlet, like Helgi and Hroar;
and by Hamlet's wife, and by the wife of Anlaf Curan,
who is partly identified with Hamlet, we can hardly hesi-
tate to draw the same sort of conclusion as would naturally
follow in a Greek story. Hamlet is more deeply involved
in this Clytemnestra-like atmosphere than any person I
know of outside Hesiod. And one cannot fail to be reminded of Oedipus and Jocasta by the fact, which is itself
of no value in the story but is preserved both in Saxo and
the *Ambales Saga,* that Amloði slept in his mother's chamber.[4]

There is something strangely characteristic in the saga
treatment of this ancient Queen-Mother, a woman under
the shadow of adultery, the shadow of incest, the shadow
of murder, who is yet left in most of the stories a motherly
and sympathetic character. Clytemnestra is an exception,
and perhaps Gormflaith. But Gaia, Rhea, and even Jocasta,
are all motherly and sympathetic. So is Gerutha, the wife
of Ørvandil and the mother of Amleth, and Amba the
mother of Ambales.[5] So is Groa, the usual wife of Ørvandil, who is probably the same person as Gerutha. "Groa,"
says Professor Rydberg, "was a tender person devoted to
the members of her family." The trait remains even in
Shakespeare. "Gertrude," says Professor Bradley, "had a
soft animal nature. . . . She loved to be happy like a
sheep in the sun, and to do her justice she loved to see
others happy, like more sheep in the sun." Just the right
character for our Mother Earth! For, of course, that is who
she is. The Greek stories speak her name openly: Gaia
and Rhea are confessed Earth-Mothers, Jocasta only a few
stages less so. One cannot apply moral disapproval to the
annual re-marriages of Mother Earth with the new Spring-
god; nor yet possibly to the impersonal and compulsory
marriages of the human queen in certain very primitive
stages of society. But later on, when life has become more

---

[4] Saxo, 88; *Ambales,* p. 119, *et ante,* ed. Gollancz.
[5] In the extant form of the *Ambales Saga* Amba's personal chastity
is preserved by a miracle; such an exception approves the rule.

self-conscious and sensitive, if once a poet or dramatist gets to thinking of the story, and tries to realise the position and feelings of this eternally traitorous wife, this eternally fostering and protecting mother, he cannot but feel in her that element of inward conflict which is the seed of great drama. She is torn between husband, lover, and son; and the avenging son, the mother-murderer, how is he torn?

English tragedy has followed the son. Yet Gerutha, Amba, Gertrude, Hermutrude, Gormflaith, Gaia, Rhea, Jocasta—there is tragedy in all of them, and it is in the main the same tragedy. Why does the most tragic of all of them, Clytemnestra, stand out of the picture?

We can only surmise. For one thing, Clytemnestra, like Gertrude in some stories, has both the normal experiences of the primitive king's wife. She both marries her husband's slayer and is slain by his avenger; and both parts of her story are equally emphasised, which is not the case with the other heroines. Their deaths are generally softened or ignored. But, apart from this, I am inclined to lay most stress on the deliberate tragic art of Aeschylus. He received perhaps from the tradition a Clytemnestra not much more articulate than Gerutha; but it needed only a turn of the wrist to change her from a silent and passive figure to a woman seething with tragic passions. If Saxo had been a man like Aeschylus, or if Shakespeare had made Gertrude his central figure instead of Hamlet, Clytemnestra would perhaps not have stood so much alone.

And what of Hamlet himself as a mythical character? I find, almost to my surprise, exactly the evidence I should have liked to find. Hamlet in Saxo is the son of Horvendillus or Ørvandil, an ancient Teutonic god connected with dawn and the spring. His great toe, for instance, is now the morning star. (It was frozen off; that is why it shines like ice.) His wife was Groa, who is said to be the Green Earth; he slew his enemy Collerus—Kollr the Hooded, or perhaps the Cold—in what Saxo calls "a sweet and spring-green spot" in a budding wood. He was slain by his brother and avenged by his son. The sort of conclusion towards which I, on my different lines, was groping had

already been drawn by several of the recognized Scandinavian authorities: notably by Professor Gollancz (who
especially calls attention to the part played by the hero's
mother), by Adolf Zinzow, and by Victor Rydberg. Professor Elton is more guarded, but his conclusions point,
on the whole, in the same direction. And the whole of the
evidence has been greatly strengthened since these words
were first published, by the appearance of Miss Phillpotts's
remarkable book, *The Elder Edda*.[6]

Thus, if these arguments are trustworthy, we finally run
the Hamlet-saga to earth in the same ground as the
Orestes-saga: in that prehistoric and world-wide ritual
battle of Summer and Winter, of Life and Death, which
has played so vast a part in the mental development of
the human race and especially, as Mr. E. K. Chambers
has shown us, in the history of mediaeval drama. Both
heroes have the notes of the winter about them rather
than summer, though both are on the side of right against
wrong. Hamlet is no joyous and triumphant slayer. He is
clad in black, he rages alone, he is the Bitter Fool who
must slay the King.[7]

IV

It seems a strange thing, this gradual shaping and reshap-
ing of a primitive folk-tale, in itself rather empty and
devoid of character, until it issues in a great tragedy which
shakes the world. Yet in Greek literature, I am sure, the
process is a common, almost a normal, one. Myth is
defined by a Greek writer as τὰ λεγόμενα ἐπὶ τοῖς δρωμέ-

---

[6] Gollancz, *Hamlet in Iceland*, Introduction; Zinzow, *Die Hamlet saga an und mit verwandten Sagen erläutert*, 1877; Rydberg, *Teutonic Mythology*, English tr. by Anderson, 1889; Elton, Appendix II to his translation of Saxo, edited by York Powell; Bertha S. Phillpotts, *The Elder Edda* (Cambridge, 1920). Rydberg goes so far as to identify Hamlet with Ørvandil's famous son Swipdag. "Two Dissertations on the Hamlet of Saxo and of Shakespeare" by R. G. Latham contain linguistic and mythological suggestions. I have not come across the works of Gubernatis mentioned in Ward, *English Dramatic Literature*, ii, 165.

[7] I believe this figure of the Fool to be capable of further analysis, but will not pursue the question here.

νοις, "the things said over a ritual act." For a certain
agricultural rite, let us suppose, you tore a cornsheaf in
pieces and scattered the grain; and to explain why you
did so, you told a myth. "There was once a young and
beautiful prince who was torn in pieces. . . ." Was he torn
by hounds or wild beasts in requital for some strange sin?
Or was he utterly innocent, torn by mad Thracian women
or devilish Titans, or the working of an unjust curse? As
the group in the village talks together, and begins to muse
and wonder and make unconscious poetry, the story gets
better and stronger and ends by being the tragedy of Pen-
theus or Hippolytus or Actaeon or Dionysus himself. Of
course, an element of history must be present also. Life was
not eventless in primitive times any more than it is now.
Things happened, and people were moved by them at the
time and talked about them afterwards. But to observe
exactly, and to remember and report exactly, is one of
the very latest and rarest of human accomplishments. By
the help of much written record and much mental train-
ing we can now manage it pretty well. But early man
was at the time too excited to observe, and afterwards too
indifferent to record, and always too much beset by fixed
forms of thought ever to take in concrete facts exactly.
(As a matter of fact, he did not even wish to do so; he
was aiming at something quite different.) In any case, the
facts, as they happened, were thrown swiftly into the same
crucible as the myths. Men did not research. They did not
keep names and dates distinct. They talked together and
wondered and followed their musings, till an historical
king of Ireland grew very like the old mythical Amloði, an
historical king of Mycenae took on part of the story of a
primitive Ouranos or Sky-King wedded to an Earth-
Mother. And in later times it was the myth that lived and
grew great rather than the history. The things that thrill
and amaze us in *Hamlet* or the *Agamemnon* are not any
historical particulars about mediaeval Elsinore or prehistoric Mycenae, but things belonging to the old stories
and the old magic rites, which stirred and thrilled our
forefathers five and six thousand years ago; set them dancing all night on the hills, tearing beasts and men in pieces,

and giving up their own bodies to a ghastly death, in hope thereby to keep the green world from dying and to be the saviours of their own people.

I am not trying to utter a paradox, or even to formulate a theory. I am not for a moment questioning or belittling the existence, or the overwhelming artistic value, of individual genius. I trust no one will suspect me of so doing. I am simply trying to understand a phenomenon which seems, before the days of the printed book and the widespread reading public, to have occurred quite normally and constantly in works of imaginative literature, and doubtless in some degree is occurring still.

What does our hypothesis imply? It seems to imply, first, a great unconscious solidarity and continuity, lasting from age to age, among all the children of the poets, both the makers and the callers-forth, both the artists and the audiences. In artistic creation, as in all the rest of life, the traditional element is far larger, the purely inventive element far smaller, than the unsophisticated man supposes.

Further, it implies that in the process of *traditio*—that is, of being handed on from generation to generation, constantly modified and expurgated, re-felt and re-thought —a subject sometimes shows a curious power of almost eternal durability. It can be vastly altered; it may seem utterly transformed. Yet some inherent quality still remains, and significant details are repeated quite unconsciously by generation after generation of poets. Nay, more. It seems to show that often there is latent in some primitive myth a wealth of detailed drama, waiting only for the dramatist of genius to discover it and draw it forth. Of course, we must not exaggerate this point. We must not say that *Hamlet* or the *Electra* is latent in the original ritual as a flower is latent in the seed. The seed, if it just gets its food, is bound to develop along a certain fixed line; the myth or ritual is not. It depends for its development on too many live people and too many changing and complex conditions. We can only say that some natural line of growth is there, and in the case before us it seems to have asserted itself both in large features and in fine details, in a rather extraordinary way. The two societies in

which the Hamlet and Orestes tragedies arose were very
dissimilar; the poets were quite different in character, and
quite independent; even the particular plays themselves
differed greatly in plot and setting and technique and most
other qualities; the only point of contact lies at their
common origin many thousand years ago, and yet the
fundamental identity still shows itself, almost unmistakable.

This conception may seem strange; but after all, in the
history of religion it is already a proved and accepted fact,
this "almost eternal durability" of primitive conceptions
and even primitive rites. Our hypothesis will imply that
what is already known to happen in religion may also
occur in imaginative drama.

If this is so, it seems only natural that those subjects,
or some of those subjects, which particularly stirred the
interest of primitive men, should still have an appeal to
certain very deep-rooted human instincts. I do not say
that they will always move us now; but, when they do,
they will tend to do so in ways which we recognize as
particularly profound and poetical. This comes in part
from their original quality; in part, I suspect, it depends
on mere repetition. We all know the emotional charm
possessed by famous and familiar words and names, even
to hearers who do not understand the words and know
little of the bearers of the names. I suspect that a charm
of that sort lies in these stories and situations, which are—
I cannot quite keep clear of metaphor—deeply implanted
in the memory of the race, stamped, as it were, upon our
physical organism. We have forgotten their faces and their
voices; we say that they are strange to us. Yet there is
that within us which leaps at the sight of them, a cry of
the blood which tells us we have known them always.

Of course, it is an essential part of the whole process of
Tradition that the mythical material is constantly casti-
gated and rekindled by comparison with real life. That is
where realism comes in, and literary skill and imagination.
An element drawn from real life was there, no doubt,
even at the beginning. The earliest myth-maker never invented in a vacuum. He really tried—in Aristotle's famous

phrase—to tell "the sort of thing that would happen"; only his conception of "what would happen" was, by our standards, a little wild. Then, as man's experience of life grew larger and calmer and more objective, his conception of "the sort of thing that would happen" grew more competent. It grew ever nearer to the truth of Nature, to its variety, to its reasonableness, to its infinite subtlety. And in the greatest ages of literature there seems to be, among other things, a power of preserving due proportion between these opposite elements—the expression of boundless primitive emotion and the subtle and delicate representation of life. In plays like *Hamlet* or the *Agamemnon* or the *Electra* we have certainly fine and flexible character-study, a varied and well-wrought story, a full command of the technical instruments of the poet and the dramatist; but we have also, I suspect, strange, unanalyzed vibration below the surface, an undercurrent of desires and fears and passions, long slumbering yet eternally familiar, which have for thousands of years lain near the root of our most intimate emotions and been wrought into the fabric of our most magical dreams. How far into past ages this stream may reach back, I dare not even surmise; but it seems as if the power of stirring it or moving with it were one of the last secrets of genius.

Editor's Note

Andrew Marvell first appeared in the Times Literary Supplement (1921), and was reprinted with two other essays by Eliot in the Hogarth Essays pamphlet Homage to John Dryden: Three Essays on Poetry of the Seventeenth Century (1924). From Selected Essays of T. S. Eliot, copyright 1932, 1936, 1950, by Harcourt, Brace and Company, Inc.

Thomas Stearns Eliot, O.M., was born in St. Louis, Missouri, in 1888, and educated at Harvard, the Sorbonne, and Oxford. He has lived in England since 1914, became a British subject in 1927, and received the Order of Merit in 1948. He founded and edited The Criterion from 1922 to 1939, and has been a director of Faber and Faber since 1923. Eliot has written on social and religious subjects in such books as The Idea of a Christian Society (1939), has published translations and editings, and has had a number of verse dramas produced. His poetry and plays are available in Complete Poems and Plays 1909–1950 (1952), and his criticism in Selected Essays, The Use of Poetry and the Use of Criticism (1933), and Essays Ancient and Modern (1936).

THREE

T. S. Eliot

Andrew Marvell

The tercentenary of the former member for Hull deserves not only the celebration proposed by that favoured borough, but a little serious reflection upon his writing. That is an act of piety, which is very different from the resurrection of a deceased reputation. Marvell has stood high for some years; his best poems are not very many, and not only must be well known, from the *Golden Treasury* and the *Oxford Book of English Verse*, but must also have been enjoyed by numerous readers. His grave needs neither rose nor rue nor laurel; there is no imaginary justice to be done; we may think about him, if there be need for thinking, for our own benefit, not his. To bring the poet back to life—the great, the perennial, task of criticism—is in this case to squeeze the drops of the essence of two or three poems; even confining ourselves to these, we may find some precious liquor unknown to the present age. Not to determine rank, but to isolate this quality, is the critical labour. The fact that of all Marvell's verse, which is itself not a great quantity, the really valuable part consists of a very few poems indicates that the unknown quality of which we speak is probably a literary rather than a personal quality; or, more truly, that it is a quality of a civilization, of a traditional habit of life. A poet like Donne, or like Baudelaire or Laforgue, may almost be considered the inventor of an attitude, a system of feeling or of morals. Donne is difficult to analyse: what appears at one time a curious personal point of view may at another time appear rather the precise concentration of a kind of feeling diffused in the air about him. Donne and his shroud,

the shroud and his motive for wearing it, are inseparable,
but they are not the same thing. The seventeenth century
sometimes seems for more than a moment to gather up
and to digest into its art all the experience of the human
mind which (from the same point of view) the later centuries seem to have been partly engaged in repudiating.
But Donne would have been an individual at any time and
place; Marvell's best verse is the product of European,
that is to say Latin, culture.

Out of that high style developed from Marlowe through
Jonson (for Shakespeare does not lend himself to these
genealogies) the seventeenth century separated two qualities: wit and magniloquence. Neither is as simple or as
apprehensible as its name seems to imply, and the two
are not in practice antithetical; both are conscious and
cultivated, and the mind which cultivates one may cultivate
the other. The actual poetry, of Marvell, of Cowley, of
Milton, and of others, is a blend in varying proportions.
And we must be on guard not to employ the terms with
too wide a comprehension; for like the other fluid terms
with which literary criticism deals, the meaning alters with
the age, and for precision we must rely to some degree
upon the literacy and good taste of the reader. The wit
of the Caroline poets is not the wit of Shakespeare, and
it is not the wit of Dryden, the great master of contempt,
or of Pope, the great master of hatred, or of Swift, the
great master of disgust. What is meant is some quality
which is common to the songs in *Comus* and Cowley's
Anacreontics and Marvell's *Horatian Ode*. It is more than
a technical accomplishment, or the vocabulary and syntax
of an epoch; it is, what we have designated tentatively as
wit, a tough reasonableness beneath the slight lyric grace.
You cannot find it in Shelley or Keats or Wordsworth; you
cannot find more than an echo of it in Landor; still less in
Tennyson or Browning; and among contemporaries Mr.
Yeats is an Irishman and Mr. Hardy is a modern English-
man—that is to say, Mr. Hardy is without it and Mr. Yeats
is outside of the tradition altogether. On the other hand, as
it certainly exists in Lafontaine, there is a large part of
it in Gautier. And of the magniloquence, the deliberate

exploitation of the possibilities of magnificence in language which Milton used and abused, there is also use and even abuse in the poetry of Baudelaire.

Wit is not a quality that we are accustomed to associate with "Puritan" literature, with Milton or with Marvell. But if so, we are at fault partly in our conception of wit and partly in our generalizations about the Puritans. And if the wit of Dryden or of Pope is not the only kind of wit in the language, the rest is not merely a little merriment or a little levity or a little impropriety or a little epigram. And, on the other hand, the sense in which a man like Marvell is a "Puritan" is restricted. The persons who opposed Charles I and the persons who supported the Commonweatlh were not all of the flock of Zeal-of-the-land Busy or the United Grand Junction Ebenezer Temperance Association. Many of them were gentlemen of the time who merely believed, with considerable show of reason, that government by a Parliament of gentlemen was better than government by a Stuart; though they were, to that extent, Liberal Practitioners, they could hardly foresee the tea-meeting and the Dissidence of Dissent. Being men of education and culture, even of travel, some of them were exposed to that spirit of the age which was coming to be the French spirit of the age. This spirit, curiously enough, was quite opposed to the tendencies latent or the forces active in Puritanism; the contest does great damage to the poetry of Milton; Marvell, an active servant of the public, but a lukewarm partisan, and a poet on a smaller scale, is far less injured by it. His line on the statue of Charles II, "It is such a King as no chisel can mend," may be set off against his criticism of the Great Rebellion: "Men . . . ought and might have trusted the King." Marvell, therefore, more a man of the century than a Puritan, speaks more clearly and unequivocally with the voice of his literary age than does Milton.

This voice speaks out uncommonly strong in the *Coy Mistress*. The theme is one of the great traditional commonplaces of European literature. It is the theme of *O mistress mine,* of *Gather ye rosebuds,* of *Go, lovely rose;* it is in the savage austerity of Lucretius and the intense

levity of Catullus. Where the wit of Marvell renews the
theme is in the variety and order of the images. In the
first of the three paragraphs Marvell plays with a fancy
which begins by pleasing and leads to astonishment.

> *Had we but world enough and time,*
> *This coyness, lady, were no crime,*
> *   . . . I would*
> *Love you ten years before the Flood,*
> *And you should, if you please, refuse*
> *Till the conversion of the Jews;*
> *My vegetable love should grow*
> *Vaster than empires and more slow. . . .*

We notice the high speed, the succession of concentrated
images, each magnifying the original fancy. When this
process has been carried to the end and summed up, the
poem turns suddenly with that surprise which has been one
of the most important means of poetic effect since Homer:

> *But at my back I always hear*
> *Time's wingèd chariot hurrying near,*
> *And yonder all before us lie*
> *Deserts of vast eternity.*

A whole civilization resides in these lines:

> *Pallida Mors aequo pulsat pede pauperum tabernas,*
> *Regumque turris. . . .*

And not only Horace but Catullus himself:

> *Nobis, cum semel occidit brevis lux,*
> *Nox est perpetua una dormienda.*

The verse of Marvell has not the grand reverberation of
Catullus's Latin; but the image of Marvell is certainly
more comprehensive and penetrates greater depths than
Horace's.

A modern poet, had he reached the height, would very
likely have closed on this moral reflection. But the three
strophes of Marvell's poem have something like a syllogistic
relation to each other. After a close approach to the
mood of Donne,

> *then worms shall try*
> *That long-preserved virginity . . .*
> *The grave's a fine and private place,*
> *But none, I think, do there embrace,*

the conclusion,

> *Let us roll all our strength and all*
> *Our sweetness up into one ball,*
> *And tear our pleasures with rough strife,*
> *Through the iron gates of life.*

It will hardly be denied that this poem contains wit; but it may not be evident that this wit forms the crescendo and diminuendo of a scale of great imaginative power. The wit is not only combined with, but fused into, the imagination. We can easily recognize a witty fancy in the successive images "my *vegetable* love," "till the conversion of the Jews"), but this fancy is not indulged, as it sometimes is by Cowley or Cleveland, for its own sake. It is structural decoration of a serious idea. In this it is superior to the fancy of *L'Allegro, Il Penseroso*, or the lighter and less successful poems of Keats. In fact, this alliance of levity and seriousness (by which the seriousness is intensified) is a characteristic of the sort of wit we are trying to identify. It is found in

> *Le squelette était invisible*
> *Au temps heureux de l'art païen!*

of Gautier, and in the *dandysme* of Baudelaire and Laforgue. It is in the poem of Catullus which has been quoted, and in the variation by Ben Jonson:

> *Cannot we deceive the eyes*
> *Of a few poor household spies?*
> *'Tis no sin love's fruits to steal,*
> *But that sweet sin to reveal,*
> *To be taken, to be seen,*
> *These have sins accounted been.*

It is in Propertius and Ovid. It is a quality of a sophisticated literature; a quality which expands in English literature just at the moment before the English mind altered; it is not a quality which we should expect Puritanism to encourage. When we come to Gray and Collins, the sophistication remains only in the language, and has disappeared from the feeling. Gray and Collins were masters, but they had lost that hold on human values, that firm grasp of human experience, which is a formidable achievement of the Elizabethan and Jacobean poets. This wisdom, cynical perhaps but untired (in Shakespeare, a terrifying clairvoyance), leads toward, and is only completed by, the religious comprehension; it leads to the point of the *Ainsi tout leur a craqué dans la main* of Bouvard and Pécuchet.

The difference between imagination and fancy, in view of this poetry of wit, is a very narrow one. Obviously, an image which is immediately and unintentionally ridiculous is merely a fancy. In the poem *Upon Appleton House,* Marvell falls in with one of these undesirable images, describing the attitude of the house toward its master:

> Yet thus the leaden house does sweat,
> And scarce endures the master great;
> But, where he comes, the swelling hall
> Stirs, and the square grows spherical;

which, whatever its intention, is more absurd than it was intended to be. Marvell also falls into the even commoner error of images which are overdeveloped or distracting; which support nothing but their own misshapen bodies:

> And now the salmon-fishers moist
> Their leathern boats begin to hoist;
> And, like Antipodes in shoes,
> Have shod their heads in their canoes.

Of this sort of image a choice collection may be found in Johnson's *Life of Cowley.* But the images in the *Coy Mistress* are not only witty, but satisfy the elucidation of Imagination given by Coleridge:

"This power . . . reveals itself in the balance or reconcilement of opposite or discordant qualities: of sameness, with difference; of the general, with the concrete; the idea with the image; the individual with the representative; the sense of novelty and freshness with old and familiar objects; a more than usual state of emotion with more than usual order; judgment ever awake and steady self-possession with enthusiasm and feeling profound or vehement. . . ."

Coleridge's statement applies also to the following verses, which are selected because of their similarity, and because they illustrate the marked caesura which Marvell often introduces in a short line:

> *The tawny mowers enter next,*
> *Who seem like Israelites to be*
> *Walking on foot through a green sea . . .*

> *And now the meadows fresher dyed,*
> *Whose grass, with moister colour dashed,*
> *Seems as green silks but newly washed . . .*

> *He hangs in shades the orange bright,*
> *Like golden lamps in a green night . . .*

> *Annihilating all that's made*
> *To a green thought in a green shade . . .*

> *Had it lived long, it would have been*
> *Lilies without, roses within.*

The whole poem, from which the last of these quotations is drawn (*The Nymph and the Fawn*), is built upon a very slight foundation, and we can imagine what some of our modern practitioners of slight themes would have made of it. But we need not descend to an invidious contemporaneity to point the difference. Here are six lines from *The Nymph and the Fawn*:

> *I have a garden of my own,*
> *But so with roses overgrown*
> *And lilies, that you would it guess*
> *To be a little wilderness;*
> *And all the spring-time of the year*
> *It only lovèd to be there.*

And here are five lines from *The Nymph's Song to Hylas* in the *Life and Death of Jason*, by William Morris:

> *I know a little garden close*
> *Set thick with lily and red rose.*
> *Where I would wander if I might*
> *From dewy dawn to dewy night,*
> *And have one with me wandering.*

So far the resemblance is more striking than the difference,
although we might just notice the vagueness of allusion
in the last line to some indefinite person, form, or phantom, compared with the more explicit reference of emotion to object which we should expect from Marvell. But
in the latter part of the poem Morris divaricates widely:

> *Yet tottering as I am, and weak,*
> *Still have I left a little breath*
> *To seek within the jaws of death*
> *An entrance to that happy place;*
> *To seek the unforgotten face*
> *Once seen, once kissed, once reft from me*
> *Anigh the murmuring of the sea.*

Here the resemblance, if there is any, is to the latter part
of *The Coy Mistress*. As for the difference, it could not
be more pronounced. The effect of Morris's charming
poem depends upon the mistiness of the feeling and the
vagueness of its object; the effect of Marvell's upon its
bright, hard precision. And this precision is not due to the
fact that Marvell is concerned with cruder or simpler or
more carnal emotions. The emotion of Morris is not more
refined or more spiritual; it is merely more vague: if any
one doubts whether the more refined or spiritual emotion
can be precise, he should study the treatment of the varieties of discarnate emotion in the *Paradiso*. A curious
result of the comparison of Morris's poem with Marvell's
is that the former, though it appears to be more serious,
is found to be the slighter; and Marvell's *Nymph and the
Fawn*, appearing more slight, is the more serious.

> *So weeps the wounded balsam; so*
> *The holy frankincense doth flow;*
> *The brotherless Heliades*
> *Melt in such amber tears as these.*

These verses have the suggestiveness of true poetry; and the verses of Morris, which are nothing if not an attempt to suggest, really suggest nothing; and we are inclined to infer that the suggestiveness is the aura around a bright clear centre, that you cannot have the aura alone. The day-dreamy feeling of Morris is essentially a slight thing; Marvell takes a slight affair, the feeling of a girl for her pet, and gives it a connexion with that inexhaustible and terrible nebula of emotion which surrounds all our exact and practical passions and mingles with them. Again, Marvell does this in a poem which, because of its formal pastoral machinery, may appear a trifling object:

CLORINDA.   *Near this, a fountain's liquid bell*
             Tinkles within the concave shell.

DAMON.   *Might a soul bathe there and be clean,*
             Or slake its drought?

where we find that a metaphor has suddenly rapt us to the image of spiritual purgation. There is here the element of *surprise,* as when Villon says:

> *Necessité faict gens mesprendre*
> *Et faim saillir le loup des boys,*

the surprise which Poe considered of the highest importance, and also the restraint and quietness of tone which make the surprise possible. And in the verses of Marvell which have been quoted there is the making the familiar strange, and the strange familiar, which Coleridge attributed to good poetry.

The effort to construct a dream-world, which alters English poetry so greatly in the nineteenth century, a dream-world utterly different from the visionary realities of the *Vita Nuova* or of the poetry of Dante's contemporaries, is a problem of which various explanations may no doubt be found; in any case, the result makes a poet of the nineteenth century, of the same size as Marvell, a more trivial and less serious figure. Marvell is no greater personality than William Morris, but he had something much more solid behind him: he had the vast and pene-

trating influence of Ben Jonson. Jonson never wrote anything purer than Marvell's *Horatian Ode;* this ode has that
same quality of wit which was diffused over the whole
Elizabethan product and concentrated in the work of
Jonson. And, as was said before, this wit which pervades
the poetry of Marvell is more Latin, more refined, than
anything that succeeded it. The great danger, as well as
the great interest and excitement, of English prose and
verse, compared with French, is that it permits and justi-
fies an exaggeration of particular qualities to the exclusion
of others. Dryden was great in wit, as Milton in magniloquence; but the former, by isolating this quality and
making it by itself into great poetry, and the latter, by
coming to dispense with it altogether, may perhaps have
injured the language. In Dryden wit becomes almost fun,
and thereby loses some contact with reality; becomes pure
fun, which French wit almost never is.

> *The midwife placed her hand on his thick skull,*
> *With this prophetic blessing: Be thou dull . . .*

> *A numerous host of dreaming saints succeed,*
> *Of the true old enthusiastic breed.*

This is audacious and splendid; it belongs to satire besides
which Marvell's *Satires* are random babbling, but it is
perhaps as exaggerated as:

> *Oft he seems to hide his face,*
> *But unexpectedly returns,*
> *And to his faithful champion hath in place*
> *Bore witness gloriously; whence Gaza mourns*
> *And all that band them to resist*
> *His uncontrollable intent.*

How oddly the sharp Dantesque phrase "whence Gaza
mourns" springs out from the brilliant contortions of Milton's sentence!

> *Who from his private gardens, where*
> *He lived reservèd and austere,*
> *(As if his highest plot*
> *To plant the bergamot)*

> *Could by industrious valour climb*
> *To ruin the great work of Time,*
> > *And cast the kingdoms old*
> > *Into another mold;*

> . . . . . .

> *The Pict no shelter now shall find*
> *Within his parti-coloured mind,*
> > *But, from this valour sad,*
> > *Shrink underneath the plaid:*

There is here an equipoise, a balance and proportion of
tones, which, while it cannot raise Marvell to the level
of Dryden or Milton, extorts an approval which these
poets do not receive from us, and bestows a pleasure at
least different in kind from any they can often give. It is
what makes Marvell a classic; or classic in a sense in
which Gray and Collins are not; for the latter, with all
their accredited purity, are comparatively poor in shades
of feeling to contrast and unite.

We are baffled in the attempt to translate the quality
indicated by the dim and antiquated term wit into the
equally unsatisfactory nomenclature of our own time. Even
Cowley is only able to define it by negatives:

> *Comely in thousand shapes appears;*
> > *Yonder we saw it plain; and here 'tis now,*
> > *Like spirits in a place, we know not how.*

It has passed out of our critical coinage altogether, and
no new term has been struck to replace it; the quality
seldom exists, and is never recognized.

> *In a true piece of Wit all things must be*
> > *Yet all things there agree;*
> *As in the Ark, join'd without force or strife,*
> *All creatures dwelt, all creatures that had life.*

> *Or as the primitive forms of all*
> > *(If we compare great things with small)*
> *Which, without discord or confusion, lie*
> *In that strange mirror of the Deity.*

So far Cowley has spoken well. But if we are to attempt
even no more than Cowley, we, placed in a retrospective
attitude, must risk much more than anxious generalizations.
With our eye still on Marvell, we can say that wit is not
erudition; it is sometimes stifled by erudition, as in much
of Milton. It is not cynicism, though it has a kind of
toughness which may be confused with cynicism by the
tender-minded. It is confused with erudition because it
belongs to an educated mind, rich in generations of experience; and it is confused with cynicism because it implies a constant inspection and criticism of experience. It
involves, probably, a recognition, implicit in the expression of every experience, of other kinds of experience
which are possible, which we find as clearly in the greatest as in poets like Marvell. Such a general statement may
seem to take us a long way from *The Nymph and the
Fawn,* or even from the *Horatian Ode;* but it is perhaps
justified by the desire to account for that precise taste of
Marvell's which finds for him the proper degree of seriousness for every subject which he treats. His errors of taste,
when he trespasses, are not sins against this virtue; they
are conceits, distended metaphors and similes, but they
never consist in taking a subject too seriously or too
lightly. This virtue of wit is not a peculiar quality of
minor poets, or of the minor poets of one age or of one
school; it is an intellectual quality which perhaps only
becomes noticeable by itself, in the work of lesser poets.
Furthermore, it is absent from the work of Wordsworth,
Shelley, and Keats, on whose poetry nineteenth-century
criticism has unconsciously been based. To the best of
their poetry wit is irrelevant:

> *Art thou pale for weariness*
> *Of climbing heaven and gazing on the earth,*
> *Wandering companionless*
> *Among the stars that have a different birth,*
> *And ever changing, like a joyless eye,*
> *That finds no object worth its constancy?*

We should find it difficult to draw any useful comparison
between these lines of Shelley and anything by Marvell.

But later poets, who would have been the better for Marvell's quality, were without it; even Browning seems oddly immature, in some way, beside Marvell. And nowadays we find occasionally good irony, or satire, which lack wit's internal equilibrium, because their voices are essentially protests against some outside sentimentality or stupidity; or we find serious poets who are afraid of acquiring wit, lest they lose intensity. The quality which Marvell had, this modest and certainly impersonal virtue —whether we call it wit or reason, or even urbanity—we have patently failed to define. By whatever name we call it, and however we define that name, it is something precious and needed and apparently extinct; it is what should preserve the reputation of Marvell. *C'était une belle âme, comme on ne fait plus à Londres.*

Editor's Note

Charlotte and Emily Brontë first appeared in *The Yale Review,* July 1925, and was reprinted in Read's *Reason and Romanticism* (1926) and *Collected Essays in Literary Criticism* (1938). Used here by permission of the author.

Sir Herbert Read was born in Kirbymoorside, Yorkshire, England, in 1893, and educated at the University of Leeds. He has been employed at the Victoria and Albert Museum, taught at the universities of Edinburgh and Liverpool, and edited *The Burlington Magazine.* He was knighted in 1953. Sir Herbert has written extensively on art, politics, and their interrelation in such books as *Art and Society* (1936), *Poetry and Anarchism* (1938), and *The Grass Roots of Art* (1947). He has published fiction, biography, autobiography, essays, and a number of volumes of verse represented in *Collected Poems* (1946). His literary criticism is available in *Collected Essays* and *The True Voice of Feeling* (1953).

FOUR

Herbert Read

Charlotte and Emily Brontë

Heredity is a factor which we cannot neglect in considering the course of any human life, but in ascribing any importance to it, we should be careful to distinguish rather sharply between intelligence or mental development, which is the product of natural selection in the race and of education in the individual, and what for want of another word we must call genius, which, when it is of any value, is intelligence directed into personal and wayward channels. It is merely the instrument of genius—the brain considered as a muscle—that is susceptible to hereditary influences. The rest is the product of environment and chance —particularly of the psychological events introduced into life by human relationships.

When we have to reckon with any degree of historical remoteness, heredity becomes a very obscure influence, and the observed facts, in a case like that of the Brontë family, are far too unreliable and unsystematic to be of much use. We see two human strains, themselves the products of incalculable forces, which unite and give issue to genius. The process, one can persist in believing, is as natural as a chemical combination, but it is impossible to reduce it to an equation. We can at the best only point to tendencies and characteristics in the parent stock and hazard that these are some of the elements responsible— and these are but vague, obvious features which it would be difficult to use with any scientific precision.

In the case of the Brontës we have, on the one side, a stock of somewhat barbarous origin, culminating in a man of determination and capability, a man who "early gave

tokens of extraordinary quickness and intelligence." Patrick
Brontë had opened a public school at the age of sixteen,
and at the age of twenty-five was still ambitious enough
to proceed to Cambridge, where he took his degree after
four years' study. Mrs. Gaskell's rather picturesque description of his passionate nature has been discredited in
some of its details, but enough authentic evidence remains
to evoke for us a grim puritanical mask, expressing, even
while it repressed, the fires beneath. Mrs. Brontë brought
characteristics which were of a more ordinary nature,
though perhaps no less essential to the result. She was
intelligent, placid, and ailing. Her delicate constitution
passed to her children, and perhaps this factor, more than
any other, determined their neurotic tendency. A neurosis,
however, generally needs more than ill health for its in-
ducement: it needs a psychic shock of some kind, and
perhaps the mother provided this also by her early death
in 1821, when Charlotte was but five and Emily three
years old. The strong instinctive link between mother and
child is never thus abruptly broken without unseen com-
pensations and reverberations. The enormous body of
childish writings still existing in Charlotte's case, but until
recently withheld for its lack of literary qualities, may
conceivably be of great significance from this point of view.
I will merely suggest that we have in Charlotte's seemingly
endless fictive evocations of the Duke of Wellington a
phantasy of a kind made familiar to us by the researches
of psycho-analysts. "Charlotte's little stories," writes Mr.
Shorter, "commence in her thirteenth year, and go on
until she is twenty-three. From thirteen to eighteen she
would seem to have had one absorbing hero—the Duke
of Wellington. Whether the stories be fairy tales or dramas
of modern life, they all alike introduce the Marquis of
Douro." [1] Interpretations of such a phantasy as this might
differ: Adler would see in it an unconscious attempt on the
part of the neurotic weakling to free herself from a feeling
of inferiority[2] by the creation of a compensating ideal of

---

[1] Clement Shorter: *The Brontës, Life and Letters* (1908), p. 72.
[2] There are many direct betrayals in Charlotte's correspondence of
this deeply-felt sense of inferiority. The following passage from the

superiority; Jung would find the unconscious origin of such a hero phantasy quite simply in a longing for the lost mother, whereas Freud would probably treat it as the sublimation of a repressed love for the father. But whatever interpretation is adopted, a sense of inferiority, of incompleteness, is seen as the essential character of the neurosis underlying the phantasy.

In the case of Emily the same causes produced a "masculine protest" of a more complex kind, showing, indeed, the typical features of what I think we must, with the psycho-analyst, regard as some kind of psychical hermaphroditism. The outward expression of this state was evident enough. In her childhood the villagers thought her more like a boy than a girl. "She should have been a man: a great navigator!" cried M. Heger, despite his horror of her intractability. Charlotte refers to "a certain harshness in her powerful and peculiar character." "Stronger than a man, simpler than a child, her nature stood alone." Yet Emily was not given to expressing herself by outward speech or action; she was sombre and reserved—was, in fact, of a shy, introspective cast; from which clue the psychologist will realize how much deeper and more powerful must have been the masculine assumptions of her mind. These found their fit expression, in due course, in *Wuthering Heights,* whose very peculiar merits show that mingling of the strong and the sweet which some critics make the criterion of all great works of the imagination, and which, in her case, was but the direct expression of her nature.

We might pass further, in illustration of our point, to the cases of Anne and Branwell. The former as an example of religious melancholy, and the latter as an example of disintegrated personality, offer familiar characteristics: they are true to type. But consideration of them is much less important, because it does not bear on a creative artist of much significance. It is sufficient to observe that

reminiscences of her school friend, Mary Taylor, is significant: "She always showed physical feebleness in everything. She ate no animal food at school. It was about this time I told her she was very ugly. Some years afterwards I told her I thought I had been very impertinent. She replied: "You did me a great deal of good, Polly, so don't repent of it.'"

though all four cases present very diverse symptoms, they
are all traceable to the one cause: the early rupture of the
maternal bond of affection and protection, the intolerance
of a stern, impassive father, the formation of inferiority
complexes in the children, and the consequent compensa-
tions by phantasy.

What it is now necessary to emphasize strongly, in concluding this psychological excursus, is that art is a triumph
over neurosis; that though it originates in a neurotic tendency, it is a coming-out-against this tendency; and that in
the case of the three sisters the sublimation was achieved.
Their art is not neurotic in kind; no art is. It is only when
we search for causes and origins (as we have a perfect
right to do) that we discover the neurosis; in the final
effect, according to the measure of its success, all is health
and harmony.

In dealing with these psychological questions we have,
I think, emphasized the kind of environment that leaves
the deepest mark on the formation of character and
genius. But we are left with the environment of place, of
locality. This influence is most in question in the case of
Emily, that "nursling of the moors," and indeed her poems
show, I think, the most intense rendering of the embodied
presence of nature that anywhere exists in English literature.

> *The earth that wakes* one *human heart to feeling*
> *Can centre both the worlds of Heaven and Hell.*

In these two lines she reaches a climax in her philosophy
of nature, and shows a depth of emotional perception
which was not exceeded even by Wordsworth.

But the immediate influence of natural scenes differs
from this general evocation of the spirit of nature. There
is about the moors of Yorkshire, where they yet remain,
a quality that works strongly on the senses. Their sparse-
ness and loneliness drive you to an intimacy with whatever life does exist there; a small thing like the scent of
bog-myrtle can kindle a keen emotion. There is a severity
in the unrelieved reach of gradual hill country; the eye
drifts into distant prospects, seeks the sky-line that is not

a line, but a subtle merging of tones; the human mind *is* perhaps heard more distinctly in this inorganic stillness— only when, however, it has learned to think, and to express its thoughts. The moors, like any other local endowment, are merely material for observation and perception, and if into their confines there happens to enter a mind of exceptional dimensions, this mind will use its environment to some purpose. Such was the case with Emily Brontë. Charlotte, writing that eloquent and penetrating Preface to the second edition of *Wuthering Heights,* expresses this fact with all her rhetorical force:

"*Wuthering Heights* was hewn in a wild workshop, with simple tools, out of homely materials. The statuary found a granite block on a solitary moor; gazing thereon, he saw how from the crag might be elicited a head, savage, swart, sinister; a form moulded with at least one element of grandeur—power. He wrought with a rude chisel, and from no model but the vision of his meditations."

We should note how objective the attitude of the artist is made. A more facile conception would have imbued the statuary with the moor's savage elements, and made the image but the reflection of an entranced imagination. But the vision of her meditations was the product of an applied mind; and that this fixed itself mainly on a rustic scene was but the result of chance limitations—limitations, however, which we do not regret, since they drove that vision so deeply into the heart of the subject.

A far more effective factor, both in the case of Emily and of Charlotte, was what we might call quite simply education, but which resolves, upon deeper analysis, into the personal influence of Constantin Heger. In Charlotte's case it seems that this aggressive intellect—masculine, fiery, compact—came opportunely to occupy the stronghold of the unconscious evacuated by the Duke of Wellington, whose lustre had no doubt waned with the growth of experience and intelligence. From the psychological point of view, that is all that need be said of a personal relationship which has been the subject of much speculation; though the intense nature that the hero worship was to assume, before the end of Charlotte's stay in Brussels, was, as I shall make out later, a determining experience in her life.

The immediate importance of this contact was its purely literary consequences. Charlotte and Emily learned the meaning of style—and style not in the English sense of picturesqueness, but in the French sense of clarity and brevity. Spirits that were romantic, or at any rate Celtic, submitted to the discipline of a strictly Latin mind—Latin in its scepticism, its dryness, and its dignity. Mrs. Gaskell printed a *devoir* of Charlotte's corrected by M. Heger, where the process may be seen in action. In the simple and halting French then at Charlotte's command we already experience the peculiar force and vividness of her impressions; but the corrections and marginal comments of M. Heger are the precepts, not of a schoolmaster, but of a master of the art of writing. "He told me," relates Mrs. Gaskell, "that one day this summer [when the Brontës had been for about four months receiving instruction from him] he read to them Victor Hugo's celebrated portrait of Mirabeau, 'mais, dans ma leçon je me bornais à ce qui concerne *Mirabeau Orateur.* C'est après l'analyse de ce morçeau, considéré surtout de point de vue du fond, de la disposition, de ce qu'on pourrait appeler *la charpente* qu' ont été faits les deux portraits que je vous donne.' He went on to say that he had pointed out to them the fault in Victor Hugo's style as being exaggeration in conception, and, at the same time, he had made them notice the extreme beauty of his 'nuances' of expression. They were then dismissed to choose the subject of a similar kind of portrait. This selection M. Heger always left to them; for 'it is necessary,' he observed, 'before sitting down to write on a subject, to have thoughts and feelings about it, I cannot tell on what subject your heart and mind have been excited. I must leave that to you.' "

When Charlotte finally left the Heger institute at Brussels, some eighteen months after the composition of the *devoir* referred to, the intense desire to write, which had been hers since childhood, assumed a more definite urgency. It was not merely that she had perfected, under the Professor's care, the methods of self-expression; she had also endured a nervous crisis of an indefinite nature but of a deep effect. She herself (in a letter to Miss Wooler in 1846) described her state as *hypochondria:* "I endured it but a year and assuredly I can never forget the concentrated anguish of certain insufferable moments, and the heavy gloom of many long hours, besides the preternatural horrors which seemed to clothe existence and nature, and which made life a continual walking nightmare. Under such circumstances the morbid nerves can know neither peace nor enjoyment; whatever touches pierces them: sensation for them is suffering." Mrs. Gaskell pictures some of the circumstances of this period. Charlotte had been left during the *grandes vacances* in the great deserted pensionnat, with only one teacher for a companion. "This teacher, a Frenchwoman, had always been uncongenial to her; but, left to each other's sole companionship, Charlotte soon discovered that her associate was more profligate, more steeped in a kind of cold, systematic sensuality, than she had before imagined it possible for a human being to be; and her whole nature revolted from this woman's society. A low nervous fever was gaining upon Miss Brontë. She had never been a good sleeper, but now she could not sleep at all. Whatever had been disagreeable, or obnoxious, to her during the day, was presented when it was over with exaggerated vividness to her disordered fancy. . . . In the daytime, driven abroad by loathing of her companion and by the weak restlessness of fever, she tried to walk herself into such a state of bodily fatigue as would induce sleep. . . . The shades of evening made her retrace her footsteps— sick for want of food, but not hungry; fatigued with long continued exercise—yet restless still, and doomed to another weary, haunted night of sleeplessness." During one such anguished progress, she found herself before a confessional in Ste. Gudule's, and, her strong Protestant prejudices succumbing to what she calls "an odd whim," she abandoned herself to that psychopathic consolation. "I was determined to confess," she writes to Emily. "I actually did confess—a real confession." The vivid use she made of the incident, in *Villette,* is only the most obvious record of

this spiritual climax; the complete pathological phase
(where sensation, as she says, was suffering) constituted,
I think, the fundamental experience upon which she built
her whole conception of imaginative reality.[3]

I have here used an epithet, "imaginative," which it is
necessary to use at all times with care and generally to
avoid. It is one of those epithets that normally cloak a
lack of thought or a failure of analysis. Nevertheless, I
think it will be found, when reduced to its definite limits,
to connote a certain process in the mind of the creative
writer for which no other more suitable term can be used.
The merely descriptive distinction between the fancy and
the imagination, which has so long served in the sphere
of literary criticism, is no longer adequate. It is not based
on any corresponding psychological distinction; and even
when the elements of fancy are excluded, we are left with
no clear boundaries within which we can confine the activities of the imagination. It is merely a distinction, as
Pater pointed out, between degrees of intensity. It would
not, however, serve any useful purpose to import into
literary criticism the purely technical conception of the
imagination current in the old psychology, however precise such a use might be. We merely want a more definite
understanding of the way in which ideas and images are
associated in that abnormal manner we term imaginative.
It was in the capture of such states of excitement that
Wordsworth quite rightly saw the function of the poet.
And although in the case of fiction the plane of conception
is different, being more relative, less absolute—a detailed
construction of dramatic events rather than a generalized

---

[3] In considering this period of her life, though I ignore, I do not
deny what the four letters from Charlotte to Constantin Heger, published by *The Times* in 1913, are a sufficient proof of: the importance
of her feelings for Professor Heger in the causation of this pathological
state. There can be no question of the existence, in her mind, of an
appalling conflict between the strength of her emotion and the considerations—social, moral, and religious—which caused her to hide,
even from herself, the nature of this emotion. The result was a decided
'complex,' and I should be disposed to agree with a psychologist who
identified her whole neurotic condition at this period with such a
specific repression. I do not consider the cause of her state too closely
because all I am concerned with is its effect upon her creative mind.

expression of states of consciousness or thought—nevertheless, the psychological mechanism is the same. True
imagination is a kind of logic; it is the capacity to deduce
from the nature of an experienced reality, the nature of
other unexperienced realities. Upon the depth and totality
of the original experience will depend the reach and
validity of the imaginative process. If the process is kept
to a quasi-logical rigidity, it may be observed that merely
one kind of experience, sufficiently realized, will suffice for
an almost unlimited progression of imaginative analogies:
the one experience will be ballast enough to carry the
author through any fictive evocation of feelings and actions. The case of Dostoevsky is very illustrative of this
truth; and the life of Charlotte Brontë is well worth consideration precisely because the process, the logic, is there
seen so uncontaminated by subsidiary influences.

Experience alone does not, of course, make the poet or
novelist; it merely qualifies him. It must be united with a
previous disposition to create an imaginary world, the
origin of which, as I have suggested, is to be found in
psychological factors at work during infancy and adoles-
cence. Charlotte early had "the desire (almost amounting
to illness) of expressing herself in some way,—writing or
drawing." [4] At school she developed a talent, under the
guise of play, of "making things out." "This habit," one of
her school friends relates, "of 'making out' interests for
themselves that most children get who have none in actual
life, was very strong in her. The whole family used to
'make out' histories, and invent characters and events. I
told her sometimes they were like growing potatoes in a
cellar. She said, sadly, 'Yes! I know we are!' " The greater
bulk of the unpublished Brontë manuscripts seems to consist of an elaborate "cycle" of stories and poems, written
over a long period of years and concerned with the politics
and chivalry of a kingdom imagined in every detail. To
revert to the old antithesis, these were works of idle fancy;
but when bleak disillusionment was added to the already
sufficiently bleak existence of these children, when expres-

[4] Mrs. Gaskell's account of conversations with Charlotte. See *Life*,
chap. xxvii.

sion became a more serious necessity as an escape from
emotional agitations too strong to be repressed with impunity, then the mere mechanism of literary expression
was ready at their command.

This is to put the matter on its deterministic level; it is
perhaps of more profit to note the conscious reactions of
Charlotte to these emotional and mental transitions. There
are two points to notice: her theory of the relation of experience to imagination; and the evolution, at her hands,
of the analytic method in fiction. The best expression of
the first point was elicited during Charlotte's brief correspondence with G. H. Lewes—a literary encounter very
characteristic of the period and about which an effect of
exquisite comedy lurks. On 6th November 1847 she wrote
in reply to a friendly letter of Lewes's, dictated by his
enthusiasm for *Jane Eyre:* "You advise me, too, not to
stray far from the ground of experience, as I become weak
when I enter the region of fiction, and you say, 'real experience is perennially interesting, and to all men.' I feel
that this is also true; but, dear sir, is not the real experience of each individual very limited? And if a writer dwells
upon that solely or principally, is he not in danger of re-
peating himself, and also of becoming an egotist? Then,
too, imagination is a strong, restless faculty, which claims
to be heard and exercised: are we to be quite deaf to her
cry, and insensate to her struggles? When she shows us
bright pictures, are we never to look at them, and try to
reproduce them? And when she is eloquent, and speaks
rapidly and urgently in our ear, are we not to write to her
dictation?"

In reading this passage we must remember that Charlotte
writes conscious of what she could but regard as a salutary
lesson in the strategy of authorship: this was the complete
failure of her first novel, *The Professor,* in which, as Mrs.
Gaskell says, "she went to the extreme of reality, depicting
characters as they had shown themselves to her in actual
life." And in the letter to Lewes already quoted, Charlotte
herself confessed: "When I first began to write, so im-
pressed was I with the truth of the principles you advocate,
that I determined to take Nature and Truth as my sole

guides, and to follow their very footprints; I restrained imagination, eschewed romance, repressed excitement; over-bright colouring, too, I avoided, and sought to produce something which should be soft, grave, and true." But the publishers would have none of it, and the convenient theory of art for art's sake not being yet a part of the literary consciousness, she had decided to modify her virtuous course. She abandoned the mere transcript of experience and adopted the imaginative process I have tried to define.[5] It is here that we must realize the essential strength of her character and genius; a weaker writer would have had recourse to the less intense forms of imaginative activity; but Charlotte, driven, perhaps, by subconscious forces, determined, in her own phrase, to be "her own woman." She determined to see justly rather than to feel kindly; and when she was almost agonized by the suggestion, emanating from the *Quarterly,* but eagerly repeated even by the kind of people she herself thought nice, that *Jane Eyre* was a "wicked book," even then she had the courage of her magnificent retort: "I am resolved not to write otherwise. *I shall bend as my powers tend."*

Her powers resided in her intuitive logic, though she rather tended to mask the incidence of her faculty. "We only suffer reality to *suggest,* never to *dictate,"* she writes to her old school friend; and some years later, with *Villette* fresh from her pen, she even went so far as to enunciate this slightly insincere maxim: "I hold that a work of fiction ought to be a work of creation: that the *real* should be sparingly introduced in pages dedicated to the *ideal."* This hardly tallies with her own criticism of *Villette:* "I greatly

[5] It is interesting to note her own subsequent and detached opinion of the qualities which, nevertheless, did result from her first method. In a letter to W. S. Williams dated 14th December 1847, she writes: "A few days since I looked over *The Professor.* I found the beginning very feeble, the whole narrative deficient in incident and in general attractiveness. Yet the middle and latter portion of the work, all that relates to Brussels, the Belgian school, etc., is as good as I can write; it contains more pith, more substance, more reality, in my judgement, than much of *Jane Eyre.* It gives, I think, a new view of a grade, an occupation, and a class of characters—all very commonplace, very insignificant in themselves, but not more so than the materials composing that portion of *Jane Eyre* which seems to please most generally."

apprehend that the weakest character in the book is the one I aimed at making the most beautiful; and, if this be the case, the fault lies in its wanting the germ of the *real*—in its being purely imaginary." We have in this latter statement, self-analysed and self-confessed, the whole secret of her strength. Her practice of fiction resolves always into a nucleus of experience and the growth, from this nucleus, of an imaginative organism "given off," as in nature, cell by cell, with inexorable continuity.

Combined with this process, a part of its mechanism, was the gift of analysis. Some years before she began to write, even before her education at Brussels, she was aware of her capabilities in this direction. She warned a rejected suitor, who wished to become her "friend," that "it has always been my habit to study the character of those amongst whom I chance to be thrown. . . . As for me, you do not know me: I am not the serious, grave, cool-headed individual you would suppose: you would think me romantic and eccentric; you would say I was satirical and severe." The two faculties of her writing are clearly foreshadowed here: imagination and analysis. There is no need to enlarge upon this second quality; it is so obviously her distinction. The consistency of its exercise—as, for example, in the character of Madame Beck—is perhaps for her date a matter for wonder. She herself remarks of Balzac: "By-and-by I seemed to enter into the mystery of his craft, and to discover, with delight, where his force lay: is it not in the analysis of motive, and in a subtle perception of the most obscure and secret workings of the mind?" But at the time of her first introduction to Balzac's work, her own gift was already fully formed. I find no evidence anywhere that she knew the work of Stendhal, or the solitary masterpiece of Benjamin Constant; but she introduced into English literature the very qualities of psychological observation and analysis by which these writers had instituted a new epoch in the literature of France.

The influence she exercised on the development of the English novel was more profound than is often acknowl-

edged: it is *Villette,* more than any work of Thackeray or
George Eliot, that we must recognize as the pioneer of an
extension of the province and function of the novelist's
art only completely worked into the tradition of the English novel by Meredith and Henry James. To her contemporaries this revolutionary element in her work was
quite evident, and though they did not stop to consider its
real nature, they disliked it strongly because it was strange.
Open-minded critics of the stamp of Lewes and Thackeray
were willing to acknowledge the power and originality of
her art, but the more average minds of the time experienced a sense of shock, deepening to outrage when it
gradually became evident that the mysterious Currer Bell
belonged to the gentler sex. The particular charge, first
raised against *Jane Eyre,* but repeated in the case of
Shirley, was one of "coarseness." What her accusers meant
by their term cannot be very vivid to our modern consciousness: all they meant would, I think, easily be included in our concept "realism." But even Mrs. Gaskell,
who by no means shared all the prudery of her age,
thought it necessary to apologize for this lapse on the part
of her heroine; and did so in these curious sentences:

"I do not deny for myself the existence of coarseness
here and there in her works, otherwise so entirely noble.
I only ask those who read them to consider her life,—
which has been openly laid bare before them,—and to say
how it could be otherwise. She saw few men; and among
these few were one or two with whom she had been ac-
quainted since early childhood,—who had shown her much
friendliness and kindness,—through whose family she had
received many pleasures,—for whose intellect she had a
great respect,—but who talked before her, if not to her,
with as little reticence as Rochester talked to Jane Eyre.
Take this in connection with her poor brother's sad life,
and the outspoken people among whom she lived,—remember her strong feeling of the duty of representing life
as it really is, not as it ought to be,—and then do her
justice for all that she was, and all that she would have
been (had God spared her), rather than censure her be-

cause circumstances forced her to touch pitch, as it were, and by it her hand was for a moment defiled." (*Life,* ch. xxvi.)

Charlotte herself could not comprehend the charge; and her unconsciousness of the very existence of what her critics so plainly realized, brings before us in all its uniqueness the amazing quality of *innocence* which distinguishes, not only her own work, but that of her sisters also. It is because the art was so innocent that it is so real. One can only account for the phenomenon by the unparalleled isolation of their lives. Though from an early age they devoured every scrap of literature that came within their reach, it is doubtful if anything of a directly inspiring kind ever came their way before Charlotte's and Emily's departure for Brussels. At Haworth they seem to have been confined to a diet of newspapers, sermons, and the Bible; and at Brussels, though in the matter of style and composition their reading there had incalculable influence, yet it seems certain that, with the possible exception of Hoffmann and Rousseau, it did not include anything that could form a model for their own efforts. At any rate, whatever the explanation, it is certain that when the three sisters solemnly and in unison sat down to compose their first serious novels, they did so without any prepossessions. They are the least influenced and most original geniuses in the whole history of the English novel. What Charlotte in her Introduction to *Wuthering Heights* wrote of the others, was equally true of herself: "Neither Ellis nor Acton was learned: they had no thoughts of filling their pitchers at the well-spring of other minds; they always wrote from the impulse of nature, the dictates of intuition, and from such stores of observation as their limited experience had enabled them to amass."

It is this quality of innocence that gives to *Wuthering Heights* its terrible and unique intensity. If I have written of Charlotte to the neglect of Emily, it is not that for one moment I make the mistake of attaching more importance to her. It is merely that in the case of Charlotte the evidence is so much more ample. The psychology of Emily is at once less complex and more profoundly hidden. She is one of the strangest geniuses in our literature, and her kinship is with Baudelaire and Poe. It is not merely that her imagination traverses the same sombre shadows, but also like these two anguished minds, she is for ever perplexed by the problem of evil—"conquered good and conquering ill." Her absorption in metaphysical problems has no parallel in the poetry of her age, and in her "Last Lines" rises to an intensity of emotional thought not surpassed in the whole range of English literature. Yet this same mind was capable of the purest lyrical utterance—in which, however, the sense of mortality seems to linger:

> *Fall, leaves, fall; die, flowers, away;*
> *Lengthen night, and shorten day!*
> *Every leaf speaks bliss to me,*
> *Fluttering from the autumn tree.*

> *I shall smile when wreaths of snow*
> *Blossom where the rose should grow;*
> *I shall sing when night's decay*
> *Ushers in a drearier day.*

Emily Brontë's poetry, which is at once explicit and profound, with sense finely annealed to cadence, is the most essential poetry ever written by a woman in the English tongue. Her mind, far more daring than Charlotte's, soared above particular creeds and attained in a few momentary manifestations those universal forms of thought common only to minds of the first order. Her best poems suffer, at present, by being bound up with much that is juvenile and occasional in kind. *Wuthering Heights* remains, the towering rock of Charlotte's metaphor, extremely definite, completely achieved, and of an amazing unity of tone.

We are left with one other element, common to Emily and Charlotte, which needs a word of notice. A certain lack of reticence had shocked the ruck of their Victorian critics; a smaller and a rarer band were disturbed by the evident rapture. It fell to Harriet Martineau, economist, moralist, agnostic, and a very typical representative of her age, to bring this criticism to a head. Despite a friendship she had formed for Charlotte, she had felt bound to air

her misgivings in *The Daily News,* and in a review of
Villette had insisted that Charlotte made love too general
and too absorbing a factor in women's lives, protesting
against the assumption that "events and characters are to
be regarded through the medium of one passion only."
Charlotte demurred, but Miss Martineau, indomitable and
pitiless, wrote to her: "I do not like the love, either the
kind or the degree of it; and its prevalence in the book
and effect on the action of it, help to explain the passages
in the reviews which you consulted me about, and seem
to afford *some* foundation for the criticisms they offered."
Charlotte retired abashed; she had but followed "the impulses of nature and the dictates of intuition." And about
this very book she had written to her publisher: "Unless I
am mistaken, the emotion of the book will be found to be
kept throughout in tolerable subjection." Emotion in subjection—that is the very definition of art! And because
Miss Martineau did not realize this, she has become a
curious paleolithic dummy, an Aunt Sally ready for our
modern ironists, whilst Charlotte still lives in her books
with all the directness of a real personality.

But it is not Miss Martineau who was destined to stand
as antitype to the Brontës: a subtler and finer antagonist
had been in the field for some time. It speaks a good deal
for Charlotte's critical perception that she realized the implications of Miss Austen's talent as soon as she became
aware of it, rather late in her life, and, though only in the
privacy of her correspondence with her publisher, she then
defined the limitations of that talent in terms which still
remain unanswerable. In a letter written in 1850 she says:
"She does her business of delineating the surface of the
lives of genteel English people curiously well. There is a
Chinese fidelity, a miniature delicacy in the painting. She
ruffles her reader by nothing vehement, disturbs him by
nothing profound. The passions are perfectly unknown to
her; she rejects even a speaking acquaintance with that
stormy sisterhood. Even to the feelings she vouchsafes no
more than an occasional graceful but distant recognition
—too frequent converse with them would ruffle the smooth
elegance of her progress. Her business is not half so much

with the human heart as with the human eyes, mouth, hands, and feet. What sees keenly, speaks aptly, moves flexibly, it suits her to study; but what throbs fast and full, though hidden, what the blood rushes through, what is the unseen seat of life and the sentient target of death—this Miss Austen ignores." The justice of that analysis remains, to confront the present sophisticated rage for Jane Austen. But it also remains the statement of an extreme position, the weakness of which would have been exceedingly patent to the precise sensibility of the author of *Pride and Prejudice*. If she had lived long enough she might have criticized *Jane Eyre* in terms of almost exact contradiction. The psychologist does not venture to take sides in such a pitched battle, but resorts to his theory of types, and sees here the dry bones of his structure take on perfect flesh. It would be difficult to discover a more exact illustration of the main distinction he draws between faculties directed inwards, to the observation of feeling, and faculties directed outwards, to the observation of external things. The psychologist must halt at this distinction, unless he suggests, as a scientific ideal, some harmony or balance of these tendencies. But the critic must pursue the matter to a judgement. It will not, for that purpose, suffice to identify the ordered conception of objective facts with the classical spirit, or the research of passion with the romantic spirit —though it is tempting in this case to think of Jane Austen, as a typical (though rare, because feminine) embodiment of classicism, and Pater seized on *Wuthering Heights,* in preference to any work of Scott's, as the "really characteristic fruit" of the spirit of romanticism. That only proves once more the inadequacy of these outworn shibboleths, since from another point of view *Wuthering Heights,* with its unerring unity of conception and its full catharsis of the emotions of pity and terror, is one of the very few occasions on which the novel has reached the dignity of classical tragedy. And, in the other case, it would be hard to concede the full meaning of classicism to Jane Austen's universe of undertones.

We return to Charlotte's phrase—emotion in subjection —and contend that this is the only normal sense in which the classical spirit should be endured. The rest is pedantry, academic closures, and the "literature of our grandfathers." To apply the distinction to Jane Austen is hardly fair: she belongs to the spirit of comedy, which has never been easily classified, always existing as a free and detached criticism of life and literature. Jane Austen, in essentials, takes her place with Congreve, if with anybody in English letters; and maybe, after all, in making her the antitype to the Brontës we are but displaying the old discordant masks side by side. Is it an equal opposition? Well, not quite. Charlotte Brontë is again the critic—"Miss Austen being, as you say, without 'sentiment,' without *poetry,* maybe *is* sensible, real (more *real* than *true*), but she cannot be great." And that might be said equally well of Congreve, or of any representative of the comic spirit. It is a question of attitude. It is, finally, a question of courage—of throwing into the attempt for truth not only intelligence, spirit, faith, but also feeling, emotion, self.

Author's Note

[text illegible/faded]

Editor's Note

Tragedy and Comedy first appeared as a chapter in *Poetry and Mathematics* (1929). Copyright, 1929, by Scott Buchanan. Reprinted by permission of the author.

Scott Buchanan was born in Sprague, Washington, in 1895, and educated at Amherst, Oxford (as a Rhodes scholar), and Harvard. He has taught Greek at Amherst and philosophy at Harvard, City College, and the University of Virginia. In association with Stringfellow Barr in 1937, Buchanan set up the Great Books program at St. John's College, Annapolis, where he served as dean for a decade. In recent years he has been active in The Foundation for World Government, and he now teaches at Springfield College and in the spring of 1956 was a guest lecturer and member of the Christian Gauss Seminar in Criticism at Princeton. He is the author of *Possibility* (1927), *Symbolic Distance* (1932), *The Doctrine of Signatures* (1938), and *Essay in Politics* (1953).

FIVE

Scott Buchanan

Tragedy and Comedy

The shift of attention in mathematics from ratios and proportions to functions has had many important consequences, or if you like, there have been corresponding shifts of attention in other fields. It has become increasingly obvious in the last few years that science is abandoning its single-minded devotion to mechanics and its appropriate methods of investigation for a new and apparently more flexible set of ideas. Some see in this an emancipation from the dogmatic determinism of physics, and jump to the analogy of the biological organism. Others fear that it is a return to the pre-mechanistic theological attitude of mind and a consequent loss of skeptical rigor. Still others think of it as an impressionistic movement in science catching up with similar movements in art. As I see it, it is another case of the Pythagorean exploitation of mathematical forms. It is the latest betrothal of mathematics and poetry.

The mathematician has again been lured to an adventure with a symbolic hobbyhorse and has discovered new routes to the absolute or infinite. After a trial journey he has come back to earth and sets a new fashion in intellectual locomotion. The new vehicle feels like an aeroplane supported only by thin air, but the view from the rider's seat is familiar even though it involves distortions of the old perspective. Newly discovered abstractions always have an exotic manner.

Pythagoras and his disciples discovered certain numerical relations. Before they knew what they were doing, they had duplicated these relations and imputed them to

geometry, calling the result magnitude. They again duplicated them and imputed them to musical instruments and
sounds and called the result harmony. The accumulation
was projected on the starry sky and the result was the
harmony of the spheres. The process was so swift, that
they condensed their language and said that the world was
a realm of numbers.

They had confused numbering numbers and numbered
numbers. As we have seen, counting involves at least two
similar series. Pythagoras saw not only two, but many
more, and then said that they were all identical with the
first. This was real and the rest of the world was confused
experience, or prime matter. He might have done otherwise. Geometrical Pythagoreans saw the multiplication of
triangles and said the world was a realm of triangles. It
is an easy trick. Take any formula, find a similar form or
some material that is plastic, select a suitable analogy, con-
dense the analogy to a metaphor, take the metaphor
literally, and you have a scientific philosophy. It has been
done with less rigorous formulae than those of arithmetic
and geometry. Thus mechanism came from the proportion,
the Daltonian atom from weights and measures of the
laboratory, the solar system from conic sections, Bohr's
atom from the solar system, Marxian theory of history
from mechanics and Christian theology.

Quite recently we have been invited to imagine movement without forces and mass, and qualities without substances. For some time the psychologist had been doing
without soul and mind, and the political scientist without
the sovereign state. The shock of all this is somewhat like
the state of mind produced by La Place's famous remark
that he did not need God in physics. This is what happens
when the mathematical physicist changes his mind, that is,
his analogies.

In the present case he has been keeping company with
the modern Pythagoreans. They have been analogizing
with functions and the physicist has been giving us his
account of their sayings. In describing functions they have
been saying that for any value of the variable there is a
corresponding value of the function. The physicist has

asked the traditional question: What varies? and the Pythagorean has answered laconically: Everything, even the function is a variable. The so-called constants are only relations governing the variations, and even these so-called constants are only arbitrarily fixed by reference to still other merely arbitrary constants. Even the numbers are thus relative.

This would have been bad news in the seventeenth century, but since that time the physicist has been watching electrical phenomena and trying to keep his accounts straight in the old terms of proportions and equations where constants were constant. But latterly the ratios have slipped and the accounts have got tangled up. The numbers seem to be elastic. Forces, masses, and weights won't stay put. The elements begin to move about on the Mendeleeff chart. The old method of calculating errors of measurement seems to signify more than human and material imperfection. It is therefore good news now that mathematics has an analogous, but clearer notion to offer to the scientist. So the physicist has translated the language of the mathematician into his own terms and has had some terms such as mass, substance, force, or cause, left over. These he threw overboard and the accounts begin to come out straight again. The mathematics is now verified by observation. The new analogies work.

The result sounds like the biologist's description of organisms. They too are forms undergoing apparently significant variation in every part. Life is an equilibrium of changes. Animals were for a time compared with machines, but with very meager results. Now the whole physical universe is compared to an organism with apparently great results. The physical universe is an organism of organisms. Or not to throw over the old tradition too quickly, the world is an organic mechanism. Biological function and mathematical function are the same. The analogy has been condensed, and the resulting metaphor is metaphysical truth. It spreads to psychology which needed it badly and, with suitable revisions, we have *Gestalten* or forms devouring the faculties of the soul, the complexes of the psyche, and the reflexes of the nervous system. It becomes a philosophy of life in emergent evolution. Pythagoras has another reincarnation in which the former rooster has become the superman.

Mathematics and poetry, as forms of thought, have a peculiar property which I have called expansiveness. They are always restless and hungry for more. Sometimes this has the aspect of the search for an absolute. In mathematics the appearance of this aspect is the sign of the completion of a symbolic episode, and the imminence of a new extension in the direction of greater generality. In poetry it is the sign of a religious and mystical peace and acquiescence. At other times expansiveness wears an air of piety to a tradition and devotes itself to the task of refinement and assimilation of detail. Both of these in terms of logic are the play of ultimate categories such as sameness and difference, one and many, and the being and not-being of negation and affirmation. A dialectical investigation of these, such as Plato made, would show that the play and consequently the expansion of ideas is unlimited except by the energy and inclination of thinking beings. Some have found in this a metaphysical secret.

There is a recurrent aphorism in philosophy that summarizes this feature of thought. It says that reality is a sphere having an infinite radius and a center at every point. I mentioned this in connection with the generalization of the notion of projective fields made by Bruno and Leibniz, and I might have added some of the dark remarks of Einstein about the shape of the universe. The saying is not wholly nonsensical; its principle of order can be stated.

The infinite sphere denotes a series of spheres each of which represents a stage of mathematical discovery. A set of assumptions is laid down and developed by deductive and intuitive methods into a system. The system so generated is a finite sphere. As soon as it is sufficiently developed, there is discovered an underlying set of assumptions with a larger system than the former as its consequence. When this is developed, it is a sphere including the former as one of its dependent parts. Modern multi-dimensional geometry thus includes Euclidean geometry. This latter sphere is in turn a subdivision of a still more inclusive sphere, and the expansive process apparently never ends. The study of comparative literature shows similarly ordered sets of allegories.

This is the cultural macrocosm. The microcosm of the individual mind is similar, and the corresponding series of spheres is an intellectual biography, a mind in the making.

We can be more explicit. The infinity of these spheres is suggestive of the number system with its densities, compactnesses, and continuities. The paradoxes of counting are solved by correlating the members of one series with those of another. We can bring a similar analogical calculus to bear on the series of mathematical and poetical spheres.

Mathematics deals with relations, and poetry deals with qualities. A sphere results when we can see the *relations* holding between *qualities*. Then the two series can be correlated. Mathematical functions find elementary values in qualities. Qualities find their relations in the functions of mathematics. Whenever this happens, a system is recognized, and it takes on a quasi-independence and reality. Often the effect in the thinker is a conviction. Belief attaches itself only to such systems. The further expansions and the wider assumptions are ignored and there is a resting point for thought in a mathematico-poetic allegory.

This is the secret of the drama which at its best undercuts the scientific and religious attitude of mind. Consequently the best metaphysical criticism of mathematics and poetry is to be found in the drama and the novel. Tragedy and comedy are the classic modes of treatment of this theme. Their analysis will exhibit it farther.

The fundamental notions in tragedy are called *hybris* and *nemesis*. The first is the attitude of arrogance or insolence that arises from blindness in human nature. The second is the eventual consequence of that blindness and arrogance, the vengeance that the ignored factor in a situation takes on man and his virtues. These are moralistic terms but the intellectualistic transformation is easy. It can be performed on the terms of Aristotle's analysis of tragedy.

A tragic character must have besides hybris, the virtue

GREEK TRAGEDY

of irony. This quality is the exercise of the capacity to discover and systematize clear ideas. It appears at first as a naïve idealism that makes it impossible to take circumstances at their face value, and expresses itself in a kind of satirical questioning, such as that of Socrates. Accompanying it is a sense of humor which condenses and dispels intervening fogs. At bottom it is a faith that there are ideas to be discovered and a conviction that the task is not easy. St. Francis and Don Quixote are additional good examples in literature. Dramatic tragedy usually discloses such a character in some advanced stage when the idea is in sight, so that action is understood as aiming to achieve its clarification. This is the situation presented in the prologue.

Action moves on exemplifying and expanding the idea. Even at this point there are at least two possible interpretations of the events. One is held by the audience who usually know the outcome already. The other is that held by the hero who is possessed of the idea to such an extent that he builds up a separate story or interpretation for himself in conformity with his ideal. Events pile up and are turned to his account by the alchemy of his own rationality. The situation becomes complicated and each event is charged with dramatic foreshadowing. The hero sees dilemmas in everything and sticks to his course in spite of the oppositions. His determination finally reaches desperation. This is the complication of the situation and the advent of hybris.

At length he is faced with some crucial and unavoidable predicament. He must decide. Using all his intellectual powers he makes the only decision possible on his interpretation of the situation. This is the crisis. In terms of mathematics and poetry, he has developed a system of relations, his idea; and the events have supplied a corresponding set of qualities. The situation is a full-rounded sphere.

Events come faster and pile themselves high on either side of his chosen path. They now have a threatening aspect for him, but there is no turning back. There is a dull inevitability about them. Finally they break and all is ruin with no compensating circumstance. This is the reversal of circumstance and catastrophe. The rounded sphere of apparent success is in a thousand pieces.

Then if he has the true quality of irony there is a recognition of what he had ignored. There comes the still small voice in the calm following the thunder and the earthquake, the voice of a god speaking not words of pity or revenge, but the decrees of necessity on his situation and his idea. Both are thrown upon a vaster background than he had envisaged, the doings of fate. In these decrees there is light and the hero recognizes himself, his idea, and his plight in terms of laws that are not for yesterday, today or tomorrow, but for always. This is the purgation.

But this may be only one episode, the first of a trilogy. The same hero, or another implicated character goes on into the new sphere with the new version of the eternal verities. No man should be judged happy until he is dead.

This pattern is the Greek view of life. It is the method of their and our science, history, and philosophy. In it poetry becomes criticism of life. It is, I believe, the final metaphysical conclusion of Greek philosophy in Plato and Aristotle.

The Greek employment of it had been humanistic in the main. The Greek tragic hero was a typical man isolated and projected on a background of fate. The late middle ages and the Renaissance substituted natural objects for the heroes of vicarious tragedies, the experiments in the laboratory. They put such objects under controlled conditions, introduced artificial complications, and waited for the answering pronouncement of fate. The crucial experiment is the crisis of an attempt to rationalize experience, that is, to force it into our analogies. Purgation and recognition are now called elimination of false hypotheses and verification. The shift is significant, but the essential tragic pattern of tragedy is still there. The popularizer of science is inviting us to reverse the change and rehumanize tragedy. There is some doubt whether he knows what he is proposing.

Tragedy proceeds by analogy and homogeneous substitution in the rationalizing thought of the hero. Events are prepared, "controlled," willed, interpreted, so as to be consistent with the idea or hypothesis. The direction of expansion is integration and generality. It ends in a cumulative catastrophe and a general purgation. Comedy seems to provide another method. It proceeds by wide variation and heterogeneous substitution. Every turn in the action marks an inconsistency discovered, a plan gone wrong, a platitude rendered paradoxical, a principle disproved, a fact caught in duplicity. There is expansion here also, but in the phase of discrimination and distinction-making. The hero of a comedy must see the point of every joke or of none, so that all the ideas may have equal opportunity for conflict and continual purgation. In a good comedy every idea must be deflated and purged by the ordeal of laughter. One laughs with or at the hero who exposes them and himself to the comic purgation.

Of course, there are many kinds of comedy, each type depending on some one of the types of heterogeneous substitution. There is the pun based on verbal substitution, the practical joke ranging from slap-stick to farcical humor based on substitutions of actions for words or ideas. Finally, there is the comedy of manners based on the substitution of ideas. This can be illustrated in mathematics.

In the study of functions and their properties it is customary to substitute trial values for one variable at a time and watch the result in the values taken on by the other variables and the whole function in consequence. By a series of such trials the limiting values are found. This is the Greek method of solving equations and was revived in analytic geometry for the purpose of isolating the general properties of equations. It is also used in the calculus and the theory of functions. McClaurin substituted zero for x in Taylor's Series and discovered the method for expanding any function by using derivative functions. The study of maxima and minima, or the greatest and least values of functions, is another application. In general the unusual or unique values are substituted. Sometimes the result is an indeterminate or nonsensical expression, and sometimes it is a transformation into another class of functions whose unsuspected relations to the original class is thus discovered. The mathematical result is, as in the comedy of literature, a clarification and definition of the properties of the ideas involved.

The main points in the comparison of the forms of tragedy and comedy, and their modern descendants in drama and fiction, also the operation of the principles of substitution and expansion that relate them, may be seen in three versions of the Œdipus story.

The first is the Sophoclean argument:

The god, Apollo, has made it known through the Oracle at Delphi that the son of Laius, King of Thebes, will kill his father and marry Jocasta, his mother. In accordance with the Greek practice with regard to the pronouncements of the Oracle Laius plans to circumvent the divine decree by having his son Œdipus exposed. A shepherd is given the commission to dispose of the child. But he is touched by pity and hands him over to the care of another shepherd, who in turn passes him on to Polybus, King of Corinth, in whose house Œdipus is reared as heir to the Corinthian throne. As a grown man he hears a rumor that he is not the son of his apparent parents. He starts to Delphi to find out his true origin. On the way he meets a royal chariot, and is pushed off the narrow road by its attendants. He attacks the occupant, kills him, and the attendants also, except one who escapes.

Proceeding on his way, in due time he nears Thebes, which is mourning the death of its king. He who can answer the riddle of the sphinx will be made king. Œdipus answers the riddle, is made king, and becomes famous for his just rule. Soon there are reports of a plague in the city of Thebes, and King Œdipus sends to the Delphic Oracle to learn its cause. The answer comes that the plague is punishment for a crime committed in the city. As soon as the offender is found and punished, the plague will disappear. The King imposes a penalty, exile, and curses the guilty. The investigation proceeds without result. Œdipus intensifies the search, and a rumor starts that he himself is the offender. He accuses his brother-in-law, Creon, of plotting to seize the throne for himself. The blind seer

Teiresias is called in to arbitrate. He confirms the rumor against Œdipus and is accused of a lying conspiracy with Creon.

Finally, the escaped attendant on Laius' chariot is called in to describe the murderer of the former king. It is still uncertain, and the shepherds are sought. They convince Œdipus that he is guilty of incest and murdering his father. He puts out his own eyes, and Jocasta hangs herself. Blind Œdipus and his daughter, Antigone, go into exile to free the city of the plague.

The comic version might go as follows:

A shepherd has come to Thebes to celebrate a short vacation from sheep-watching. He is making merry with wine and old friends. They tell him about the death of the king and encourage him to answer the riddle of the sphinx. In his state of inebriation and spiritual ecstasy he accidentally hits upon the right answer. He is taken to the court and made king of Thebes, by this time sober and embarrassed. He marries Jocasta.

In the course of time the ceremonies and royal duties begin to bore him. He plans to escape. The plague comes to Thebes. He sends an old shepherd friend as messenger to Delphi, instructing him before he leaves what his report is to be. The shepherd returns and says that the King is Œdipus, Laius' son, who escaped exposure, and has fulfilled the prophecy that he would kill his father and marry his mother. There is danger that the King and Queen will be stoned by the people.

Meanwhile Jocasta has fallen in love with the shepherd and is also bored with court life. The herald reports that she has hanged herself, and as they carry out a dummy corpse to show the people, the King and Queen escape by another route to the hills where they tend sheep in peace.

A modern novel:

King Laius of Thebes is loved by his people for his strong and just administration of the laws, but he has a bad temper. In a fit of temper brought on by some insubordination of his own six-year-old son, Œdipus, he bursts a blood vessel and dies. A regency is declared until Œdipus is old enough to take on his father's duties. Creon,

the brother of Jocasta, the queen, becomes regent. Œdipus
is sent to be educated at the Persian court.

At the age of twenty-one he returns, a man of the
world, but in ill health. He is loved by the people because
they think his ill health is due to his grief for his father,
also because he reminds them of his father in his passion
for justice. He marries the Princess of the house of
Corinth, who also wins the hearts of the people because
she resembles Jocasta, their former queen.

Some years later there is a plague in Thebes. The people
are going blind. Œdipus' wife is a victim and dies. The
oracle is consulted and its answer is that the cause of the
blindness is a mysterious Persian disease that has spread
from the palace itself to the town. Œdipus hands over the
throne to Haemon, the son of Creon, with whom Antigone,
Œdipus' daughter, is in love. Antigone will not marry him
for fear of continuing the plague. Œdipus grows blind,
and Antigone devotes the rest of her life to caring for her
father in a country home near Thebes. Haemon comes
often to see her.

Œdipus dies calling for his mother and the sun.

*   *   *   *

Critical philosophy is the highest type of intellectual
comedy, and Plato is the best comic poet of philosophy.
It is said that Plato as a youth wrote comedies for the
Olympic prizes. The plays are lost, but the marks of the
comic poet are to be found in his dialogues. For in them
we find all the types of humor bent to the somewhat tragic
purpose of a moral philosophy. He is a master of heterogeneous substitution, and in the mouth of Socrates such
substitutions get the sparkling expression that comedy
should provide.

All the persons of the drama speak in character. In the
early dialogues Socrates is talking with Sophists of one
sort or another. He catches them making comic substitutions without a smile, usually aping a tragic *deus ex
machina* in their manner and matter. He takes up the
game and carries it to the extremes where the pun or
witticism can be seen. These first dialogues should be read

with one eye on the contemporary comic poet George Bernard Shaw in whom the same Platonic blend of comedy and tragedy is articulate.

In the *Republic* Plato is exposing the Pythagorean secrets of the Delphic Oracle which is the Greek analogue of our modern research foundations. It expounded the mathematical and poetic secrets of the universe in moral precepts for the people. In the later dialogues the theory of ideas, a common doctrine of the day and the pet device of Socrates to confound his opponents, undergoes the ordeal by laughter. The humor becomes more intellectual and abstract, and the sparkle becomes the play of philosophic insights. Poetry and mathematics meet and part in perfect freedom and lack of mutual embarrassment. Most of the dialogues end with an epilogue, the first part of which is mathematics, and the second part of which a poetic myth. Many have misunderstood these endings and taken the myth as the final interpretation of the mathematics. They do Plato a great injustice. His only conclusions are the clear and distinct ideas that his comic treatment reveals in unsuspected turns of the dialogues.

But comedy plays with the ideas to which tragedy has given birth. It is never the discoverer or creator. Plato's philosophy never quite frees its doctrines from their traditional origins, although it does give them an ideal dimension. The play of ideas is always hedged about with the darkness and mystery of tragic issues. This is inevitable. There probably never was a pure comedy or tragedy. The drama is often spoiled by a bad mixture of the two. Ibsen tried to fill comic situations with fate. Comic characters strut across the stage inflating the comedy, the play of local customs and popular science, with a pseudo-seriousness. This is the tragicomedy of the melodrama and contains a sentimental faith and a preaching hero. It is an unconscious parody on tragic purgation.

Ibsen on the other hand is an authentic historian, and the times he describes are not remote from the present. Most of us live with the mixture of poetry and mathematics in our heads which makes our understanding melodramatic. Our romanticism and our realism are seldom purged. One reason for this is that science is being preached to us before it is understood by the preachers. We apply it without irony and study it without humor. The consequence is sentimentalism in our action and mystification at the denouement.

It is this situation that has aroused the present controversy over the popularization of science. It is a typical crisis in the life of reason. Reason oscillates between tragic pain and comic disillusionment. The popularizer is speaking seriously for the method of the laboratory. He is the stage manager for the world and wishes people to act and speak by the book of science. If his management were successful there would be the crisis in civilization which he foretells and fears. Whether there are enough tragic heroes to give it a high seriousness, nobody knows. But it seems at present that the actors have missed the spirit of the play. Most of them are melodramatic heroes and villains who now and then suffer comic relief. There are here and there signs of the play of clear and distinct ideas that go with comedy. There are a few individuals with insight and love of ideas, who understand without believing. But on the whole science is not yet a tradition within which one can play. The result is a confusion of mathematics and poetry in experience that I pointed out at the beginning.

It would be a pleasant prospect if this essay were an introduction to a *De Rerum Natura* or a *Divine Comedy*. When such a work is worthily done it will be clear what the difference between tragedy and comedy is. It will then be possible to decide what to do with modern scientific opinion. It is said that the function of theology has always been to spiritualize the sacraments, that is, to discover and formulate their symbolic function and to reduce popular belief in their causal efficacy to its proper status. The function of philosophical criticism is to intellectualize scientific method, that is, to discover and formulate its symbolic significance and to reduce popular belief in its causal efficacy to its proper status. With regard to the symbolic function of science and its conclusions, at present it can only be said that they are wavering shadows of those clear and distinct ideas without which experience is neither good nor true. Their present mathematical and poetic embodiments are intimations of some such immortality.

Editor's Note

Ivor Armstrong Richards was born in Sandbach, Cheshire, England, in 1893, and educated at Magdalene College, Cambridge, where he became a Fellow in 1926. He has taught at Cambridge, Tsing Hua University in Peking, and Harvard. With C. K. Ogden, Richards published *The Meaning of Meaning* (1922) and has been active in the Basic English movement. He is now Chairman of the Board of Language Research, Inc. His literary criticism includes *Principles of Literary Criticism* (1924), *Science and Poetry* (1926), *Practical Criticism* (1929), *Mencius on the Mind* (1932), and *Coleridge on Imagination* (1935).

SIX

I. A. Richards

Fifteen Lines from Landor

Suppose that a gale is sweeping over a forest, the trees respond with their varied notes according to all the possible differences in their cavities. What need would there be to pass a judgment on their multitudinous notes or declare that some and not others are the voice of the gale?

—CHUANG TZU

"Poetry gives most pleasure," said Coleridge, "when only generally and not perfectly understood. . . . From this cause it is that what I call metaphysical poetry gives me so much delight." (*Anima Poetæ*, p. 5) The remark, like so many of S.T.C.'s other jottings deserves more attention and development than it has received.[1] To treat it adequately would require a complete theory of the kinds of understanding and the world is not yet ripe for that. But some immediate advance can be made by a close study of the actual processes of understanding poetry. I shall first describe a method for this study, then present some of its results, and then speculate upon the inferences that may be drawn from these as regards Coleridge's *dictum*, our reading habits, and criticism in general.

We can take any passage of poetry for which "perfect understanding" is not likely to be too frequent and invite a number of readers (about whom we should, ideally, know as much as we can) to give, in any fashion they please, an

[1] The qualification published by Miss Kathleen Coburn (*Inquiring Spirit*, p. 55): "When no criticism is pretended to, and the Mind in its simplicity gives itself up to a Poem as to a work of nature, Poetry gives . . ." should be borne in mind, but hardly lessens the subversive force of the remark.

account of what they understand by it. In practice, we have to ask for a paraphrase and exposition leaving it to them to decide which parts require exposition. It is best for this purpose to eliminate, so far as possible, the question "Is the passage good or bad poetry?" and to invite answers only to the question "What does it mean?" (Or, "What is it, as a system of meanings?"); which is a different question from "What does it say?"

These accounts, if the writers have been at all successful, are sets of signs from which we then have to conjecture their various readings of the passage. Here is where the difficulties and dangers of the method occur. What we take as their readings of the passage are only our interpretations of accounts which will as a rule be very inadequate and sometimes very misleading. However, in a large number of accounts of the same passage, we shall usually discover instructive groupings and very different accounts often throw helpful light on one another. Through this rather hazardous work of interpretation we arrive at a representative collection of readings. These, in the ideal case—in which all our own interpretations were correct and the accounts themselves sufficient—would be a collection of specimens of high significance for biology. They would show the history of a set of interpretations, the points at which variation occurs, and the types of variation—the stages in the growth and the occasions for mishap of the most important human function. But ours is not the ideal case, we must be content to use our readings more tentatively and concern ourselves with simpler, which here means less analysed, problems.

A passage which has provided interestingly varied readings is the following (Landor, *Gebir,* iii, 4–18):

> *Tho' panting in the play-hour of my youth*
> *I drank of Avon too, a dangerous draught,*
> *That rous'd within the feverish thirst of song,*
> *Yet never may I trespass o'er the stream*
> *Of jealous Acheron, nor alive descend*
> *The silent and unsearchable abodes*
> *Of Erebus and Night, nor unchastized*
> *Lead up long-absent heroes into day.*

When on the pausing theatre of earth
Eve's shadowy curtain falls, can any man
Bring back the far off intercepted hills,
Grasp the round rock-built turret, or arrest
The glittering spires that pierce the brow of Heav'n?
Rather can any with outstripping voice
The parting Sun's gigantic strides recall?

The readers who supplied the accounts of its meaning that I am about to use were men and women studying English Literature at Cambridge or Harvard and Radcliffe. The authorship of the passage was not told them, and no one guessed it.

May I strongly recommend those who wish to gain all the insight that the following specimen interpretations can afford, to take paper and pencil and write out their own paraphrase before reading further. Without intimate familiarity with the specific problem the adventures of other readers lose their instructive power.

For convenience, we may break the passage into three sections, Lines 1–3, 4–8, 9–15, though a more complete study would, of course, trace connections between individuals' peculiarities of interpretation in all three sections. Each section is evidently susceptible of more varied interpretations when taken by itself than when taken with the rest of the passage, and a first difference between good and bad readers can be stated simply in terms of the number of relevant items that they can bring and hold together as co-operating signs. These items in such a passage as this will be of several sorts:

1. The plain literal senses of the words and sentences.

2. The metaphoric senses. These, in most cases, are multiple; within the range of transference from the literal sense (supposing there to be only one) are a number of other senses with various relations to it. Which of these relations serves as the ground of the metaphor, and thus which of the possible metaphoric senses is taken, depends upon what is happening at many other points in the interpretative process. More than one metaphoric sense (and more than one literal sense) *may* be taken by a reader

simultaneously, and may need to be taken, as Mr. Empson has, perhaps overwhelmingly, demonstrated.

3. Feeling. Attitudes of the poet to his sense (literal or metaphoric). We may call these *emotive overtones*, if we are careful not to overlook the fact that they are not less important than sense in guiding interpretation.

4. Tone, the poet's manner of address to his reader.

5. Signs of his own critical attitude to his work, of his confidence or diffidence about the success of his intricate endeavour.

6. Signs of his intention which may be larger than can be implemented by the items so far enumerated. For example, omissions, or a choice of form, or of highly developed metaphor in preference to plain sense, may come under this heading.[2]

It is noteworthy that feeling, e.g., will often prescribe words for the sake of metaphoric senses that are superfluous to the main sense-articulation of the passage, but which control feeling. The connections and transactions between these items may be, and frequently are, *inexplicit*, made without any conscious recognition of them by the reader (or by the poet).

Almost word by word the process of interpretation can be seen—from our accounts—to bifurcate according to the sets of items, of all these sorts, that are taken together.

SECTION ONE

Tho' panting in the play-hour of my youth

1.1   In an idle hour of my youth being restless for something to do.

1.11 Although as a boy in brief pauses of my play.

1.12 When, in my youth, I needed spiritual refreshment.

1.13 Searching in my youth for aesthetic comfort.

1.2   Although at the time in my youth when I frequented plays.

1.21 I too was enthralled by dramatic poetry—as enthralled as a child at the theatre.

---

[2] For further discussions of these items and their possible interrelationships, see *Practical Criticism*, Appendix A.

1.3   When eager and careless, in the irresponsibility of youth.

> *I drank of Avon too, a dangerous draught,*
> *That rous'd within a feverish thirst of song,*

1.4   I (like Shakespeare) drank of the River Avon.

1.41   "Avon too" may mean "Avon as well as other poets," or "I have done what other people have done," or "of the same rich draughts that Shakespeare drank." The third is the least likely, the first the most.

1.42   He became inspired to write poetry, by drinking of the River Avon, our local Helicon, which had inspired Shakespeare.

1.43   Although I read Shakespeare also (as well as doing other things).

1.44   By "thirst of song" is meant "thirst of singing."

1.45   There is something definitely comic in the thought of overindulgence in the reading of Shakespeare as an act of youthful heedlessness.

1.5   I drank in the spirit of the countryside.

1.51   The beauty of the River Avon aroused in me the desire for self-expression.

1.6   Although overcome by passions in my youth, I thought deeply and thinking maddened me.

1.61   In the days of his youth when life was still a game, tho' a hard one, the writer turned to Shakespeare to refresh his spirits, a questionable resort because the study of poetry is as likely to be discouraging as refreshing. . . .

Hitherto I have not commented upon these specimens of interpretation. I am not here concerned to defend or arraign them as products of our educational system. They are facts of natural science to be inquired into as best we may. The last example is sufficiently curious to be quoted in entirety. It continues:

> He hopes that his soul may never be so discouraged as to experience the deep pangs of torture of which it is capable and which, once started, are never quite soothed away. That while yet able to enjoy life he

may not find his convictions shattered, his mind groping in Despair for Truth where all is confusion and
where Truth cannot be found. That he may not revive
from the past stories of tragic heroes to bring dismay
into the hearts of others.

Whether such a reader is likely to benefit from a university, or how he came there, are questions for another
occasion. Here the medical interest of studies of interpretation is more to the purpose. Such an extreme case
brings out clearly something which is very frequently apparent in accounts given of the meaning of almost any
passage—that personal preoccupations are strong enough
to override everything and twist any pointers into directions governed by the reader's own volitional situation. We
shall see further examples, in what follows, of these ex-
traneous interventions, factors of interpretation which
prevent communication from occurring. Their theoretical
importance is that they show how, in normal communication, similar volitional factors (but not irrelevant ones)
are at work.

SECTION TWO

Yet never may I trespass o'er the stream
Of jealous Acheron, nor alive descend
The silent and unsearchable abodes
Of Erebus and Night, nor unchastized
Lead up long-absent heroes into day.

The duplicity of *may* ("I cannot," "I hope I shall not")
acted as a main pivot, but both what the poet could not
do and what he would not do varied widely and for
equally diverse reasons:

CANNOT

2.11 He cannot go into the past, into the place of death,
      nor search out again the heroes—poets—that have
      died.

2.12 True intimacy with the spirit of such a past hero (as
      Shakespeare) is naturally denied us.

2.121 He feels that he can never do more than catch glimpses of this beauty, that he can never know the man through his works. . . . The last two lines (13–15) obviously refer to Shakespeare alone.

2.13 I concluded that I could never write of the other world (as Dante), nor treat, without much criticism, of old epic heroes.

2.131 Now I realize that I can never recover in their fulness the exploits and characters of the heroes of poetry just as I cannot look upon the dead.

2.14 I shall never be able to write any poetry myself.

2.15 But I shall never live to solve the secrets which those dead heroes knew. (Cf. comment on 1.61?)

2.151 But never will I be able to make convincing and immortal the phenomena of life, the hidden secrets of the universe. (Cf. comment on 1.61).

2.152 I cannot pierce beyond Death, or in life discover its secrets; nor can I, with impunity (an unnecessary phrase: he couldn't do it at all), call up again the heroes of the past.

2.16 Yet even Shakespeare I found difficult enough. How much the less then may I attempt to fathom the writings of the Ancients whose works must ever remain a closed book to me.

2.17 Yet I shall never arrive at this so desirable and far off land.

2.18 All the poem seems to mean as a whole is that the gentleman liked poetry and wished he could shake the hand of Shakespeare and perhaps get his autograph.

2.19 But I should not be able—even if I had the cheek to try—to accompany Homer, Virgil or Dante to Hell. That sort of thing is over now.

WOULD NOT

2.21 Yet I should never want to go down to Hades alive.

2.211 I have never wanted to learn to play music which would help me, like Orpheus, to cross Acheron and bring back dead heroes from Hell.

2.22   Yet may I never descend in my lifetime to the practice of dragging to light the deeds, perhaps unworthy, of heroes long dead.

2.221 He tried to write of dead heroes and evil-doers.

2.23   Yet may I never try to do impossible things.

2.231 Not that I wish to invent impossible stories of my adventures in Hades.

2.24   He hopes that he will never, in choosing subjects for his writing, go back to classical material or any material characteristic of another age.

2.241 Yet may I never write of Greek mythology, for to do this sort of thing properly one must live in the times when Greek mythology was believed in.

2.242 I did not want to write of past deeds and classical lore, because I found that I could not handle such subjects worthily.

2.25   I hope I may never, like epic writers, lose touch with life, to trespass over Acheron which would be jealous of my enjoyment of mundane pleasures.

2.251 I realize that the epic writer, the man who merges an exact philosophy of life with the study and enjoyment of living things has failed to perceive that man cannot go beyond expediency. (Cf. 1.61?)

2.26   The rest of the poem, after the first three lines, expresses the idea of the vanished sunlight of youth. It is a wistful retrospection toward a youth now worn out. In contrast with youth is the darkness of the underworld, an underworld from which the speaker is unable to draw back the friends of his youth. He can draw them back, but he is *chastized*. He then is pained by his past excesses.

2.261 Yet having crossed over into this realm of age and dark, I can never re-emerge with my youth into the day of joy.

The "Regret for vanished youth" and the "occultism" (2.15, 2.151) prepossessions are, as we shall see, very persistent.

My documentation is becoming somewhat extensive, but I am omitting numerous varieties, several species, and

even some genera. It must be remembered that any of
these readers might discuss at length Landor's merits or
defects as a poet, and even the qualities of this passage—
in the pages of the *Criterion,* for example—without ever
discovering the discrepancies of their readings. Landor,
after all, is not thought to be an unusually cryptic poet. It
is a stimulating exercise to attempt to imagine a similar
display of readings of one of the Editor's poems, or of
Mr. Yeats' *Byzantium.* Among other things it might
stimulate the desire to pursue the theory of interpretation
further.

SECTION THREE

When on the pausing theatre of earth
Eve's shadowy curtain falls, can any man
Bring back the far off intercepted hills,
Grasp the round rock-built turret, or arrest
The glittering spires that pierce the brow of Heav'n?
Rather can any with outstripping voice
The parting Sun's gigantic strides recall?

Great difficulty was clearly felt (except by those who
had read Sections One and Two with unusual sagacity) in
bringing Section Three into living connection with them.
And odd interpretations of the earlier sections led to attempts to force parallel strangenesses into Section Three.
I shall cite only a few special cases.

But even those who left the last section quite uncon-
nected with the rest indulged at times in equally remarkable conjectures:

3.1 When, in an interval of life on earth, a woman's
    shadow falls like a curtain on a stage, can any man
    do anything?

The Freudian possibilities in the interpretation of the remaining lines, after this auspicious start, escaped, however, this reader.

The apparent variation in the visual images (it may be
only in the phrasing) evoked by "Eve's shadowy curtain"
raises an interesting point of critical detail.

3.2   By night's dark curtains.
3.21   Like a black curtain.

A reader who is unaware of discrepancy of effect here will
receive little from poetry. And apart from all accidents of
imagery the senses of *black* and *shadowy* support totally
distinct feelings.

Attempts to connect "pausing theatre" with "play-hour"
in part explain some of the following:

3.3   When one's life is drawing to a close.
3.31   At the end of the world's play.
3.32   When the darkness of death falls on humanity.

A pause, however, usually implies a continuation.

Allegories of several kinds were drawn out:

3.33   When the curtain of age falls upon his life, can any
       man bring back the far off hills that were his goal,
       hold fast to the turret of youthful certainties, or
       stay the disappearing spires of great ambitions.
       Rather can any man recall his glorious but setting
       youth?
3.331 When one has reached the end of life, after ex-
       periencing its manifestations can he bring back the
       spontaneity, the convictions, the ambitions of his
       youth?
3.332 The last seven lines seem to ask whether, as age
       comes on, any man is able to recapture the poignant
       visions of youth and express them in song. The
       mood appears similar to that of Wordsworth's *Inti-
       mations,* the light of common day into which the
       Wordsworth vision fades being here represented by
       the fall of evening.
3.333 "Intercepted hills"—I think this means the dreams
       of youth.
3.34   The meaning here resolves itself into a doubt
       whether *any* man, tho' he be a Shakespeare, can
       remember the things of life, symbolized by hill,
       turret, spires, and sun, after he has died.
3.341 If in these lines the writer is alluding to man's exile
       from Eden, barring him from Paradise, one would

have no quarrel with the poet. Perhaps his meaning is that by his own sins he is rendered incapable.

3.35 Can any man when death has taken it from the world, revive and keep alive past greatness?

3.4 Although the huge landscape seems to be standing still as I write—what with Christianity and one thing and another—you cannot do that sort of thing now any more than bring the landscape back this side of the dusk, or stop the Pagan sun from setting (Continuation from 2.19).

3.41 How in this twilight of the ages can man bring back and picture vividly the far off times—the old stories of Mount Olympus as the abode of the gods, or of the rock-built turrets of Greece or Rome, or of the glittering Cathedrals of the middle ages? The underlying plea is for poetry to turn from the far off past towards the present.

3.42 No man can fully recapture the spirit of a bygone age.

Most preferred much more literal readings, but not necessarily safer ones:

3.5 As fruitless as for a man to contrive the approach of the horizon or other inaccessible and architectural phenomena.

3.51 Can any one cause the circular turret to leave its rock and approach.

3.52 Stop the glittering spires from piercing Heaven.

3.521 Tried to write of long-dead evil doers, but found it as impossible as it is to grasp the smooth surface of a stone turret or prevent a spire from reaching heavenward.

3.522 Crush the glittering spires?

3.523 Extinguish the stars in the sky?

3.524 Prevent the glistering stars that threaten the brow of heaven?

Some of these last, since they occur after twelve lines of hard reading, may perhaps be set down as effects of fatigue. A majority of readers were content to take the last seven lines as a decorated platitude of the flattest kind.

It is difficult, in giving such a display of interpretation, to avoid the impression that a mere teaching scandal is being exploited, that the utterances of pre-eminent dolts are being elicited and put forward with undue prominence, in brief, that I have been collecting "howlers." I have, however, not yet met anyone who thought so whose own critical endeavours would not have added lustre to that aspect of any collection. But it may be useful—to correct this impression that the writers of these paraphrases are not normal readers—to consider briefly a few equivalent examples of interpretations by more mature students. They will help us to remember that the most eminent poets and critics, most justly esteemed authorities, most brilliantly perceptive persons, do not unflaggingly maintain a very much higher level than these undergraduates. I take my examples at random with a feeling that choice is invidious and a firm opinion that equally good examples will be found in any expository work which comes sufficiently near its subject-matter to run any risks. If I begin with Coleridge, I shall not be suspected of intending any disparagement of the authors I cite from:

It is a well-known fact, that bright colours in motion both make and leave the strongest impressions on the eye. Nothing is more likely, too, than that a vivid image or visual spectrum, thus originated, may become the link of association in recalling the feelings and images that had accompanied the original impression. But if we describe this in such lines, as

> They flash upon the inward eye,
> Which is the bliss of solitude;

in what words shall we describe the joy of retrospection, when the images and virtuous actions of a whole well-spent life, pass before that conscience which is indeed the *inward* eye: which is indeed *"the bliss of solitude"*? (*Biographia Literaria,* Chapter xxii. It is worth remarking that of Coleridge's three examples of Wordsworth's *"mental* bombast," this and the third show an equally wilful twist in the interpretation and that the second, from *The Gypsies,* is hardly by Coleridge's own showing an example of *excess* of thought to the circumstance and the occasion. I discuss these unhappy noddings further in *Coleridge on Imagination*.)

Professor Garrod on the *Ode to Psyche* may follow:

Keats will be the priest of Psyche, priest and choir and shrine and grove; she shall have a fane "in some untrodden region of the mind," and shall enjoy

> *all soft delight*
> *That shadowy thought shall win.*

There shall be a "bright torch" burning for her, and the casement shall be open to let her in at night. I do not find that any commentator has seized the significance of this symbolism. The open window and the lighted torch—they are to admit and attract the timorous *moth-goddess,* who symbolizes melancholy love. (*Keats,* p. 98.)

If it were not Psyche but Cupid, "the warm Love," who is to be let in, the slowness of the commentators would not be surprising.

An example from Rupert Brooke will round off this little collection. After pointing out that Webster's

> So perfect shall be thy happiness, that, as men at sea think land and trees and ships go that way they go, so both heaven and earth shall seem to go your journey.

was derived from Montaigne:

> As they who travel by sea, to whom mountains, fields, towns, heaven and earth, seem to go the same motion, and keep the same course they do

he adds a footnote: "Note, though, that Montaigne has made a slip. They really appear to be moving in the *opposite* direction to yourself. Webster takes the idea over, mistake and all." Those who are not clear, in this case, as to who was mistaken may try the experiment of watching *distant* objects on their next railway journey.

I may now, under the shelter of these examples, offer a paraphrase exposition of my own for the Landor passage, a venture—after so many shipwrecks surveyed—calling for some resolution.

Young, eager, idle, active, irresponsible (*panting*, further, has a very large number of metaphoric implications—it is a typical "wheel" metaphor, the spokes being different relations to a more or less connected rim), made thirsty, heated, needing rest, refreshment (with some others of the symbolic senses of water); I read Shakespeare and underwent the influences which lead a man to write and read poetry. *Too*, can here couple almost any of the sense items: I, like Shakespeare; I, like others; Avon as well as other influences; Shakespeare as well. . . . *Drank of Avon* is a "wheel within wheel" metaphor, revolving, in one set of motions, together with *panting* and, in another set of motions, together with *dangerous draught* and *feverish thirst*. The influence is thirst-arousing, perhaps salt, intoxicant, alternative. (These motions bring in a very mixed and fleeting throng of feelings.)

Yet it is impossible, not allowed (feeling of injustice suffered, or of regret alone, as the emphasis is moved from *I* back to *never*) to me—whatever my merits (in a matter where "even a little seems a lot" and "the greatest is unworthy")—to

1. Perform the "Orphic" functions of the Poet,
2. Write in the spirit or purpose or manner, and on the subjects, of Homer, Virgil, Dante, Shakespeare.

The specific form of the metaphor here loads the statement with feelings of loss and inevitability—the vanishing of a possibility of the mind.

An act in human history is over, it comes to an end like a day. What was known in it—the distances and heights, the symbols of man's strength and security, his hope and religion—cannot be recaptured (as symbols, *hills, turrets,* and *spires,* like the suggested water of line two, have powers upon feeling independent of any specific interpretations that may be stressed by individual readers, they carry a general feeling for which any detailed exposition would be chiefly a rationalization). Can any poet now restore *those* powers of poetry (Apollo, Animism, Belief) that are themselves now closing a cycle?

The exercise of penning such a set of indications brings out, much better than any reading, the kind of elusiveness such meanings enjoy. The mental process—the developing understanding—is what we need to catch, and the words of an account are suited chiefly to the catching of parts of the product. They artificially precipitate much that in the normal reading of the poem remains in solution—but not therefore, if invisible, inactive. This explains some of the oddities in the accounts. The reader who is experimenting with alternative formulations has already, in the words of the poem, a better set of signs than he—being ordinarily no very good poet—is likely to be able to contrive. And he cannot, in the present state of this subject, take the other course and write as a man of science. What he gives us will not, as a rule, state anything that he has found and we must not read him—though the temptation is persistent and strong—as though his sentences were statements. As such they would often be absurd; as signs, though inadequate, they may show us something of what has been happening.

"Poetry gives most pleasure when only generally and not perfectly understood." "Perfect" understanding might here be a product, something which a sufficiently delicate and elaborate account might represent, an end-state of thought and feeling to which understanding had led. It would obviously be possible to make up a rough scale with specimens of poetry arranged according to the degree to which their meanings settled down finally and remained fixed. We might then find that this scale agreed often with our usual rankings. Some would find this so, others not.

Whether this were so or not, one moral of immense critical importance emerges undeniably from any close study of the process of interpretation, of understanding, of reading. Like most critical morals it is hardly a novelty, though its observance would have novel results. It is this,

ALL "READINGS" ARE "REMAKINGS":

that a judgment seemingly about a poem is primarily evidence about a reading of it. There are ways of reading almost any poem so as to make it magnificent or ludicrous. Opinions about it to either effect really tell us how it has been read. Every critical opinion is an ellipsis; a conditional assertion with the conditional part omitted. Fully expanded it would state that if a mind of a certain sort, under certain conditions (stage of its development, width of its recoverable experience, height of its temporary vigilance, direction of its temporary interest, etc.), has, at scores, or hundreds, or thousands of points in the growth of its response to certain words, taken certain courses; then such and such. But, as a rule, it seems to be immediately about a certain fictional public object, a projected experience, the poem. It pretends to be, and is usually taken to be, a categoric assertion, discussible as though it were in simple logical relations, of agreement or contradiction and so on, with other assertions of the same type. But these also are collapsed conditional statements. Marvellously alike though we are, it would be fantastic to suggest that our interpretations are often sufficiently similar for critical discussions to yield *the kind of profit we profess to expect.* But they may yield a different profit in increased knowledge of, and skill with, ourselves and others.

It may seem that on this view the difference between good and bad reading has gone; that there is no sense left for "correct" as applied to interpretations. This would be a mistake. We can always give a sense to a word if we want one, and here we more than want, we *need* a sense for "correct," or rather, we need several. One for occasions when we are asking about communication, another for semantics, another for orthology, another for general critical purposes, and yet another for the comparison of readings. To take this last only, the *tests,* we should ordinarily say, for the correctness of any interpretation of a set of complex signs are its internal coherence and its coherence with all else that is relevant. But this is an unnecessarily fictitious way of talking. We can say instead that this inner and outer coherence is the correctness. When an interpretation hangs together (without conflict-

A STANDARD FOR INTERPRETATION:

ing with anything else: history, literary tradition, etc.) we call it correct—when it takes into account all the items given for interpretation and orders the other items, by which it interprets them, in the most acceptable manner. There are problems behind such a formulation. Correct interpretations of bad and good writing will not hang together in the same specific ways, for example, but though these problems are large ones there seems nothing to prevent an inquiry which would be repaying. We may not have "the correct interpretation" of a passage and we probably won't have it and we might not recognize it for such if we had it; in this our definition agrees nicely with the ordinary use of "correct"—which perhaps follows some such definition as "corresponding to what was in the poet's mind." But ours has this advantage, that we need not, in judging correctness, attempt, even by fiction, to trespass across Acheron.

* *. *

The reader may be glad to have the opening three lines of *Gebir*, III—omitted by me in this experiment to heighten the difficulty:

> *O for the spirit of that matchless man*
> *Whom nature led throughout her whole domain,*
> *While he, embodied, breath'd etherial air.*

I do not think that their presence would have made much difference to the comments.

Editor's Note

*A*lice in Wonderland: The Child as Swain first appeared in *Some Versions of Pastoral* (1935) by William Empson, issued in America as *English Pastoral Poetry* (1938). All rights reserved. Reprinted by permission of the publisher, New Directions.

William Empson was born in Howden, Yorkshire, England, in 1906, and educated at Cambridge, where he took a degree in mathematics and did graduate study in English literature under I. A. Richards. He has taught at the Bunrika Daigaku in Toyko (where this essay was written) and at the Peking National University, and now teaches at Sheffield University. Empson is the author of several volumes of poetry, represented in *Collected Poems* (1955), and of three volumes of criticism: *Seven Types of Ambiguity* (1930), *Some Versions of Pastoral,* and *The Structure of Complex Words* (1951).

SEVEN

William Empson

Alice in Wonderland:
The Child as Swain

It must seem a curious thing that there has been so little serious criticism of the Alices, and that so many critics, with so militant and eager an air of good taste, have explained that they would not think of attempting it. Even Mr. De La Mare's book, which made many good points, is queerly evasive in tone. There seems to be a feeling that real criticism would involve psycho-analysis, and that the results would be so improper as to destroy the atmosphere of the books altogether. Dodgson was too conscious a writer to be caught out so easily. For instance it is an obvious bit of interpretation to say that the Queen of Hearts is a symbol of "uncontrolled animal passion" seen through the clear but blank eyes of sexlessness; obvious, and the sort of thing critics are now so sure would be in bad taste; Dodgson said it himself, to the actress who took the part when the thing was acted. The books are so frankly about growing up that there is no great discovery in translating them into Freudian terms; it seems only the proper exegesis of a classic even where it would be a shock to the author. On the whole the results of the analysis, when put into drawing-room language, are his conscious opinions; and if there was no other satisfactory outlet for his feelings but the special one fixed in his books the same is true in a degree of any original artist. I shall use psycho-analysis where it seems relevant, and feel I had better begin by saying what use it is supposed to be. Its business here is not to discover a neurosis peculiar to Dodgson. The essential idea behind the books is a shift onto the child, which Dodgson did not invent, of the obscure tradition of pastoral. The formula is now *"child-become-judge,"* and if Dodgson identifies himself with the child so does the writer of the primary sort of pastoral with his magnified version of the swain. (He took an excellent photograph, much admired by Tennyson, of Alice Liddell as a ragged beggar-girl, which seems a sort of example of the connection.) I should say indeed that this version was more open to neurosis than the older ones; it is less hopeful and more a return into oneself. The analysis should show how this works in general. But there are other things to be said about such a version of pastoral; its use of the device prior to irony lets it make covert judgments about any matter the author was interested in.

There is a tantalising one about Darwinism. The first Neanderthal skull was found in 1856. *The Origin of Species* (1859) came out six years before *Wonderland,* three before its conception, and was very much in the air, a pervading bad smell. It is hard to say how far Dodgson under cover of nonsense was using ideas of which his set disapproved; he wrote some hysterical passages against vivisection and has a curious remark to the effect that chemistry professors had better not have laboratories, but was open to new ideas and doubted the eternity of hell. The 1860 meeting of the British Association, at which Huxley started his career as publicist and gave that resounding snub to Bishop Wilberforce, was held at Oxford where Dodgson was already in residence. He had met Tennyson in '56, and we hear of Tennyson lecturing him later on the likeness of monkeys' and men's skulls.

The only passage that I feel sure involves evolution comes at the beginning of *Wonderland* (the most spontaneous and "subconscious" part of the books) when Alice gets out of the bath of tears that has magically released her from the underground chamber; it is made clear (for instance about watering-places) that the salt water is the sea from which life arose; as a bodily product it is also the amniotic fluid (there are other forces at work here); ontogeny then repeats phylogeny, and a whole Noah's Ark gets out of the sea with her. In Dodgson's own illustration as well as Tenniel's there is the disturbing head of a monkey and in the text there is an extinct bird. Our minds having thus been forced back onto the history of species there is a reading of history from the period when the Mouse "came over" with the Conqueror; questions of race turn into the questions of breeding in which Dodgson was more frankly interested, and there are obscure snubs for people who boast about their ancestors. We then have the Caucus Race (the word had associations for Dodgson with local politics; he says somewhere, "I never go to a Caucus without reluctance"), in which you begin running when you like and leave off when you like, and all win. The subtlety of this is that it supports Natural Selection (in the offensive way the nineteenth century did) to show the absurdity of democracy, and supports democracy (or at any rate liberty) to show the absurdity of Natural Selection. The race is not to the swift because idealism will not let it be to the swift, and because life, as we are told in the final poem, is at random and a dream. But there is no weakening of human values in this generosity; all the animals win, and Alice because she is Man has therefore to give them comfits, but though they demand this they do not fail to recognise that she is superior. They give her her own elegant thimble, the symbol of her labour, because she too has won, and because the highest among you shall be the servant of all. This is a solid piece of symbolism; the politically minded scientists preaching progress through "selection" and *laissez-faire* are confronted with the full anarchy of Christ. And the pretence of infantilism allows it a certain grim honesty; Alice is a little ridiculous and discomfited, under cover of charm, and would prefer a more aristocratic system.

In the *Looking-Glass* too there are ideas about progress at an early stage of the journey of growing up. Alice goes quickly through the first square by railway, in a carriage full of animals in a state of excitement about the progress of business and machinery; the only man is Disraeli dressed in newspapers—the new man who gets on by self-advertisement, the newspaper-fed man who believes in progress, possibly even the rational dress of the future.

> . . . to her great surprise, they all *thought* in chorus (I hope you understand what *thinking in chorus* means—for I must confess that *I* don't), "Better say nothing at all. Language is worth a thousand pounds a word."
>
> "I shall dream of a thousand pounds to-night, I know I shall," thought Alice.
>
> All this time the Guard was looking at her, first through a telescope, then through a microscope, and then through an opera-glass. At last he said, "You're travelling the wrong way," and shut up the window and went away.

This seems to be a prophecy; Huxley in the Romanes lecture of 1893, and less clearly beforehand, said that the human sense of right must judge and often be opposed to the progress imposed by Nature, but at this time he was still looking through the glasses.

> But the gentleman dressed in white paper leaned forwards and whispered in her ear, "Never mind what they all say, my dear, but take a return ticket every time the train stops."

In 1861 "many Tory members considered that the prime minister was a better representative of conservative opinions than the leader of the opposition" (*D.N.B.*). This seems to be the double outlook of Disraeli's conservatism, too subtle to inspire action. I think he turns up again as the unicorn when the Lion and the Unicorn are fighting for the Crown; they make a great dust and nuisance, treat the commonsense Alice as entirely mythical, and are very frightening to the poor king to whom the Crown really belongs.

> "Indeed I shan't," Alice said rather impatiently. "I don't belong to this railway journey at all—I was in a wood just now—and I wish I could get back there!"

When she gets back to the wood it is different; it is Nature in the raw, with no names, and she is afraid of it. She still thinks the animals are right to stay there; even when they know their names "they wouldn't answer at all, if they were wise." (They might do well to write nonsense books under an assumed name, and refuse to answer even to that.) All this is a very Kafka piece of symbolism, less at ease than the preceding one; *Wonderland* is a dream, but the *Looking-Glass* is self-consciousness. But both are topical; whether you call the result allegory or "pure nonsense" it depends on ideas about progress and industrialisation, and there is room for exegesis on the matter.

The beginning of modern child-sentiment may be placed at the obscure edition of *Mother Goose's Melodies* (John Newbury, 1760), with "maxims" very probably by Goldsmith. The important thing is not the rhymes (Boston boasts an edition of 1719. My impression is that they improved as time went on) but the appended maxims, which take a sophisticated pleasure in them. Most are sensible proverbs which the child had better know anyway; their charm (mainly for the adult) comes from the unexpected view of the story you must take if they are not to be irrelevant.

Amphion's Song of Eurydice.

I won't be my Father's Jack,
I won't be my Father's Jill,
I won't be the Fiddler's Wife,
And I will have music when I will.

T'other little Tune,
T'other little Tune,
Prithee Love play me
T'other little Tune.

MAXIM.—Those Arts are the most valuable which are of the greatest Use.

It seems to be the fiddler whose art has been useful in controlling her, but then again she may have discovered the art of wheedling the fiddler. The pomp of the maxim and the childishness of the rhyme make a mock-pastoral

compound. The pleasure in children here is obviously a
derivative of the pleasure in Macheath; the children are
"little rogues."

> *Bow wow wow*
> *Whose dog art Thou?*
> *Little Tom Tinker's Dog.*
> *Bow wow wow.*

Tom Tinker's Dog is a very good Dog; and an
honester Dog than his Master.

Honest ("free from hypocrisy" or the patronising tone to
a social inferior) and *dog* ("you young dog") have their
Beggar's Opera feelings here; it is not even clear whether
Tom is a young vagabond or a child.

This is a pleasant example because one can trace the
question back. Pope engraved a couplet "on the collar of
a dog which I gave to His Royal Highness"—a friendly
act as from one gentleman to another resident in the
neighbourhood.

> *I am his Highness' dog at Kew.*
> *Pray tell me, sir, whose dog are you?*

Presumably Frederick himself would be the first to read
it. The joke carries a certain praise for the underdog; the
point is not that men are slaves but that they find it suits
them and remain good-humoured. The dog is proud of
being the prince's dog and expects no one to take offence
at the question. There is also a hearty independence in its
lack of respect for the inquirer. Pope took this from Sir
William Temple, where it is said by a fool: "I am the
Lord Chamberlain's fool. And whose are you?" was his
answer to the nobleman. It is a neat case of the slow
shift of this sentiment from fool to rogue to child.

Alice, I think, is more of a "little rogue" than it is usual
to say, or than Dodgson himself thought in later years:

> loving as a dog . . . and gentle as a fawn; then
> courteous,—courteous to *all,* high or low, grand or
> grotesque, King or Caterpillar . . . trustful, with an
> absolute trust. . . .

and so on. It depends what you expect of a child of seven.

> . . . she had quite a long argument with the Lory, who at last turned sulky, and would only say, "I am older than you, and must know better"; and this Alice would not allow without knowing how old it was, and as the Lory positively refused to tell its age, there was no more to be said.

Alice had to be made to speak up to bring out the points —here the point is a sense of the fundamental oddity of life given by the fact that different animals become grown-up at different ages; but still if you accept the Lory as a grown-up this is rather a pert child. She is often the underdog speaking up for itself.

A quite separate feeling about children, which is yet at the back of the pertness here and in the Goldsmith, since it is needed if the pertness is to be charming, may be seen in its clearest form in Wordsworth and Coleridge; it is the whole point of the *Ode to Intimations* and even of *We are Seven*. The child has not yet been put wrong by civilisation, and all grown-ups have been. It may well be true that Dodgson envied the child because it was sexless, and Wordsworth because he knew that he was destroying his native poetry by the smugness of his life, but neither theory explains why this feeling about children arose when it did and became so general. There is much of it in Vaughan after the Civil War, but as a general tendency it appeared when the eighteenth-century settlement had come to seem narrow and unescapable; one might connect it with the end of duelling; also when the scientific sort of truth had been generally accepted as the main and real one. It strengthened as the aristocracy became more puritan. It depends on a feeling, whatever may have caused that in its turn, that no way of building up character, no intellectual system, can bring out all that is inherent in the human spirit, and therefore that there is more in the child than any man has been able to keep. (The child is a microcosm like Donne's world, and Alice too is a stoic.) This runs through all Victorian and Romantic literature;

the world of the adult made it hard to be an artist, and
they kept a sort of tap-root going down to their experience
as children. Artists like Wordsworth and Coleridge, who
accepted this fact and used it, naturally come to seem the
most interesting and in a way the most sincere writers of
the period. Their idea of the child, that it is in the right
relation to Nature, not dividing what should be unified,
that its intuitive judgment contains what poetry and philosophy must spend their time labouring to recover, was
accepted by Dodgson and a main part of his feeling. He
quotes Wordsworth on this point in the "Easter Greeting"
—the child feels its life in every limb; Dodgson advises
it, with an infelicitous memory of the original poem, to
give its attention to death from time to time. That the
dream books are

> *Like Pilgrim's withered wreaths of flowers*
> *Plucked in a far-off land*

is a fine expression of Wordsworth's sense both of the
poetry of childhood and of his advancing sterility. And
the moment when she finds herself dancing with Tweedle-
dum and Tweedledee, so that it is difficult to introduce
herself afterwards, is a successful interruption of Wordsworthian sentiment into his normal style.

> . . . she took hold of both hands at once; the next
> moment they were dancing round in a ring. This
> seemed quite natural (she remembered afterwards),
> and she was not even surprised to hear music playing:
> it seemed to come from the tree under which they
> were dancing, and it was done (as well as she could
> make out) by the branches rubbing one against an-
> other, like fiddles and fiddle-sticks. . . . "I don't
> know when I began it, but somehow I felt as if I had
> been singing it a long long time."

This is presented as like the odd behaviour of comic
objects such as soup-tureens, but it is a directer version of
the idea of the child's unity with nature. She has been
singing a long long time because she sang with no temporal limits in that imperial palace whence she came. Yet

it is the frank selfishness of the brothers, who being little boys are horrid, are made into a satire on war, and will only give her the hands free from hugging each other, that forces her into the ring with them that produces eternity. Even here this puts a subtle doubt into the eternities open to the child.

For Dodgson will only go half-way with the sentiment of the child's unity with nature, and has another purpose for his heroine; she is the free and independent mind. Not that this is contradictory; because she is right about life she is independent from all the other characters who are wrong. But it is important to him because it enables him to clash the Wordsworth sentiments with the other main tradition about children derived from rogue-sentiment. (For both, no doubt, he had to go some way back; the intervening sentiment about children is that the great thing is to repress their Original Sin, and I suppose, though he would not have much liked it, he was among the obscure influences that led to the cult of games in the public schools.)

One might say that the Alices differ from other versions of pastoral in lacking the sense of glory. Normally the idea of including all sorts of men in yourself brings in an idea of reconciling yourself with nature and therefore gaining power over it. The Alices are more self-protective; the dream cuts out the real world and the delicacy of the mood is felt to cut out the lower classes. This is true enough, but when Humpty Dumpty says that glory means a nice knock-down argument he is not far from the central feeling of the book. There is a real feeling of isolation and yet just that is taken as the source of power.

The obvious parody of Wordsworth is the poem of the White Knight, an important figure for whom Dodgson is willing to break the language of humour into the language of sentiment. It takes off *Resolution and Independence,* a genuine pastoral poem if ever there was one; the endurance of the leechgatherer gives Wordsworth strength to face the pain of the world. Dodgson was fond of saying that one parodied the best poems, or anyway that parody showed no lack of admiration, but a certain bitterness is

inherent in parody; if the meaning is not "This poem is
absurd" it must be "In my present mood of emotional
sterility the poem will not work, or I am afraid to let it
work, on *me*." The parody here will have no truck with
the dignity of the leechgatherer, but the point of that
is to make the unworldly dreaminess of the Knight more
absurd; there may even be a reproach for Wordsworth in
the lack of consideration that makes him go on asking
the same question. One feels that the Knight has probably
imagined most of the old man's answers, or anyway that
the old man was playing up to the fool who questioned
him. At any rate there is a complete shift of interest from
the virtues of the leechgatherer onto the childish but profound virtues of his questioner.

The main basis of the joke is the idea of absurd inventions of new foods. Dodgson was well-informed about
food, kept his old menus and was wine-taster to the
College; but ate very little, suspected the High Table of
overeating, and would see no reason to deny that he connected overeating with other forms of sensuality. One
reason for the importance of rich food here is that it is
the child's symbol for all luxuries reserved for grown-ups.
I take it that the fascination of Soup and of the Mock
Turtle who sings about it was that soup is mainly eaten
at dinner, the excitingly grown-up meal eaten after the
child has gone to bed. When Alice talks about her dinner
she presumably means lunch, and it is rather a boast
when she says she has already met whiting. In the White
Knight's song and conversation these little jokes based on
fear of sensuality are put to a further use; he becomes the
scientist, the inventor, whose mind is nobly but absurdly
detached from interest in the pleasures of the senses and
even from "good sense."

"How *can* you go on talking so quietly, head downwards?" Alice asked, as she dragged him out by the
feet, and laid him in a heap on the bank.

The Knight looked surprised at the question. "What
does it matter where my body happens to be?" he
said. "My mind goes on working all the same. In fact,

the more head downwards I am, the more I keep inventing new things."

"Now the cleverest thing that I ever did," he went on after a pause, "was inventing a new pudding during the meat-course."

This required extreme detachment; the word "clever" has become a signal that the mind is being admired for such a reason. The more absurd the assumptions of the thinking, for instance those of scientific materialism, the more vigorous the thought based upon it. "Life is so strange that his results have the more chance of being valuable because his assumptions are absurd, but we must not forget that they are so." This indeed is as near the truth as one need get about scientific determinism.

One reason for the moral grandeur of the Knight, then, is that he stands for the Victorian scientist, who was felt to have invented a new kind of Roman virtue; earnestly, patiently, carefully (it annoyed Samuel Butler to have these words used so continually about scientists) without sensuality, without self-seeking, without claiming any but a fragment of knowledge, he goes on labouring at his absurd but fruitful conceptions. But the parody makes him stand also for the poet, and Wordsworth would have been pleased by this; he considered that the poet was essentially one who revived our sense of the original facts of nature, and should use scientific ideas where he could; poetry was the impassioned expression of the face of all science; Wordsworth was as successful in putting life into the abstract words of science as into "the plain language of men," and many of the Lyrical Ballads are best understood as psychological notes written in a form that saves one from forgetting their actuality. The Knight has the same readiness to accept new ideas and ways of life, such as the sciences were imposing, without ceasing to be good and in his way sensible, as Alice herself shows for instance when in falling down the rabbit-hole she plans a polite entry into the Antipodes and is careful not to drop the marmalade onto the inhabitants. It is the childishness of the Knight that lets him combine the virtues of the poet and the scientist, and one must expect a creature so finely suited to life to be absurd because life itself is absurd.

The talking animal convention and the changes of relative size appear in so different a children's book as *Gulliver;* they evidently make some direct appeal to the child whatever more sophisticated ideas are piled onto them. Children feel at home with animals conceived as human; the animal can be made affectionate without its making serious emotional demands on them, does not want to educate them, is at least unconventional in the sense that it does not impose its conventions, and does not make a secret of the processes of nature. So the talking animals here are a child-world; the rule about them is that they are always friendly though childishly frank to Alice while she is small, and when she is big (suggesting grown-up) always opposed to her, or by her, or both. But talking animals in children's books had been turned to didactic purposes ever since Aesop; the schoolmastering tone in which the animals talk nonsense to Alice is partly a parody of this—they are really childish but try not to look it. On the other hand, this tone is so supported by the way they can order her about, the firm and surprising way their minds work, the abstract topics they work on, the useless rules they accept with so much conviction, that we take them as real grown-ups contrasted with unsophisticated childhood. "The grown-up world is as odd as the child-world, and both are a dream." This ambivalence seems to correspond to Dodgson's own attitude to children; he, like Alice, wanted to get the advantages of being childish and grown-up at once. In real life this seems to have at least occasional disadvantages both ways; one remembers the little girl who screamed and demanded to be taken from the lunch-table because she knew she couldn't solve his puzzles (not, apparently, a usual, but one would think a natural reaction to his mode of approach)—she clearly thought him too grown-up; whereas in the scenes of jealousy with his little girls' parents the grown-ups must have thought him quite enough of a child. He made a success of the process, and it seems clear that it did none of the little girls any harm, but one cannot help cocking one's eye at it as a way of life.

The changes of size are more complex. In Gulliver they are the impersonal eye; to change size and nothing else makes you feel "this makes one see things as they are in themselves." It excites Wonder but of a scientific sort. Swift used it for satire on science or from a horrified interest in it, and to give a sort of scientific authority to his deductions, that men seen as small are spiritually petty and seen as large physically loathsome. And it is the small observer, like the child, who does least to alter what he sees and therefore sees most truly. (The definition of potential, in all but the most rigid textbooks of electricity, contents itself with talking about the force on a *small* charge which doesn't alter the field *much*. The objection that the small alteration in the field might be proportional to the small force does not occur easily to the reader.) To mix this with a pious child's type of Wonder made science seem less irreligious and gave you a feeling that you were being good because educating a child; Faraday's talks for children on the chemical history of a candle came out in 1861, so the method was in the air. But these are special uses of a material rich in itself. Children like to think of being so small that they could hide from grown-ups and so big that they could control them, and to do this dramatises the great topic of growing up, which both Alices keep to consistently. In the same way the charm of Jabberwocky is that it is a code language, the language with which grown-ups hide things from children or children from grown-ups. Also the words are such good tongue-gestures, in Sir Richard Paget's phrase, that they seem to carry their own meaning; this carries a hint of the paradox that the conventions are natural.

Both books also keep to the topic of death—the first two jokes about death in *Wonderland* come on pages 3 and 4—and for the child this may be a natural connection; I remember believing I should have to die in order to grow up, and thinking the prospect very disagreeable. There seems to be a connection in Dodgson's mind between the death of childhood and the development of sex, which might be pursued into many of the details of the books. Alice will die if the Red King wakes up, partly because she is a dream-product of the author and partly because the pawn is put back in its box at the end of the game. He is the absent husband of the Red Queen who is a governess, and the end of the book comes when Alice defeats the Red Queen and "mates" the King. Everything seems to break up because she arrives at a piece of *knowledge,* that all the poems are about fish. I should say the idea was somehow at work at the end of *Wonderland* too. The trial is meant to be a mystery; Alice is told to leave the court, as if a child ought not to hear the evidence, and yet they expect her to give evidence herself.

"What do you know about this business?" the King said to Alice.

"Nothing," said Alice.

"Nothing *whatever?*" persisted the King.

"Nothing whatever," said Alice.

"That's very important," the King said, turning to the jury. They were just beginning to write this down on their slates, when the White Rabbit interrupted: *"Un*important, your Majesty means, of course," he said in a very respectful tone, but frowning and making faces as he spoke.

*"Un*important, of course, I meant," the King hastily said, and went on to himself in an undertone, "important—unimportant—unimportant—important—" as if he were trying which word sounded best.

There is no such stress in the passage as would make one feel there must be something behind it, and certainly it is funny enough as it stands. But I think Dodgson felt it was important that Alice should be innocent of all knowledge of what the Knave of Hearts (a flashy-looking lady's-man in the picture) is likely to have been doing, and also important that she should not be told she is innocent. That is why the king, always a well-intentioned man, is embarrassed. At the same time Dodgson feels that Alice is right in thinking "it doesn't matter a bit" which word the jury write down; she is too stable in her detach-

ment to be embarrassed, these things will not interest her,
and in a way she includes them all in herself. And it is
the refusal to let her stay that makes her revolt and break
the dream. It is tempting to read an example of this idea
into the poem that introduces the *Looking-Glass.*

> *Come, hearken then, ere voice of dread,*
> *With bitter summons laden,*
> *Shall summon to unwelcome bed*
> *A melancholy maiden.*

After all the marriage-bed was more likely to be the end
of the maiden than the grave, and the metaphor firmly implied treats them as identical.

The last example is obviously more a joke against
Dodgson than anything else, and though the connection
between death and the development of sex is I think at
work it is not the main point of the conflict about growing up. Alice is given a magical control over her growth
by the traditionally symbolic caterpillar, a creature which
has to go through a sort of death to become grown-up,
and then seems a more spiritual creature. It refuses to
agree with Alice that this process is at all peculiar, and
clearly her own life will be somehow like it, but the main
idea is not its development of sex. The butterfly implied
may be the girl when she is "out" or her soul when in
heaven, to which she is now nearer than she will be when
she is "out"; she must walk to it by walking away from
it. Alice knows several reasons why she should object to
growing up, and does not at all like being an obvious
angel, a head out of contact with its body that has to come
down from the sky, and gets mistaken for the Paradisal
serpent of the knowledge of good and evil, and by the
pigeon of the Annunciation, too. But she only makes herself smaller for reasons of tact or proportion; the triumphant close of *Wonderland* is that she has outgrown her
fancies and can afford to wake and despise them. The
Looking-Glass is less of a dream-product, less concentrated
on the child's situation, and (once started) less full of
changes of size; but it has the same end; the governess
shrinks to a kitten when Alice has grown from a pawn to

a queen, and can shake her. Both these clearly stand for
becoming grown-up and yet in part are a revolt against
grown-up behavior; there is the same ambivalence as about
the talking animals. Whether children often find this symbolism as interesting as Carroll did is another thing; there
are recorded cases of tears at such a betrayal of the reality
of the story. I remember feeling that the ends of the books
were a sort of necessary assertion that the grown-up world
was after all the proper one; one did not object to that in
principle, but would no more turn to those parts from
preference than to the "Easter Greeting to Every Child
that Loves Alice" (Gothic type).

To make the dream-story from which *Wonderland* was
elaborated seem Freudian one has only to tell it. A fall
through a deep hole into the secrets of Mother Earth
produces a new enclosed soul wondering who it is, what
will be its position in the world, and how it can get out.
It is in a long low hall, part of the palace of the Queen of
Hearts (a neat touch), from which it can only get out to
the fresh air and the fountains through a hole frighteningly
too small. Strange changes, caused by the way it is nour-
ished there, happen to it in this place, but always when it
is big it cannot get out and when it is small it is not
allowed to; for one thing, being a little girl, it has no key.
The nightmare theme of the birth-trauma, that she grows
too big for the room and is almost crushed by it, is not
only used here but repeated more painfully after she
seems to have got out; the rabbit sends her sternly into
its house and some food there makes her grow again. In
Dodgson's own drawing of Alice when cramped into the
room with one foot up the chimney, kicking out the hate-
ful thing that tries to come down (she takes away its
pencil when it is a juror), she is much more obviously
in the foetus position than in Tenniel's. The White Rabbit
is Mr. Spooner to whom the spoonerisms happened, an
undergraduate in 1862, but its business here is as a pet for
children which they may be allowed to breed. Not that
the clearness of the framework makes the interpretation
simple; Alice peering through the hole into the garden
may be wanting a return to the womb as well as an escape

from it; she is fond, we are told, of taking both sides of an argument when talking to herself, and the whole book balances between the luscious nonsense-world of fantasy and the ironic nonsense-world of fact.

I said that the sea of tears she swims in was the amniotic fluid, which is much too simple. You may take it as Lethe in which the souls were bathed before re-birth (and it is their own tears; they forget, as we forget our childhood, through the repression of pain) or as the "solution" of an intellectual contradiction through Intuition and a return to the Unconscious. Anyway it is a sordid image made pretty; one need not read Dodgson's satirical verses against babies to see how much he would dislike a child wallowing in its tears in real life. The fondness of small girls for doing this has to be faced early in attempting to prefer them, possibly to small boys, certainly to grown-ups; to a man idealising children as free from the falsity of a rich emotional life their displays of emotion must be particularly disconcerting. The celibate may be forced to observe them, on the floor of a railway carriage for example, after a storm of fury, dabbling in their ooze; covertly snuggling against mamma while each still pretends to ignore the other. The symbolic pleasure of dabbling seems based on an idea that the liquid itself is the bad temper which they have got rid of by the storm and yet are still hugging, or that they are not quite impotent since they have at least "done" this much about the situation. The acid quality of the style shows that Dodgson does not entirely like having to love creatures whose narcissism takes this form, but he does not want simply to forget it as he too would like a relief from "ill-temper"; he sterilises it from the start by giving it a charming myth. The love for narcissists itself seems mainly based on a desire to keep oneself safely detached, which is the essential notion here.

The symbolic completeness of Alice's experience is I think important. She runs the whole gamut; she is a father in getting down the hole, a foetus at the bottom, and can only be born by becoming a mother and producing her own amniotic fluid. Whether his mind played the trick of putting this into the story or not he has the feelings that would correspond to it. A desire to include all sexuality in the girl child, the least obviously sexed of human creatures, the one that keeps its sex in the safest place, was an important part of their fascination for him. He is partly imagining himself as the girl-child (with these comforting characteristics) partly as its father (these together make *it* a father) partly as its lover—so it might be a mother—but then of course it is clever and detached enough to do everything for itself. He told one of his little girls a story about cats wearing gloves over their claws: "For you see, 'gloves' have got 'love' inside them—there's none outside, you know." So far from its dependence, the child's independence is the important thing, and the theme behind that is the self-centred emotional life imposed by the detached intelligence.

The famous cat is a very direct symbol of this ideal of intellectual detachment; all cats are detached, and since this one grins it is the amused observer. It can disappear because it can abstract itself from its surroundings into a more interesting inner world; it appears only as a head because it is almost a disembodied intelligence, and only as a grin because it can impose an atmosphere without being present. In frightening the king by the allowable act of looking at him it displays the soul-force of Mr. Gandhi; it is unbeheadable because its soul cannot be killed; and its influence brings about a short amnesty in the divided nature of the Queen and Duchess. Its cleverness makes it formidable—it has very long claws and a great many teeth—but Alice is particularly at home with it; she is the same sort of thing.

The Gnat gives a more touching picture of Dodgson; he treats nowhere more directly of his actual relations with the child. He feels he is liable to nag at it, as a gnat would, and the gnat turns out, as he is, to be alarmingly big as a friend for the child, but at first it sounds tiny because he means so little to her. It tries to amuse her by rather frightening accounts of other dangerous insects, other grown-ups. It is reduced to tears by the melancholy of its own jokes, which it usually can't bear to finish; only if Alice had made them, as it keeps egging her on to do,

would they be at all interesting. That at least would show
the child had paid some sort of attention, and he could
go away and repeat them to other people. The desire
to have jokes made all the time, he feels, is a painful and
obvious confession of spiritual discomfort, and the freedom of Alice from such a feeling makes her unapproach-
able.

"Don't tease so," said Alice, looking about in vain
to see where the voice came from; "if you're so anxious to have a joke made, why don't you make one
yourself?"

The little voice sighed deeply: it was *very* unhappy,
evidently, and Alice would have said something pity-
ing to comfort it, "if it would only sigh like other
people!" she thought. But this was such a wonderfully
small sigh, that she wouldn't have heard it at all, if
it hadn't come *quite* close to her ear. The consequence of this was that it tickled her ear very much,
and quite took off her thoughts from the unhappiness
of the poor little creature.

"I know you are a friend," the little voice went on;
*"a dear friend, and an old friend. And you won't
hurt me, though I am an insect."*

"What kind of insect?" Alice inquired a little anx-
iously. What she really wanted to know was, whether
it could sting or not, but she thought this wouldn't
be quite a civil question to ask.

"What, then you don't—" the little voice began. . . .

"Don't know who I am! Does anybody not know who
I am?" He is afraid that even so innocent a love as his,
like all love, may be cruel, and yet it is she who is able
to hurt him, if only through his vanity. The implications
of these few pages are so painful that the ironical calm
of the close, when she kills it, seems delightfully gay and
strong. The Gnat is suggesting to her that she would like
to remain purely a creature of Nature and stay in the
wood where there are no names.

". . . That's a joke. I wish *you* had made it."

"Why do you wish *I* had made it?" Alice asked.
"It's a very bad one."

But the Gnat only sighed deeply, while two large
tears came rolling down its cheeks.

"You shouldn't make jokes," Alice said, "if it
makes you so unhappy."

Then came another of those melancholy little
sighs, and this time the poor Gnat really seemed to
have sighed itself away, for, when Alice looked up,
there was nothing whatever to be seen on the twig,
and, as she was getting quite chilly with sitting so
long, she got up and walked on.

The overpunctuation and the flat assonance of "long—
on" add to the effect. There is something charmingly prim
and well-meaning about the way she sweeps aside the
feelings that she can't deal with. One need not suppose
that Dodgson ever performed this scene, which he can
imagine so clearly, but there is too much self-knowledge
here to make the game of psycho-analysis seem merely
good fun.

The scene in which the Duchess has become friendly
to Alice at the garden-party shows Alice no longer separate from her creator; it is clear that Dodgson would be
as irritated as she is by the incident, and is putting himself in her place. The obvious way to read it is as the
middle-aged woman trying to flirt with the chaste young
man.

"The game seems to be going on rather better
now," she said.

" 'Tis so," said the Duchess; "and the moral of it
is—'Oh, 'tis love, 'tis love, that makes the world go
round!' "

"Somebody said," whispered Alice, "that it's done
by everybody minding their own business!"

"Ah, well! It means much the same thing," said
the Duchess, digging her sharp little chin into Alice's
shoulder as she added, "and the moral of *that* is—

'Take care of the sense, and the sounds will take care
of themselves.' "

"How fond she is of finding morals in things,"
Alice thought to herself.

Both are true because the generous and the selfish kinds
of love have the same name; the Duchess seems to take
the view of the political economists, that the greatest
public good is produced by the greatest private selfishness.
All this talk about "morals" makes Alice suspicious; also
she is carrying a flamingo, a pink bird with a long neck.
"The chief difficulty Alice found at first was in managing
her flamingo . . . it *would* twist itself round and look up
in her face."

"I dare say you're wondering why I don't put my
arm round your waist," the Duchess said after a
pause: "the reason is, that I'm doubtful about the
temper of your flamingo. Shall I try the experiment?"

"He might bite," Alice cautiously replied, not feeling at all anxious to have the experiment tried.

"Very true," said the Duchess: "flamingoes and
mustard both bite. And the moral of that is—'Birds
of a feather flock together.' "

Mustard may be classed with the pepper that made her
"ill-tempered" when she had so much of it in the soup,
so that flamingoes and mustard become the desires of
the two sexes. No doubt Dodgson would be indignant
at having this meaning read into his symbols, but the
meaning itself, if he had been intending to talk about the
matter, is just what he would have wished to say.

The Duchess then jumps away to another aspect of
the selfishness of our nature.

"It's a mineral, I *think*," said Alice.

"Of course it is," said the Duchess, who seemed
ready to agree to everything that Alice said; "there's
a large mustard-mine near here. And the moral of
that is—'The more there is of mine, the less there is
of yours.' "

One could put the same meanings in again, but a new
one has come forward: "Industrialism is as merely greedy
as sex; all we get from it is a sharper distinction between
rich and poor." They go off into riddles about sincerity
and how one can grow into what one would seem to be.

This sort of "analysis" is a peep at machinery; the
question for criticism is what is done with the machine.
The purpose of a dream on the Freudian theory is simply
to keep you in an undisturbed state so that you can go
on sleeping; in the course of this practical work you may
produce something of more general value, but not only
of one sort. Alice has, I understand, become a patron
saint of the Surrealists, but they do not go in for Comic
Primness, a sort of reserve of force, which is her chief
charm. Wyndham Lewis avoided putting her beside Proust
and Lorelei to be danced on as a debilitating child-cult
(though she is a bit of pragmatist too); the present-day
reader is more likely to complain of her complacence. In
this sort of child-cult the child, though a means of imaginative escape, becomes the critic; Alice is the most reasonable and responsible person in the book. This is meant as
charmingly pathetic about her as well as satire about her
elders, and there is some implication that the sane man
can take no other view of the world, even for controlling
it, than the child does; but this is kept a good distance
from sentimental infantilism. There is always some doubt
about the meaning of a man who says he wants to be like
a child, because he may want to be like it in having fresh
and vivid feelings and senses, in not knowing, expecting,
or desiring evil, in not having an analytical mind, in
having no sexual desires recognisable as such, or out of
a desire to be mothered and evade responsibility. He is
usually mixing them up—Christ's praise of children, given
perhaps for reasons I have failed to list, has made it a
respected thing to say, and it has been said often and
loosely—but he can make his own mixture; Lewis's invec-
tive hardly shows which he is attacking. The praise of
the child in the Alices mainly depends on a distaste not
only for sexuality but for all the distortions of vision that
go with a rich emotional life; the opposite idea needs

to be set against this, that you can only understand people
or even things by having such a life in yourself to be
their mirror; but the idea itself is very respectable. So
far as it is typical of the scientist the books are an expression of the scientific attitude (*e.g.* the bread-and-
butter fly) or a sort of satire on it that treats it as inevitable.

The most obvious aspect of the complacence is the
snobbery. It is clear that Alice is not only a very well-
brought-up but a very well-to-do little girl; if she has
grown into Mabel, so that she will have to go and live
in that poky little house and have next to no toys to play
with, she will refuse to come out of her rabbit-hole at
all. One is only surprised that she is allowed to meet
Mabel. All through the books odd objects of luxury are
viewed rather as Wordsworth viewed mountains; meaning-
less, but grand and irremovable; objects of myth. The
whiting, the talking leg of mutton, the soup-tureen, the
tea-tray in the sky, are obvious examples. The shift from
the idea of the child's unity with nature is amusingly complete; a mere change in the objects viewed makes it at one
with the conventions. But this is still not far from Wordsworth, who made his mountains into symbols of the stable
and moral society living among them. In part the joke of
this stands for the sincerity of the child that criticises the
folly of convention, but Alice is very respectful to conventions and interested to learn new ones; indeed the discussions about the rules of the game of conversation, those
stern comments on the isolation of humanity, put the tone
so strongly in favour of the conventions that one feels
there is nothing else in the world. There is a strange
clash on this topic about the three little sisters discussed
at the Mad Teaparty, who lived on treacle. "They couldn't
have done that, you know," Alice gently remarked, "they'd
have been ill." "So they were," said the Dormouse, "*very*
ill." The creatures are always self-centred and argumentative, to stand for the detachment of the intellect
from emotion, which is necessary to it and yet makes it
childish. Then the remark stands both for the danger of
taking as one's guide the natural desires ("this is the sort

of thing little girls would do if they were left alone") and for a pathetic example of a martyrdom to the conventions; the little girls did not mind *how* ill they were made by living on treacle, because it was their rule, and they knew it was expected of them. (That they are refined girls is clear from the fact that they do allegorical sketches.) There is an obscure connection here with the belief of the period that a really nice girl is "delicate" (the profound sentences implied by the combination of meanings in this word are (*a*) "you cannot get a woman to be refined unless you make her ill" and more darkly (*b*) "she is desirable because corpse-like"); Dodgson was always shocked to find that his little girls had appetites, because it made them seem less pure. The passage about the bread-and-butter fly brings this out more frankly, with something of the wilful grimness of Webster. It was a creature of such high refinement that it could only live on weak tea with cream in it (tea being the caller's meal, sacred to the fair, with nothing gross about it).

A new difficulty came into Alice's head.

> "Supposing it couldn't find any?" she suggested.
>
> "Then it would die, of course."
>
> "But that must happen very often," Alice remarked thoughtfully.
>
> "It always happens," said the Gnat.
>
> After this, Alice was silent for a minute or two, pondering.

There need be no gloating over the child's innocence here, as in Barrie; anybody might ponder. Alice has just suggested that flies burn themselves to death in candles out of a martyr's ambition to become Snapdragon flies. The talk goes on to losing one's name, which is the next stage on her journey, and brings freedom but is like death; the girl may lose her personality by growing up into the life of convention, and her virginity (like her surname) by marriage; or she may lose her "good name" when she loses the conventions "in the woods"—the animals, etc., there have no names because they are out of reach of the controlling reason; or when she develops sex she must neither understand nor name her feelings. The Gnat is weeping and Alice is afraid of the wood but determined to go on. "It always dies of thirst" or "it always dies in the end, as do we all"; "the life of highest refinement is the most deathly, yet what else is one to aim at when life is so brief, and when there is so little in it of any value." A certain ghoulishness in the atmosphere of this, of which the tight-lacing may have been a product or partial cause,[1] comes out very strongly in Henry James; the decadents pounced on it for their own purposes but could not put more death-wishes into it than these respectables had done already.

The blend of child-cult and snobbery that Alice shares with Oscar Wilde is indeed much more bouncing and cheerful; the theme here is that it is proper for the well-meaning and innocent girl to be worldly, because she, like the world, should know the value of her condition. "When we were girls we were brought up to know nothing, and very interesting it was"; "mamma, whose ideas on education are remarkably strict, has brought me up to be extremely short-sighted; so do you mind my looking at you through my glasses?" This joke seems to have come in after the Restoration dramatists as innocence recovered its social value; there are touches in Farquhar and it is strong in the *Beggar's Opera*. Sheridan has full control of it for Mrs. Malaprop.

> I don't think so much learning becomes a young woman. . . . But, Sir Anthony, I would send her, at nine years old, to a boarding school, in order to learn a little ingenuity and artifice. Then, sir, she should have a supercilious knowledge in accounts; and as she grew up, I would have her instructed in geometry, that she might learn something of the contagious countries; but above all, Sir Anthony, she should be mistress of orthodoxy, that she might not mis-spell, and mispronounce words so shamefully as girls

[1] It was getting worse when the Alices were written. In what Mr. Hugh Kingsmill calls "the fatal fifties" skirts were so big that the small waist was not much needed for contrast, so it can't be blamed for the literary works of that decade.

usually do; and likewise that she might reprehend the true meaning of what she is saying.

Dodgson has an imitation of this which may show, what many of his appreciators seem anxious to deny, that even *Wonderland* contains straight satire. The Mock Turtle was taught at school

> Reeling and Writing, of course, to begin with, and then the different branches of Arithmetic—Ambition, Distraction, Uglification, and Derision . . . Mystery, ancient and modern, with Seaography; then Drawling —the Drawling-master used to come once a week; *he* taught us Drawling, Stretching, and Fainting in Coils.

Children are to enjoy the jokes as against education, grown-ups as against a smart and too expensive education. Alice was not one of the climbers taught like this, and remarks firmly elsewhere that manners are not learnt from lessons. But she willingly receives social advice like "curtsey while you're thinking what to say, it saves time," and the doctrine that you must walk away from a queen if you really want to meet her has more point when said of the greed of the climber than of the unselfseeking curiosity of the small girl. Or it applies to both, and allows the climber a sense of purity and simplicity; I think this was a source of charm whether Dodgson meant it or not. Alice's own social assumptions are more subtle and all-pervading; she always seems to raise the tone of the company she enters, and to find this all the easier because the creatures are so rude to her. A central idea here is that the perfect lady can gain all the advantages of contempt without soiling herself by expressing or even feeling it.

> This time there could be no mistake about it; it was neither more nor less than a pig, and she felt that it would be quite absurd for her to carry it any further. So she set the little creature down, and felt quite relieved to see it trot quietly away into the wood. "If it had grown up," she said to herself, "it would have made a dreadfully ugly child, but it makes

rather a handsome pig, I think." And she began
thinking over other children she knew, who might do
very well as pigs, and was just saying to herself, "if
only one knew the right way to change them—"
when she was a little startled by seeing the Cheshire
Cat on the bough of a tree a few yards off.

The Cat only grinned when it saw Alice. It looked
good-natured, she thought: still it had very long claws
and a great many teeth, so she felt that it ought to be
treated with respect.

The effect of cuddling these mellow evasive phrases—
"a good deal"—"do very well as"—whose vagueness can
convey so rich an irony and so complete a detachment,
while making so firm a claim to show charming good-will,
is very close to that of Wilde's comedy. So is the hint of
a delicious slavishness behind the primness, and contrasting with the irony, of the last phrase. (But then Dodgson
feels the cat deserves respect as the detached intelligence
—he is enjoying the idea that Alice and other social
figures have got to respect Dodgson.) I think there is a
feeling that the aristocrat is essentially like the child because it is his business to make claims in advance of his
immediate personal merits; the child is not strong yet, and
the aristocrat only as part of a system; the best he can do
if actually asked for his credentials, since it would be
indecent to produce his pedigree, is to display charm and
hope it will appear unconscious, like the good young girl.
Wilde's version of this leaves rather a bad taste in the
mouth because it is slavish; it has something of the naïve
snobbery of the high-class servant. Whistler meant this by
the most crashing of his insults—"Oscar now stands forth
unveiled as his own 'gentleman'"—when Wilde took
shelter from a charge of plagiarism behind the claim that
a gentleman does not attend to coarse abuse.

Slavish, for one thing, because they were always juggling
between what they themselves thought wicked and what
the society they addressed thought wicked, talking about
sin when they meant scandal. The thrill of *Pen, Pencil and
Poison* is in the covert comparison between Wilde himself

and the poisoner, and Wilde certainly did not think his sexual habits as wicked as killing a friend to annoy an insurance company. By their very hints that they deserved notice as sinners they pretended to accept all the moral ideas of society, because they wanted to succeed in it, and yet society only took them seriously because they were connected with an intellectual movement which refused to accept some of those ideas. The Byronic theme of the man unable to accept the moral ideas of his society and yet torn by his feelings about them is real and permanent, but to base it on intellectual dishonesty is to short-circuit it; and leads to a claim that the life of highest refinement must be allowed a certain avid infantile petulance.

Alice is not a slave like this; she is almost too sure that she is good and right. The grown-up is egged on to imitate her not as a privileged decadent but as a privileged eccentric, a Victorian figure that we must be sorry to lose. The eccentric though kind and noble would be alarming from the strength of his virtues if he were less funny; Dodgson saw to it that this underlying feeling about his monsters was brought out firmly by Tenniel, who had been trained on drawing very serious things like the British Lion weeping over Gordon, for Punch. Their massive and romantic nobility is, I think, an important element in the effect; Dodgson did not get it in his own drawings (nor, by the way, did he give all the young men eunuchoid legs) but no doubt he would have done if he had been able. I should connect this weighty background with the tone of worldly goodness, of universal but not stupid charity, in Alice's remarks about the pig: "I shall do my best even for you; of course one will suffer, because you are not worth the efforts spent on you; but I have no temptation to be uncharitable to you because I am too far above you to need to put you in your place"— this is what her tone would develop into; a genuine readiness for self-sacrifice and a more genuine sense of power.

The qualities held in so subtle a suspension in Alice are shown in full blast in the two queens. It is clear that this sort of moral superiority involves a painful isolation, similar to those involved in the intellectual way of life and the life of chastity, which are here associated with it. The reference to *Maud* (1855) brings this out. It was a shocking book; mockery was deserved; and its improper freedom was parodied by the flowers at the beginning of the *Looking-Glass*. A taint of fussiness hangs over this sort of essay, but the parodies were assumed to be obvious (children who aren't forced to learn Dr. Watts can't get the same thrill from parodies of him as the original children did) and even this parody is not as obvious as it was. There is no doubt that the flowers are much funnier if you compare them with their indestructible originals.

> *whenever a March-wind sighs*
> *He sets the jewel-print of your feet*
> *In violets blue as your eyes . . .*
> *the pimpernel dozed on the lea;*
> *But the rose was awake all night for your sake,*
> *Knowing your promise to me;*
> *The lilies and roses were all awake . . .*
> *Queen rose of the rose-bud garden of girls. . . .*
>
> *There has fallen a splendid tear*
> *From the passion-flower at the gate.*
> *She is coming, my dove, my dear;*
> *She is coming, my life, my fate;*
> *The red rose cries, "She is near, she is near";*
> *And the white rose weeps, "She is late";*
> *The larkspur listens, "I hear, I hear";*
> *And the lily whispers, "I wait."*

"It isn't manners for us to begin, you know," said the Rose, "and I really was wondering when you'd speak." . . . "How is it that you all talk so nicely?" Alice said, hoping to get it into a better temper by a compliment. . . . "In most gardens," the Tiger-Lily said, "they make the beds too soft, so that the flowers are always asleep." This sounded a very good reason, and Alice was quite pleased to know it. "I never thought of that before!" she said. "It's *my* opinion you never think *at all*," the Rose said in rather a

severe tone. "I never saw anybody that looked
stupider," a Violet said, so suddenly, that Alice quite
jumped; for it hadn't spoken before. . . . "She's coming!" cried the Larkspur. "I hear her footstep, thump,
thump, along the gravel-walk!" Alice looked round
eagerly, and found that it was the Red Queen—

the concentrated essence, Dodgson was to explain, of all
governesses. The Tiger-Lily was originally a Passion-
Flower, but it was explained to Dodgson in time that the
passion meant was not that of sexual desire (which he
relates to ill-temper) but of Christ; a brilliant recovery
was made after the shock of this, for *Tiger-Lily* includes
both the alarming fierceness of ideal passion (chaste till
now) and the ill-temper of the life of virtue and self-
sacrifice typified by the governess (chaste always). So that
in effect he includes all the flowers Tennyson named. The
willow-tree that said Bough-Wough doesn't come in the
poem, but it is a symbol of hopeless love anyway. The
pink daisies turn white out of fear, as the white ones turn
pink in the poem out of admiration. I don't know how
far we ought to notice the remark about beds, which implies that they should be hard because even passion demands the virtues of asceticism (they are also the earthy
beds of the grave); it fits in very well with the ideas at
work, but does not seem a thing Dodgson would have
said in clearer language.

But though he shied from the Christian association in
the complex idea wanted from "Passion-Flower" the
flowers make another one very firmly.

"But that's not *your* fault," the Rose added kindly:
"you're beginning to fade, you know—and then one
can't help one's petals getting a little untidy." Alice
didn't like this idea at all: so, to change the subject,
she asked "Does she ever come out here?" "I daresay
you'll see her soon," said the Rose. "She's one of the
thorny kind." "Where does she wear the thorns?"
Alice asked with some curiosity. "Why, all round her
head, of course," the Rose replied. "I was wondering

you hadn't got some too. I thought it was the regular rule."

Death is never far out of sight in the books. The Rose cannot help standing for desire but its thorns here stand for the ill-temper not so much of passion as of chastity, that of the governess or that involved in ideal love. Then the thorns round the Queen's head, the "regular rule" for suffering humanity, not yet assumed by the child, stand for the Passion, the self-sacrifice of the most ideal and most generous love, which produces ugliness and ill-temper.

The joke of making romantic love ridiculous by applying it to undesired middle-aged women is less to be respected than the joke of the hopelessness of idealism. W. S. Gilbert uses it for the same timid facetiousness but more offensively. This perhaps specially nineteenth-century trick is played about all the women in the Alices—the Ugly Duchess who had the aphrodisiac in the soup (pepper, as Alice pointed out, produces "ill-temper") was the same person as the Queen in the first draft ("Queen of Hearts and Marchioness of Mock Turtles") so that the Queen's sentence of her is the suicide of disruptive passion. The Mock Turtle, who is half beef in the picture, with a cloven hoof, suffers from the calf-love of a turtle-dove; he went to a bad school and is excited about dancing. (He is also weeping for his lost childhood, which Dodgson sympathised with while blaming its exaggeration, and Alice thought very queer; this keeps it from being direct satire.) So love is also ridiculous in young men; it is felt that these two cover the whole field (Dodgson was about thirty at the time) so that granted these points the world is safe for chastity. The danger was from middle-aged women because young women could be treated as pure like Alice. Nor indeed is this mere convention; Gilbert was relying on one of the more permanent jokes played by nature on civilisation, that unless somewhat primitive methods are employed the specific desires of refined women may appear too late. So far as the chaste man uses this fact, and the

fact that men are hurt by permanent chastity less than
women, in order to insult women, no fuss that he may
make about baby women will make him dignified. Dodgson keeps the theme fairly agreeable by connecting it
with the more general one of self-sacrifice—which may be
useless or harmful, even when spontaneous or part of a
reasonable convention, which then makes the sacrificer
ridiculous and crippled, but which even then makes him
deserve respect and may give him unexpected sources of
power. The man playing at child-cult arrives at Sex War
here (as usual since, but the comic Lear didn't), but not
to the death nor with all weapons.

The same ideas are behind the White Queen, the emotional as against the practical idealist. It seems clear that
the Apologia (1864) is in sight when she believes the impossible for half an hour before breakfast, to keep in
practice; I should interpret the two examples she gives as
immortality and putting back the clock of history, also
Mass occurs before breakfast. All through the Wool and
Water chapter (milk and water but not nourishing, and
gritty to the teeth) she is Oxford; the life of learning
rather than of dogmatic religion. Every one recognises
the local shop, the sham fights, the rowing, the academic
old sheep, and the way it laughs scornfully when Alice
doesn't know the technical slang of rowing; and there
are some general reflections on education. The teacher
wilfully puts the egg a long way off, so that you have to
walk after it yourself, and meanwhile it turns into something else; and when you have "paid for" the education
its effects, then first known, must be accepted as part of
you whether they are good or bad. Oxford as dreamy may
be half satire half acceptance of Arnold's "adorable
dreamer" purple patch (1865).

Once at least in each book a cry of loneliness goes up
from Alice at the oddity beyond sympathy or communication of the world she has entered—whether that in
which the child is shut by weakness, or the adult by the
renunciations necessary both for the ideal and the worldly
way of life (the strength of the snobbery is to imply that
these are the same). It seems strangely terrible that the

answers of the White Queen, on the second of these occasions, should be so unanswerable.

> By this time it was getting light. "The crow must have flown away, I think," said Alice: "I'm so glad it's gone. I thought it was the night coming on."

Even in the rhyme the crow may be fear of death. The rhymes, like those other main structural materials, chess and cards, are useful because, being fixed, trivial, odd, and stirring to the imagination, they affect one as conventions of the dream world, and this sets the tone about conventions.

> "I wish I could manage to be glad!" the Queen said. "Only I never can remember the rule. You must be very happy, living in this wood, and being glad whenever you like."

So another wood has turned out to be Nature. This use of "that's a rule" is Sheridan's in *The Critic;* the pathos of its futility is that it is an attempt of reason to do the work of emotion and escape the dangers of the emotional approach to life. There may be a glance at the Oxford Movement and dogma. Perhaps chiefly a satire on the complacence of the fashion of slumming, the remark seems to spread out into the whole beauty and pathos of the ideas of pastoral; by its very universality her vague sympathy becomes an obscure self-indulgence.

> "Only it is so very lonely here!" Alice said in a melancholy voice; and at the thought of her loneliness two large tears came rolling down her cheeks.
> "Oh, don't go on like that," cried the poor Queen, wringing her hands in despair. "Consider what a great girl you are. Consider what a long way you've come to-day. Consider what o'clock it is. Consider anything, only don't cry!"
> Alice could not help laughing at this, even in the midst of her tears. "Can you keep from crying by considering things?" she asked.
> "That's the way it's done," the Queen said with

great decision; "nobody can do two things at once, you know. Let's consider your age to begin with—how old are you?"

We are back at once to the crucial topic of age and the fear of death, and pass to the effectiveness of practice in helping one to believe the impossible; for example that the ageing Queen is so old that she would be dead. The helplessness of the intellect, which claims to rule so much, is granted under cover of the counter-claim that since it makes you impersonal you can forget pain with it; we do not believe this about the queen chiefly because she has not enough understanding of other people. The jerk of the return to age, and the assumption that this is a field for polite lying, make the work of the intellect only the game of conversation. Humpty Dumpty has the same embarrassing trick for arguing away a suggestion of loneliness. Indeed about all the rationalism of Alice and her acquaintances there hangs a suggestion that there are after all questions of pure thought, academic thought whose altruism is recognised and paid for, though meant only for the upper classes to whom the conventions are in any case natural habit; like that suggestion that the scientist is sure to be a gentleman and has plenty of space which is the fascination of Kew Gardens.

The Queen is a very inclusive figure. "Looking before and after" with the plaintive tone of universal altruism she lives chiefly backwards, in history; the necessary darkness of growth, the mysteries of self-knowledge, the self-contradictions of the will, the antinomies of philosophy, the very Looking-Glass itself, impose this; nor is it mere weakness to attempt to resolve them only in the direct impulse of the child. Gathering the more dream-rushes her love for man becomes the more universal, herself the more like a porcupine. Knitting with more and more needles she tries to control life by a more and more complex intellectual apparatus—the "progress" of Herbert Spencer; any one shelf of the shop is empty, but there is always something very interesting—the "atmosphere" of the place is so interesting—which moves up as you look at it from shelf to shelf; there is jam only in the future and our traditional past, and the test made by Alice, who sent value through the ceiling as if it were quite used to it, shows that progress can never reach value, because its habitation and name is heaven. The Queen's scheme of social reform, which is to punish those who are not respectable before their crimes are committed, seems to be another of these jokes about progress:

"But if you *hadn't* done them," the Queen said, "that would have been better still; better, and better, and better!" Her voice went higher with each "better" till it got to quite a squeak at last.

There is a similar attack in the Walrus and the Carpenter, who are depressed by the spectacle of unimproved nature and engage in charitable work among oysters. The Carpenter is a Castle and the Walrus, who could eat so many more because he was crying behind his handkerchief, was a Bishop, in the scheme at the beginning of the book. But in saying so one must be struck by the depth at which the satire is hidden; the queerness of the incident and the characters takes on a Wordsworthian grandeur and aridity, and the landscape defined by the tricks of facetiousness takes on the remote and staring beauty of the ideas of the insane. It is odd to find that Tenniel went on to illustrate Poe in the same manner; Dodgson is often doing what Poe wanted to do, and can do it the more easily because he can safely introduce the absurd. The Idiot Boy of Wordsworth is too milky a moonlit creature to be at home with Nature as she was deplored by the Carpenter, and much of the technique of the rudeness of the Mad Hatter has been learned from Hamlet. It is the groundbass of this kinship with insanity, I think, that makes it so clear that the books are not trifling, and the cool courage with which Alice accepts madmen that gives them their strength.

This talk about the snobbery of the Alices may seem a mere attack, but a little acid may help to remove the slime with which they have been encrusted. The two main ideas behind the snobbery, that virtue and intelligence are alike lonely, and that good manners are therefore important though an absurd confession of human limitations, do not depend on a local class system; they would be recognised in a degree by any tolerable society. And if in a degree their opposites must also be recognised, so they are here; there are solid enough statements of the shams of altruism and convention and their horrors when genuine; it is the forces of this conflict that make a clash violent enough to end both the dreams. In *Wonderland* this is mysteriously mixed up with the trial of the Knave of Hearts, the thief of love, but at the end of the second book the symbolism is franker and more simple. She is a grown queen and has acquired the conventional dignities of her insane world; suddenly she admits their insanity, refuses to be a grown queen, and destroys them.

> "I can't stand this any longer!" she cried, as she seized the table-cloth in both hands: one good pull, and plates, dishes, guests, and candles came crashing down together in a heap on the floor.

The guests are inanimate and the crawling self-stultifying machinery of luxury has taken on a hideous life of its own. It is the High Table of Christ Church that we must think of here. The gentleman is not the slave of his conventions because at need he could destroy them; and yet, even if he did this, and all the more because he does not, he must adopt while despising it the attitude to them of the child.

Editor's Note

D. *H. Lawrence: A Study of the Bourgeois Artist* first appeared in *Studies in a Dying Culture* (1938) by Christopher Caudwell. Reprinted by permission of the publisher, John Lane The Bodley Head.

Christopher St. John Sprigg was born in Putney, England, in 1907, and educated at Ealing Priory School. He worked at journalism, editing, and publishing. Sprigg was killed in the Spanish Civil War in 1937, fighting in a machine-gun section of the International Brigade on the side of the Loyalists. Under his own name he wrote detective novels, psychological fiction, and books on aviation. Under his pseudonym, "Christopher Caudwell," he published one book of literary criticism, *Illusion and Reality* (1937). Four books have since been published posthumously: *Studies in a Dying Culture, The Crisis in Physics* (1939), *Poems* (1939), and *Further Studies in a Dying Culture* (1949).

EIGHT

Christopher Caudwell

D. H. Lawrence:
A Study of the Bourgeois Artist

What is the function of the artist? Any artist such as Lawrence, who aims to be "more than" an artist, necessarily raises this question. It is supposed to be the teaching of Marxism that art for art's sake is an illusion and that art must be propaganda. This is, however, making the usual bourgeois simplification of a complex matter.

Art is a social function. This is not a Marxist demand, but arises from the very way in which art forms are defined. Only those things are recognised as art forms which have a conscious social function. The phantasies of a dreamer are not art. They only become art when they are given music, forms or words, when they are clothed in socially recognised symbols, and of course in the process there is a modification. The phantasies are modified by the social dress; the language as a whole acquires new associations and context. No chance sounds constitute music, but sounds selected from a socially recognised scale and played on socially developed instruments.

It is not for Marxism therefore to demand that art play a social function or to attack the conception of "art for art's sake," for art only *is* art, and recognisable as such, in so far as it plays a social function. What is of importance to art, Marxism and society is the question: *What social function is art playing?* This in turn depends on the type of society in which it is secreted.

In bourgeois society social relations are denied in the form of relations between men, and take the form of a relation between man and a thing, a property relation, which, because it is a dominating relation, is believed to make man free. But this is an illusion. The property relation is only a disguise for relations which now become unconscious and therefore anarchic but are still between man and man and in particular between exploiter and exploited.

The artist in bourgeois culture is asked to do the same thing. He is asked to regard the art work as a finished commodity and the process of art as a relation between himself and the work, which then disappears into the market. There is a further relation between the art work and the buyer, but with this he can hardly be immediately concerned. The whole pressure of bourgeois society is to make him regard the art work as hypostatised and his relation to it as primarily that of a producer for the market.

This will have two results.

(i) The mere fact that he has to earn his living by the sale of the concrete hypostatised entity as a property right —copyright, picture, statue—may drive him to estimate his work as an artist by the market chances which produce a high total return for these property rights. This leads to the commercialisation or vulgarisation of art.

(ii) But art is not in any case a relation to a thing, it is a relation between men, between artist and audience, and the art work is only like a machine which they must both grasp as part of the process. The commercialisation of art may revolt the sincere artist, but the tragedy is that he revolts against it still within the limitations of bourgeois culture. He attempts to forget the market completely and concentrate on his relation to the art work, which now becomes still further hypostatised as an entity-in-itself. Because the art work is now completely an end-in-itself, and even the market is forgotten, the art process becomes an extremely individualistic relation. The social values inherent in the art form, such as syntax, tradition, rules, technique, form, accepted tonal scale, now seem to have little value, for the art work more and more exists for the individual alone. The art work is necessarily always the product of a tension between old conscious social formulations—the art "form"—and new individual experience made conscious—the art "content" or the artist's "message." This is the synthesis, the specifically hard task of creation. But the hypostatisation of the art work as the goal makes old conscious social formulations less and less important, and individual experience more and more dominating. As a result art becomes more and more formless, personal, and individualistic, culminating in Dadaism, surréalism and "Steining."

Thus bourgeois art disintegrates under the tension of two forces, both arising from the same feature of bourgeois culture. On the one hand there is production for the market—vulgarisation, commercialisation. On the other there is hypostatisation of the art work as the goal of the art process, and the relation between art work and individual as paramount. This necessarily leads to a dissolution of those social values which make the art in question a social relation, and therefore ultimately results in the art work's ceasing to be an art work and becoming a mere private phantasy.

All bourgeois art during the last two centuries shows the steady development of this bifurcation. As long as the social values inherent in an art form are not disintegrated —e.g. up to say 1910—the artist who hypostatises the art form and despises the market can produce good art. After that, it becomes steadily more difficult. Needless to say, the complete acceptance of the market, being a refusal to regard any part of the art process as a social process, is even more incompetent to produce great art. Anything which helps the artist to escape from the bourgeois trap and become conscious of social relations inherent in art, will help to delay the rot. For this reason the novel is the last surviving literary art form in bourgeois culture, for in it, for reasons explained elsewhere, the social relations inherent in the art process are overt. Dorothy Richardson, James Joyce, and Proust, all in different ways are the last blossoms of the bourgeois novel, for with them the novel begins to disappear as an objective study of social relations and becomes a study of the subject's experience in society.

It is then only a step for the thing experienced to disappear and, as in Gertrude Stein, for complete "me-ness" to reign.

It is inevitable that at this stage the conception of the artist as a pure "artist" must cease to exist. For commercialised art has become intolerably base and negated itself. And equally art for art's sake (that is, the ignoring of the market and concentration on the perfect art work as a goal in itself) has negated itself, for the art form has ceased to exist, and what was art has become private phantasy. It is for this reason that sincere artists, such as Lawrence, Gide, Romain Rolland, Romains and so on, cannot be content with the beautiful art work, but seem to desert the practice of art for social theory and become novelists of ideas, literary prophets and propaganda novelists. They represent the efforts of bourgeois art, exploded into individualistic phantasy and commercialised muck, to become once more a social process and so be reborn. Whether such art is or can be great art is beside the point, since it is inevitably the pre-requisite for art becoming art again, just as it is beside the point whether the transition from bourgeoisdom to communism is itself smooth or happy or beautiful or free, since it is the inevitable step if bourgeois anarchy and misery is to be healed and society to become happy and free.

But what is art as a social process? What is art, not as a mere art work or a means of earning a living, but in itself, the part it plays in society? I have dealt fully with this point elsewhere, and need only briefly recapitulate now.

The personal phantasy or day-dream is not art, however beautiful. Nor is the beautiful sunset. Both are only the raw material of art. It is the property of art that it makes mimic pictures of reality which we accept as illusory. We do not suppose the events of a novel really happen, that a landscape shown on a painting can be walked upon—yet it has a measure of reality.

The mimic representation, by the technique appropriate to the art in question, causes the social representation to sweat out of its pores an affective emanation. The emanation is *in* us, *in* our affective reaction with the elements of the representation. Given in the representation are not only the affects, but, simultaneously, their organisation in an affective *attitude* towards the piece of reality symbolised in the mimicry. This affective attitude is bitten in by a general heightening of consciousness and increase in self-value, due to the non-motor nature of the innervations aroused, which seems therefore all to pass into an affective irradiation of consciousness. This affective attitude is not permanent, as is the intellectual attitude towards reality aroused by a cogent scientific argument, but still—because of the mnemic characteristics of an organism—it remains as an *experience* and must, therefore, in proportion to the amount of conscious poignancy accompanying the experience and the nature of the experience, modify the subject's general attitude towards life itself. This modification tends to make life more interesting to the organism, hence the survival value of art. But viewed from society's standpoint, art is the fashioning of the affective consciousness of its members, the conditioning of their instincts.

Language, simply because it is the most general instrument for communicating views of reality, whether affective and cognitive, has a particularly fluid range of representations of reality. Hence the suppleness and scope of literary art; the novel, the drama, the poem, the short story, and the essay. It can draw upon all the symbolic pictures of reality made by scientific, historical and discursive intellectual processes. Art can only achieve its purpose if the pictures themselves are made simultaneously to produce affect and organisation. Then, even as the artist holds up to us the piece of reality, it seems already glowing with affective colouring.

Reality constitutes for us our environment; and our environment, which is chiefly social, alters continuously— sometimes barely perceptibly, sometimes at dizzy speeds. The socially accepted pictures we make in words of reality cannot change as if they were reflections in a mirror. An object is reflected in a mirror. If the object moves the reflection moves. But in language reality is symbolised in unchanging words, which give a false stability and permanence to the object they represent. Thus they instantaneously photograph reality rather than reflect it. This frigid character of language is regrettable but it has its utilitarian purposes. It is probably the only way in which man, with his linear consciousness, can get a grip of fluid reality. Language, as it develops, shows more and more of this false permanence, till we arrive at the Platonic Ideas, Eternal and Perfect Words. Their eternity and perfection is simply the permanence of print and paper. If you coin a word or write a symbol to describe an entity or event, the word will remain "eternally" unchanged even while the entity has changed and the event is no longer present. This permanence is part of the inescapable nature of symbolism, which is expressed in the rules of logic. It is one of the strange freaks of the human mind that it has supposed that reality must obey the rules of logic, whereas the correct view is that symbolism by its very nature has certain rules, expressed in the laws of logic, and these are nothing to do with the process of reality, but represent the nature of the symbolic process itself.

The artist experiences this discrepancy between language and reality as follows: he has had an intense experience of a rose and wishes to communicate his experience to his fellows in words. He wishes to say, "I saw a rose." But "rose" has a definite social meaning, or group of meanings, and we are to suppose that he has had an experience with the rose which does not correspond to any of society's previous experiences of roses, embodied in the world and its history. His experience of the rose is therefore the negation of the word "rose," it is "not-rose"—all that in his experience which is not expressed in the current social meaning of the word "rose." He therefore says—"I saw a rose like"—and there follows a metaphor, or there is an adjective—"a heavenly rose," or a euphemism—"I saw a flowery blush," and in each case there is a synthesis, for his new experience has become socially fused into society's old experiences and both have been changed in the process. His own experience has taken colour from all past meanings of the word "rose," for these will be present in men's minds when they read his poem, and the word "rose" will have taken colour from his individual experience, for his poem will in future be in men's minds when they encounter the word "rose."

But why was the poet's experience different from society's tradition? Because that cross-section of his environment which we call his individual life-experience was different. But if we take all society's art as a whole, i.e. the sum of individual cross-sections, we get on the one hand the whole experience of the environment averaged out, and also the average man, or average genotype. Now the constant genesis of new art must mean that the environment is changing, so that man's individual experiences are changing, and he is constantly finding inherited social conscious formulations inadequate and requiring resynthesis. Thus if art forms remain unchanged and traditional, as in Chinese civilisation, it is evident that the environment—social relations—are static. If they decay the environment is on the down-grade, as with current bourgeois culture. If they improve, the reverse is the case. But the artist's value is not in *self*-expression. If so, why should he struggle to achieve the synthesis in which old social formulations are fused with his individual experience? Why not disregard social formalities and express himself direct as one does by shouting, leaping, and cries? Because, to begin with, it is the old bourgeois illusion to suppose there is such a thing as pure individual expression. It is not even that the artist nobly forces his self-expression into a social mould for the benefit of society. Both attitudes are simply expressions of the old bourgeois fallacy that man is free in freely giving vent to his instincts. In fact the artist does not express himself in art forms, he finds himself therein. He does not adulterate his free self-expression to make it socially current, he finds free self-expression only in the social relations embodied in art. The value of art to the artist then is this, that it makes him free. It appears to him of value as a self-expression, but in fact it is not the expression of a self but the discovery of a self. It is the creation of a self. In synthesising experience with society's, in pressing his inner self into the mould of social relations, he not only creates a new mould, a socially valuable product, but he also moulds and creates his own self. The mute inglorious Milton is a fallacy. Miltons are made not born.

The value of art to society is that by it an emotional adaptation is possible. Man's instincts are pressed in art against the altered mould of reality, and by a specific organisation of the emotions thus generated, there is a new attitude, an *adaptation*.

All art is produced by this tension between changing social relations and outmoded consciousness. The very reason why new art is created, why the old art does not satisfy either artist or appreciator, is because it seems somehow out of gear with the present. Old art always has meaning for us, because the instincts, the source of the affects, do not change, because a new system of social relations does not exclude but includes the old, and because new art too includes the traditions of the art that has gone before. But it is not enough. We must have new art.

And new art results from tension. This tension takes two forms. (i) One is productive—the evolutionary form. The tension between productive relations and productive forces secures the advance of society as a whole, simply by producing in an even more pronounced form the contradiction which was the source of the dynamism. Thus bourgeois culture by continually dissolving the relations between men for relations to a thing, and thus hypostatising the market, procured the growth of industrial capitalism. And, in the sphere of art it produced the increasing individualism which, seen at its best in Shakespeare, was a positive value, but pushed to its limit finally spelt the complete breakdown of art in surréalism, Dadaism and Steinism.

(ii) The tension now becomes revolutionary. For productive relations are a brake on productive forces and the tension between them, instead of altering productive relations in the direction of giving better outlet to productive forces, has the opposite effect. It drives productive relations on still further into negation, increases the tension, and prepares the explosion which will shatter the old productive relations and enable them to be rebuilt anew—not arbitrarily, but according to a pattern which will itself be given by the circumstances of the tension. Thus in art the tension between individualism and the increasing complexity and catastrophes of the artist's environment, between the free following of dream and the rude blows of anarchic reality, wakes the artist from his dream and forces him in spite of himself to look at the world, not merely as an artist, but also as a man, as a citizen, as a sociologist. It forces him to be interested in things not strictly germane to art;—politics, economics, science, and philosophy, just as it did during the early bourgeois Renaissance, producing "all-round men" like Leonardo da Vinci. Whether this is good for art or not is beside the point. Bourgeois art like bourgeois culture is moribund and this process is an inevitable concomitant of the stage proceeding art's rebirth. And because of this intervening period, the new art when it emerges will be art more conscious of itself as part of the whole social process, will be *communist* art. This explains why all modern artists of any significance such as Lawrence, Gide, Aragon, Dos Passos, Eliot and so on, cannot be content to be "pure" artists, but must also be prophets, thinkers, philosophers, and politicians, men interested in life and social reality as a whole. They are conscious of having a message. This is the inevitable effect on art of a revolutionary period, and it is not possible to escape from it into "pure" art, into the ivory tower, for now there is no pure art; that phase is either over or not yet begun.

But at a revolution two paths are possible. So indeed they are in evolution—one can either stay still and be classical, academic and null, or go forward. But at a time of revolution it is not possible to stay still, one must either go forward, or back. To us this choice appears as a choice between Communism and Fascism, either to create the future or to go back to old primitive values, to mythology, racialism, nationalism, hero-worship, and *participation mystique*. This Fascist art is like the regression of the neurotic to a previous level of adaptation.

It is Lawrence's importance as an artist that he was well aware of the fact that the pure artist cannot exist to-day, and that the artist must inevitably be a man hating cash relationships and the market, and profoundly interested in the relations between persons. Moreover, he must be a man not merely profoundly interested in the relations between persons as they are, but interested in changing them, dissatisfied with them as they are, and wanting newer and fuller values in personal relationships.

But it is Lawrence's final tragedy that his solution was ultimately Fascist and not Communist. It was regressive. Lawrence wanted us to return to the past, to the "Mother." He sees human discontent as the yearning of the solar plexus for the umbilical connexion, and he demands the substitution for sharp sexual love of the unconscious fleshy identification of foetus with mother. All this was symbolic of regression, of neurosis, of the return to the primitive.

Lawrence felt that the Europe of to-day was moribund; and he turned therefore to other forms of existence, in Mexico, Etruria and Sicily, where he found or thought he found systems of social relations in which life flowed more easily and more meaningfully. The life of Bourgeois Europe seemed to him permeated with possessiveness and rationalising, so that it had got out of gear with the simple needs of the body. In a thousand forms he repeats this indictment of a civilisation which consciously *and just because it is conscious*—sins against the instinctive currents which are man's primal source of energy. It is a mistake to suppose that Lawrence preaches the gospel of sex. Bourgeois Europe has had its bellyful of sex, and a sex cult would not now attract the interest and emotional support which Lawrence's teaching received. Lawrence's gospel was purely sociological. Even sex was too conscious for him.

"Anybody who calls my novel (*Lady Chatterley's Lover*) a dirty sexual novel, is a liar. It's not even a sexual novel: it's a phallic. Sex is a thing that exists in the head, its reactions are cerebral, and its processes mental. Whereas the phallic reality is warm and spontaneous——"

Again he wrote:

"What ails me is the absolute frustration of my primitive societal instinct . . . I think societal instinct much deeper than the sex instinct—and societal repression much more devastating. There is no repression of the sexual individual comparable to the repression of the societal man in me, by the individual ego, my own and everybody else's. I am weary even of my own individuality, and simply nauseated by other people's."

One more analysis by him of the evil in bourgeois culture: (In the Cornish people)—

"the old race is still revealed, a race which believed in the darkness, in magic, and in the magic transcendency of one man over another which is fascinating. Also there is left some of the old sensuousness of the darkness and warmth and passionateness of the blood, sudden, incalculable. Whereas they are like insects, gone cold, living only for money, for *dirt*. They are foul in this. They ought to die."

Now here is a clear artistic, i.e. *emotional*, analysis of the decay of bourgeois social relations. They live for money, the societal instinct is repressed, even the sex relations have become cold and infected. Survivals of barbaric social relations between men (the "magic transcendency" of man over man) stand out as valuable in a culture where these relations have become relations between man and a thing, *man and dirt*.

But Lawrence does not look for a cause in social relations themselves, but in man's consciousness of them. The solution of the individual's needs is then plainly to be found in a return to instinctive living. But how are we to return to instinctive living? By casting off consciousness; we must return along the path we have come. But intellectualism consists in this, that we give either linguistically, plastically, or mentally, a symbolic projection to portions of reality, and consciousness or thinking consists simply in shuffling these images or verbal products. If therefore we are to cast off intellectualism and consciousness we must abandon all symbolism and rationalisation *tout court,* we must *be,* and no longer think, even in images. Yet on the contrary Lawrence again and again *consciously* formulates his creed in intellectual terms or terms of imagery. But this is self-contradiction, for how can we be led intellectually and consciously *back* from consciousness? It is our consciousness that Lawrence attempts to extend and heighten even at the moment he urges us to abandon it.

Consciousness can only be abandoned in action, and the first action of Fascism is the crushing of culture and the burning of the books. It is impossible therefore for an artist and thinker to be a consistent Fascist. He can only be like Lawrence, a self-contradictory one, who appeals to the consciousness of men to abandon consciousness.

There is a confusion here due to equating consciousness with thinking and unconsciousness with feeling. This is wrong. Both are conscious. No one ever had or could have an unconscious affect or emotion. Feeling indeed is what makes the unconscious memory-traces conscious, and heats them into thoughts. All of us, in times of deep feeling, whether artistic or emotional feeling, are aware of heightened consciousness almost like a white light in us so intense and clear is it. But Lawrence never clearly saw this, and constantly equates unconsciousness with feeling and consciousness with intellect. For example:

"My great religion is a belief in the blood, in the flesh, as being wiser than the intellect. We can go wrong in our minds. But what our blood feels and believes and says is always true. The intellect is only a bit and a bridle. What do I care about knowledge? All I want is to answer to my blood, direct, without fumbling intervention of mind, or moral, or what not. I conceive a man's body as a kind of flame, like a candle flame forever upright and yet flowing: and the intellect is just the light that is shed on the things around, coming God knows how from out of practically nowhere, and being *itself,* whatever there is around it that it lights up. We have got so ridiculously mindful, that we never know that we ourselves are anything—we think there are only the objects we shine upon. And there the poor flame goes on burning ignored, to produce this light. And instead of chasing the mystery in the fugitive, half-lighted things outside us, we ought to look at ourselves and say, 'My God, I am myself!' That is why I like to live in Italy. The people are so unconscious. They only feel and want, they don't know. We know too much. No, we only *think* we know such a lot. A flame isn't a flame because it lights up two, or twenty objects on a table. It's a flame because it is itself. And we have forgotten ourselves."

Feeling and thinking play into each other's hands and heighten each other. Man feels more deeply than the slug because he thinks more. Why did Lawrence make this error of supposing them essentially exclusive, and equate feeling with unconsciousness? Once again, the answer is in the nature of current society. All feeling and all thinking must contain something of each other to form part of consciousness at all. But it is possible to distinguish certain conscious phenomena as chiefly feeling, or vice versa. "Pure" feelings, any more than "Pure" thoughts, do not exist at all, since the first would be a mere instinctive tendency, the second nothing but a mnemic trace. Both would be unconscious and evidenced therefore only in behaviour. Lawrence might mean that feeling has wilted under modern conditions and that we must expand the feeling basis of our consciousness.

We know this of feelings (and affects generally) that they come into consciousness associated with innate responses or—more loosely—that they seem to be born of the modification, by experience and in action of the "instincts." Instinct going out in unmodified action, in mechanical response to a stimulus, is without *feeling*, it is pure automatism. Only when it becomes modified by memory traces or stifled by action does it become conscious and appear as feeling. The more intelligent the animal, the more its behaviour is modifiable by experience, the more feeling it displays. This extra display of feeling is *because* it is more intelligent, more conscious, less swayed by heredity, more subject to personal experience. Modification of innate responses by experience simply implies that previous behaviour leaves a mnemic trace on the neurones, chiefly of the cortex. These when innervated produce a new pattern, whose modification takes in the cortical sphere the form of thoughts and, in the visceral and thalamic sphere, the form of feelings or emotional dynamism. The different proportion of the components decides whether we call them thoughts or feelings. Even the simplest thought is irradiated with affect, and even the simplest emotion is accompanied by a thought, not necessarily verbalised but of some such character as "I am hurt," or "A pain." It is because thought and feeling arise from the same modification of innate responses, by experience, that the growth of intelligence, i.e. of the *capacity* for modification of behaviour by experience, is accompanied by a steadily increasing emotional complexity, richness, and deepness. It is plain that the growth of civilisation in *Homo Sapiens* has been accompanied by a steady increase in sensibility to pain and pleasure. This is the famous "sensitiveness" of civilised man, the "luxury" of high cultures, which is also manifested in their art and their vocabulary. Primitive peoples on the other hand show a marked deficiency in their sensibility, not only to refined emotions but even the cruder ones. The extremely erotic character of savage dances is not due, as some observers naïvely suppose, to the emotional erethism of the natives, but to the reverse, that in them the erotic impulses, owing to their deficient sensibility, can only be aroused by violent stimulation, whereas a slight stimulus will set off the hair-trigger emotions of civilised people. The same phenomenon is shown in primitive insensibility to pain. Consequently if we are to return down the path we have come from, back to primitiveness, to the blood, to the flesh, it is not only to less and cruder thought but also to less and cruder feeling, to a lessened consciousness in which feeling and thought, precisely because they are less rich and complex, will be more intimately mingled, until finally, as they both blend completely and become one, they vanish and nothing is left but unconscious *behaviour*. But how can this goal be of value to an artist, save on condition he denies himself the very law of his being? Art is not unconscious behaviour, it is conscious feeling.

It is, however, possible to broaden feeling without altering thought or losing consciousness, by altering the ratio between them in modern civilisation. That is precisely the purpose of art, for the artist makes use always of just those verbal or pictorial images of reality which are more charged with feeling than cognition, and he organises them in such a way that the affects re-inforce each other and fuse to a glowing mass. Consequently, he who believes that at all costs the feeling element must be broadened in present-day consciousness, must preach and secure, not the contraction of all consciousness, but the widening of feeling consciousness. This is art's mission. Art is the technique of affective manipulation in relation to reality. Lawrence was doing what I suppose him to have wished to do, just when he was artist pure and simple, sensitively recording the spirit of a place or the emotions of real people—in his early work. In proportion as he became a prophet, preaching a gospel intellectually, he departed from that goal.

How did he come to make first the initial *sortie* in favour of feeling, and then the contradictory error, deserting art for preaching? He came to the first conclusion because feeling is impoverished by modern bourgeois culture. Social relations, by ceasing to be between man and man and adhering to a thing, become emptied of tenderness. Man feels himself deprived of love. His whole instinct revolts against this. He feels a vast maladaption to his environment. Lawrence perceives this clearly when he talks about the repression of the societal instinct.

But things have gone so far that no tinkering with social relations, no adaptation of the instincts to the environment by means of art, will cure this. Social relations themselves must be rebuilt. The artist is bound for the sake of his integrity to become thinker and revolutionary. Lawrence therefore was bound not to be content with pure art, with widening feeling consciousness in the old circle. He had to try and recast social relations and proceed to a solution. But there is only one revolutionary solution. Social relations must be altered, not so as to contract consciousness but so as to widen it. The higher feeling must be found, not in a lower but as always in a higher level of culture.

Naturally consciousness seems in bourgeois culture now, as in all periods of decay, full of defects with which being struggles, and this seems like unconsciousness crippled by consciousness. Those defects in bourgeois social relations all arise from the cash nexus which replaces all other social ties, so that society seems held together, not by mutual love or tenderness or obligation, but simply by profit. Money makes the bourgeois world go round and this means that selfishness is the hinge on which bourgeois society turns, for money is a dominating relation to an owned thing. This commercialisation of all social relations invades the most intimate of emotions, and the relations of the sexes are affected by the differing economic situations of man and woman. The notion of private property, aggravated by its importance and overwhelming power in bourgeois relations, extends to love itself. Because economic relations in capitalism are simply each man struggling for himself in the impersonal market, the world seems torn apart with the black forces of envy, covetousness and hate, which mix with and make ambivalent even the most "altruistic" emotions.

But it is simplifying the drama to make it a struggle between contemporary consciousness and old being. It is a conflict between productive relations and productive powers, between the contemporary formulations of consciousness, and all the possibilities of future being including consciousness latent in society and struggling to be released from their bonds. Bourgeois defects are implicit in bourgeois civilisation and therefore in bourgeois consciousness. Hence man wants to turn against the intellect, for it seems that the intellect is his enemy, and indeed it is, if by intellect we mean the bourgeois intellect. But it can only be fought with intellect. To deny intellect is to assist the forces of conservatism. In hundreds of diverse forms we see to-day the useless European revolt against intellectualism.

In any civilisation the rôle of consciousness is to modify instinctive responses so that they flow smoothly into the mill of social relations and turn it. Instinct not money really turns the social mill, though in the bourgeois world instinctive relations can only operate along the money channel. Hence when social relations come to be a brake on society's forces, there is felt a conflict between the social relations and the instincts. It seems as if the feelings were out of gear, as if the world was uncomfortable and hurt the feelings and repressed them. It seems as if the instincts, and the feelings, those products of the instincts, were being penalised by the environment, and that, therefore, the instincts and feelings must be "given their due," must be exalted even if it means breaking up and abandoning the civilised environment for a more primitive one. To-day this exaltation of the instincts is seen in all demands for a return to deeper "feeling" as with Lawrence, and in all worships of unconscious "mentation," as with the surréalists, Hemingways, and Fascists. In individuals this mechanism is infantile regression, seen in its pathological form in the neuroses.

Now these mechanisms involve the discovery of a real defect. Social being *is* held back by social consciousness; the instincts *are* thwarted and the feelings *are* made poor by the environment. But the remedy is wrong. The neurotic cannot, as we know, be cured by infantile regression. All it does for him is to secure him unconsciousness and take from him painful thoughts, at the price of a lowering of consciousness and an impoverishing of values. Civilisation cannot be cured by going back along the path to the primitive, it can only become at a lower level more unconscious of its decay. Just as the neurotic's return to childhood solutions of problems is unhealthier than childhood, so a civilisation's return to a primitive solution is unhealthier than primitive life itself. The very history between makes such solutions unreal. To the primitive these problems have never existed. To the regressive they have existed but he has repressed them. It is into the wilderness these people would lead us. They preach, not new vigour, but old decadence.

What then is the cure? We know that both in the case of the neurotic and the civilisation, the cure is a more strenuous and creative act than the invalid's relapse into the womb of that unconsciousness from which we emerged. Our task is to be performed, not in an air heavy and fetid with mysteries and dead symbolism like that of a cavern used for old obscene rites, but in the open air.

We are not to return to the old but it is into the new we must go; and the new does not exist, we must bring it into being. The child would love to return to the womb, but it must become adult and face the strenuous and bracing tasks of life. We are not to abandon consciousness but to expand it, to deepen and purge feeling and break up and recast thought, and this new consciousness does not exist in any thing's keeping either Mexicans or Yogis or the "blood" but we must make it ourselves. In this struggle with reality in which instincts, feeling and thought all partake and interact, the instincts themselves will be changed, and emerging in consciousness as new thought and new feeling, will once again feel themselves in harmony with the new environment they have created. Social relations must be changed so that love returns to the earth and man is not only wiser but more full of emotion. This is not a task which one prophet can perform in one Gospel, but since the whole fabric of social relations are to be changed, every human being must in some sort participate in the change, be either for it or against it, and be victorious if he is for it and be defeated if he is against it.

Why did Lawrence, faced with the problem, fail of a solution? He failed because while hating bourgeois culture he never succeeded in escaping from its limitations. Here in him, too, we see the same old lie. Man is "free" in so far as his "free" instincts, the "blood," the "flesh," are given an outlet. Man is free not through but *in spite of* social relations.

If one believes this—which, as we have seen, is the deepest and most ineradicable bourgeois illusion, all others are built on this—one must, if one is hurt by bourgeois social relations, see security and freedom only in casting them off, and returning to a primitive state with less "constraints." One must necessarily believe freedom and happiness can be found by one's own individual action. One will not believe freedom and happiness can only be found through social relations, by co-operating with others to change them, but there is always something one can do, fly to Mexico, find the right woman or the right friends, and so discover salvation. One will never see the truth, that one can only find salvation for oneself by finding it for all others at the same time.

Lawrence therefore could never escape from this essential selfishness—not a petty selfishness but the selfishness which is the pattern of bourgeois culture and is revealed in pacifism, Protestantism, and all varieties of salvation obtained by individual action. The world to which Lawrence wished to return is not really the world of primitives who are in fact bound by more rigid relations than those of bourgeois Europe. It is the old bourgeois pastoral heaven of the "natural man" born everywhere in chains, which does not exist. It does not exist because it is self-contradictory, and because it is self-contradictory the bourgeois world in striving for it more clearly produces the opposite, as in moving towards an object in a mirror we move away from the real object. Lawrence's gospel therefore only forms part of the self-destructive element in bourgeois culture.

Lawrence for all his gifts suffered from the old *petit bourgeois* errors. Like Wells, he strove to climb upwards into the world of bourgeois culture; being more artistic than Wells and born in a later era, it could not be the security and power of that already sick class that appealed to him. It was their cultural values. He succeeded in entering that world and drinking deeply of all its tremendous intellectual and æsthetic riches, only to find them riches turning into dust. The shock of that disillusion, added to the pain endured in that climb, filled him finally with a hatred for bourgeois values. He could criticise them relentlessly and bitterly, but he could provide no solution for the whole set of his life; all that long difficult climb of his into the bourgeois sunshine ensured that he remained a bourgeois. His was always bourgeois culture, conscious of its decay, criticising itself and with no solution except to go back to a time when things were different and so undo all the development that had brought bourgeois culture to this pass.

Had he been born later, had that sunlit world never appealed to him so irresistibly, he might have seen that it was the proletariat—to whom he was so near at the start of his climb—that was the dynamic force of the future. Not only would he then have had a standpoint outside bourgeois culture from which to criticise it, but from that position he would have been able to find the true solution—in the future, not the past. But Lawrence remained to the end a man incapable of that subordination of self to others, of co-operation, of solidarity as a class, which is the characteristic of the proletariat. He remained the individualist, the bourgeois revolutionary angrily working out his own salvation, critical of all, alone in possession of grace. He rid himself of every bourgeois illusion but the important one. He saw finally neither the world nor himself as it really was. He saw the march of events as a bourgeois tragedy, which is true but unimportant. The important thing, which was absolutely closed to him, was that it was also a proletarian renaissance.

Everywhere to-day will be found the conscious or unconscious followers of Lawrence—the pacifists, the snug little hedonists, the conscientious sexualists, the well-meaning Liberals, the idealists, all seeking the impossible solution, salvation through the free act of the individual will amid decay and disaster. They may find a temporary solution, a momentary happiness, although I judge Lawrence to have found neither. But it is of its nature unstable, for external events to which they have regressively adjusted themselves, beget incessantly new horrors and undreamed-of disasters. What avails such pinchbeck constructs during the screaming horror of a War? One may stop one's ears and hide oneself in Cornwall like Lawrence, but the cry of one's millions of suffering fellow-humans reaches one's ears and tortures one. And, the War at last survived, there come new horrors. The eating disintegra-

tion of the slump. Nazism outpouring a flood of barbarism
and horror. And what next? Armaments piling up like an
accumulating catastrophe, mass neurosis, nations like mad
dogs. All this seems gratuitous, horrible, cosmic to such
people, unaware of the causes. How can the bourgeois
still pretend to be free, to find salvation individually? Only
by sinking himself in still cruder illusions, by denying art,
science, emotion, even ultimately life itself. Humanism,
the creation of bourgeois culture, finally separates from it.
Against the sky stands Capitalism without a rag to cover
it, naked in its terror. And humanism, leaving it, or rather,
forcibly thrust aside, must either pass into the ranks of the
proletariat or, going quietly into a corner, cut its throat.
Lawrence did not live to face this final issue, which would
necessarily make straw of his philosophy and his teaching.

Editor's Note

Narcissus as Narcissus first appeared in *The Virginia Quarterly Review,* Winter 1938. Reprinted in *Reason in Madness* (1941), *On the Limits of Poetry* (1948), and *The Man of Letters in the Modern World* (1955). The version used here is from *On the Limits of Poetry* by Allen Tate, by permission of the publisher, Alan Swallow. Copyright 1948 by Allen Tate.

Allen Tate was born in Winchester, Kentucky, in 1899, and educated at Georgetown, the University of Virginia, and Vanderbilt, where he studied under John Crowe Ransom. He has been an editor of *The Fugitive, Hound and Horn,* and *The Sewanee Review,* and has taught at Southwestern University, the Woman's College of the University of North Carolina, Princeton, and New York University. He is now at the University of Minnesota. Tate has published biographies, a novel, and a number of books of verse, collected in *Poems: 1922–47.* His other books of criticism include *Reactionary Essays on Poetry and Ideas* (1936), *The Hovering Fly* (1949), and *The Forlorn Demon* (1953).

NINE

Allen Tate

Narcissus as Narcissus

On this first occasion, which will probably be the last, of my writing about my own verse, I could plead in excuse the example of Edgar Allan Poe, who wrote about himself in an essay called "The Philosophy of Composition." But in our age the appeal to authority is weak, and I am of my age. What I happen to know about the poem that I shall discuss is limited. I remember merely my intention in writing it; I do not know whether the poem is good; and I do not know its obscure origins.

How does one happen to write a poem: where does it come from? That is the question asked by the psychologists or the geneticists of poetry. Of late I have not read any of the genetic theories very attentively: years ago I read one by Mr. Conrad Aiken; another, I think, by Mr. Robert Graves; but I have forgotten them. I am not ridiculing verbal mechanisms, dreams, or repressions as origins of poetry; all three of them and more besides may have a great deal to do with it. Other psychological theories say a good deal about compensation. A poem is an indirect effort of a shaky man to justify himself to happier men, or to present a superior account of his relation to a world that allows him but little certainty, and would allow equally little to the happier men if they did not wear blinders—according to the poet. For example, a poet might be a man who could not get enough self-justification out of being an automobile salesman (whose certainty is a fixed quota of cars every month) to rest comfortably upon it. So the poet, who wants to be something that he cannot be, and is a failure in plain life, makes up fictitious versions of his

predicament that are interesting even to other persons because nobody is a perfect automobile salesman. Everybody, alas, suffers a little. . . . I constantly read this kind
of criticism of my own verse. According to its doctors, my
one intransigent desire is to have been a Confederate general, and because I could not or would not become anything else, I set up for poet and began to invent fictions
about the personal ambitions that my society has no use
for.

Although a theory may not be "true," it may make certain insights available for a while; and I have deemed it
proper to notice theories of the genetic variety because a
poet talking about himself is often expected, as the best
authority, to explain the origins of his poems. But persons
interested in origins are seldom quick to use them. Poets,
in their way, are practical men; they are interested in results. What is the poem, after it is written? That is the
question. Not where it came from, or why. The Why and
Where can never get beyond the guessing stage because,
in the language of those who think it can, poetry cannot
be brought to "laboratory conditions." The only real evidence that any critic may bring before his gaze is the
finished poem. For some reason most critics have a hard
time fixing their minds directly under their noses, and before they see the object that is there they use a telescope
upon the horizon to see where it came from. They are
wood cutters who do their job by finding out where the
ore came from in the iron of the steel of the blade of the
ax that Jack built. I do not say that this procedure is without its own contributory insights; but the insights are
merely contributory and should not replace the poem,
which is the object upon which they must be focused. A
poem may be an instance of morality, of social conditions,
of psychological history; it may instance all its qualities,
but never one of them alone, nor any two or three; never
less than all.

Genetic theories, I gather, have been cherished aca-
demically with detachment. Among "critics" they have
been useless and not quite disinterested: I have myself

found them applicable to the work of poets whom I do not like. That is the easiest way.

I say all this because it seems to me that my verse or anybody else's is merely a way of knowing something: if the poem is a real creation, it is a kind of knowledge that we did not possess before. It is not knowledge "about" something else; the poem is the fullness of that knowledge. We know the particular poem, not what it says that we can restate. In a manner of speaking, the poem is its own knower, neither poet nor reader knowing anything that the poem says apart from the words of the poem. I have expressed this view elsewhere in other terms, and it has been accused of aestheticism or art for art's sake. But let the reader recall the historic position of Catholicism: *nulla salus extra ecclesiam*. That must be religion*ism*. There is probably nothing wrong with art for art's sake if we take the phrase seriously, and not take it to mean the kind of poetry written in England forty years ago. Religion always ought to transcend any of its particular uses; and likewise the true art-for-art's-sake view can be held only by persons who are always looking for things that they can respect apart from use (though they may be useful), like poems, fly-rods, and formal gardens. . . . These are negative postulates, and I am going to illustrate them with some commentary on a poem called "Ode to the Confederate Dead."

II

That poem is "about" solipsism, a philosophical doctrine which says that we create the world in the act of perceiving it; or about Narcissism, or any other *ism* that denotes the failure of the human personality to function objectively in nature and society. Society (and "nature" as modern society constructs it) appears to offer limited fields for the exercise of the whole man, who wastes his energy piecemeal over separate functions that ought to come under a unity of being. (Until the last generation, only certain women were whores, having been set aside as special

instances of sex amid a social scheme that held the general
belief that sex must be part of a whole; now the general
belief is that sex must be special.) Without unity we get
the remarkable self-consciousness of our age. Everybody
is talking about this evil, and a great many persons know
what ought to be done to correct it. As a citizen I have my
own prescription, but as a poet I am concerned with the
experience of "solipsism." And an experience *of* it is not
quite the same thing as a philosophical statement *about* it.

I should have trouble connecting solipsism and the Confederate dead in a rational argument; I should make a fool
of myself in the discussion, because I know no more of the
Confederate dead or of solipsism than hundreds of other
people. (Possibly less: the dead Confederates may be pre-
sumed to have a certain privacy; and as for solipsism, I
blush in the presence of philosophers, who know all about
Bishop Berkeley; I use the term here in its strict etymol-
ogy.) And if I call this interest in one's ego Narcissism,
I make myself a logical ignoramus, and I take liberties
with mythology. I use Narcissism to mean only preoccupation with self; it may be either love or hate. But a good
psychiatrist knows that it means self-love only, and otherwise he can talk about it more coherently, knows more
about it than I shall ever hope or desire to know. He
would look at me professionally if I uttered the remark
that the modern squirrel cage of our sensibility, the extreme introspection of our time, has anything whatever
to do with the Confederate dead.

But when the doctor looks at literature it is a question
whether he sees it: the sea boils and pigs have wings
because in poetry all things are possible—if you are man
enough. They are possible because in poetry the disparate
elements are not combined in logic, which can join things
only under certain categories and under the law of contradiction; they are combined in poetry rather as experience,
and experience has decided to ignore logic, except perhaps
as another field of experience. Experience means conflict,
our natures being what they are, and conflict means
drama. Dramatic experience is not logical; it may be sub-
dued to the kind of coherence that we indicate when we

speak, in criticism, of form. Indeed, as experience, this conflict is always a logical contradiction, or philosophically an antinomy. Serious poetry deals with the fundamental conflicts that cannot be logically resolved: we can state the conflicts rationally, but reason does not relieve us of them. Their only final coherence is the formal re-creation of art, which "freezes" the experience as permanently as a logical formula, but without, like the formula, leaving all but the logic out.

Narcissism and the Confederate dead cannot be connected logically, or even historically; even were the connection an historical fact, they would not stand connected as art, for no one experiences raw history. The proof of the connection must lie, if anywhere, in the experienced conflict which is the poem itself. Since one set of references for the conflict is the historic Confederates, the poem, if it is successful, is a certain section of history made into experience, but only on this occasion, and on these terms: even the author of the poem has no experience of its history apart from the occasion and the terms.

It will be understood that I do not claim even a partial success in the junction of the two "ideas" in the poem that I am about to discuss. I am describing an intention, and the labor of revising the poem—a labor spread over ten years—fairly exposes the lack of confidence that I have felt and still feel in it. All the tests of its success in style and versification would come in the end to a single test, an answer, yes or no, to the question: Assuming that the Confederates and Narcissus are not yoked together by mere violence, has the poet convinced the reader that, on the specific occasion of this poem, there is a necessary yet hitherto undetected relation between them? By necessary I mean dramatically relevant, a relation "discovered" in terms of the particular occasion, not historically argued or philosophically deduced. Should the question that I have just asked be answered yes, then this poem or any other with its specific problem could be said to have form: what was previously a merely felt quality of life has been raised to the level of experience—it has become specific, local, dramatic, "formal"—that is to say, *in*-formed.

III

The structure of the Ode is simple. Figure to yourself
a man stopping at the gate of a Confederate graveyard
on a late autumn afternoon. The leaves are falling; his
first impressions bring him the "rumor of mortality"; and
the desolation barely allows him, at the beginning of the
second stanza, the conventionally heroic surmise that the
dead will enrich the earth, "where these memories grow."
From those quoted words to the end of that passage he
pauses for a baroque meditation on the ravages of time,
concluding with the figure of the "blind crab." This creature has mobility but no direction; energy but, from the
human point of view, no purposeful world to use it in: in
the entire poem there are only two explicit symbols for
the locked-in ego; the crab is the first and less explicit
symbol, a mere hint, a planting of the idea that will become overt in its second instance—the jaguar towards
the end. The crab is the first intimation of the nature of
the moral conflict upon which the drama of the poem
develops: the cut-off-ness of the modern "intellectual man"
from the world.

The next long passage or "strophe," beginning "You
know who have waited by the wall," states the other term
of the conflict. It is the theme of heroism, not merely
moral heroism, but heroism in the grand style, elevating
even death from mere physical dissolution into a formal
ritual: this heroism is a formal ebullience of the human
spirit in an entire society, not private, romantic illusion—
something better than moral heroism, great as that may
be, for moral heroism, being personal and individual,
may be achieved by certain men in all ages, even ages of
decadence. But the late Hart Crane's commentary, in a
letter, is better than any I can make; he described the
theme as the "theme of chivalry, a tradition of excess
(not literally excess, rather active faith) which cannot be
perpetuated in the fragmentary cosmos of today—'those
desires which should be yours tomorrow,' but which, you
know, will not persist nor find any way into action."

The structure then is the objective frame for the tension between the two themes, "active faith" which has decayed, and the "fragmentary cosmos" which surrounds us. (I must repeat here that this is not a philosophical thesis; it is an analytical statement of a conflict that is concrete within the poem.) In contemplating the heroic theme the man at the gate never quite commits himself to the illusion of its availability to him. The most that he can allow himself is the fancy that the blowing leaves are charging soldiers, but he rigorously returns to the refrain: "Only the wind"—or the "leaves flying." I suppose it is a commentary on our age that the man at the gate never quite achieves the illusion that the leaves are heroic men, so that he may identify himself with them, as Keats and Shelley too easily and too beautifully did with nightingales and west winds. More than this, he cautions himself, reminds himself repeatedly of his subjective prison, his solipsism, by breaking off the half-illusion and coming back to the refrain of wind and leaves—a refrain that, as Hart Crane said, is necessary to the "subjective continuity."

These two themes struggle for mastery up to the passage,

> *We shall say only the leaves whispering*
> *In the improbable mist of nightfall—*

which is near the end. It will be observed that the passage begins with a phrase taken from the wind-leaves refrain—the signal that it has won. The refrain has been fused with the main stream of the man's reflections, dominating them; and he cannot return even to an ironic vision of the heroes. There is nothing but death, the mere naturalism of death at that—spiritual extinction in the decay of the body. Autumn and the leaves are death; the men who exemplified in a grand style an "active faith" are dead; there are only the leaves.

Shall we then worship death . . .

> *. . . set up the grave*
> *In the house? The ravenous grave . . .*

that will take us before our time? The question is not answered, although as a kind of morbid romanticism it
might, if answered affirmatively, provide the man with an
illusory escape from his solipsism; but he cannot accept it.
Nor has he been able to live in his immediate world, the
fragmentary cosmos. There is no practical solution, no
solution offered for the edification of moralists. (To those
who may identify the man at the gate with the author of
the poem I would say: He differs from the author in not
accepting a "practical solution," for the author's personal
dilemma is perhaps not quite so exclusive as that of the
meditating man.) The main intention of the poem has
been to make dramatically visible the conflict, to concentrate it, to present it, in Mr. R. P. Blackmur's phrase, as
"experienced form"—not as a logical dilemma.

The closing image, that of the serpent, is the ancient
symbol of time, and I tried to give it the credibility of the
commonplace by placing it in a mulberry bush—with the
faint hope that the silkworm would somehow be implicit.
But time is also death. If that is so, then space, or the
Becoming, is life; and I believe there is not a single
spatial symbol in the poem. "Sea-space" is allowed the
"blind crab"; but the sea, as appears plainly in the passage beginning, "Now that the salt of their blood . . ." is
life only in so far as it is the source of the lowest forms
of life, the source perhaps of all life, but life undifferentiated, halfway between life and death. This passage is a
contrasting inversion of the conventional

> . . . *inexhaustible bodies that are not*
> *Dead, but feed the grass . . .*

the reduction of the earlier, literary conceit to a more
naturalistic figure derived from modern biological speculation. These "buried Caesars" will not bloom in the hya-
cinth but will only make saltier the sea.

The wind-leaves refrain was added to the poem in 1930,
nearly five years after the first draft was written. I felt
that the danger of adding it was small because, implicit in
the long strophes of meditation, the ironic commentary
on the vanished heroes was already there, giving the poem

such dramatic tension as it had in the earlier version. The refrain makes the commentary more explicit, more visibly dramatic, and renders quite plain, as Hart Crane intimated, the subjective character of the imagery throughout. But there was another reason for it, besides the increased visualization that it imparts to the dramatic conflict. It "times" the poem better, offers the reader frequent pauses in the development of the two themes, allows him occasions of assimilation; and on the whole—this was my hope and intention—the refrain makes the poem seem longer than it is and thus eases the concentration of imagery—without, I hope, sacrificing a possible effect of concentration.

IV

I have been asked why I called the poem an ode. I first called it an elegy. It is an ode only in the sense in which Cowley in the seventeenth century misunderstood the real structure of the Pindaric ode. Not only are the meter and rhyme without fixed pattern, but in another feature the poem is even further removed from Pindar than Abraham Cowley was: a purely subjective meditation would not even in Cowley's age have been called an ode. I suppose in so calling it I intended an irony: the scene of the poem is not a public celebration, it is a lone man by a gate.

The dominant rhythm is "mounting," the dominant meter iambic pentameter varied with six-, four-, and three-stressed lines; but this was not planned in advance for variety. I adapted the meter to the effect desired at the moment. The model for the irregular rhyming was "Lycidas," but other models could have served. The rhymes in a given strophe I tried to adjust to the rhythm and the texture of feeling and image. For example, take this passage in the second strophe:

Autumn is desolation in the plot
Of a thousand acres where these memories grow
From the inexhaustible bodies that are not
Dead, but feed the grass row after rich row.
Think of the autumns that have come and gone!—

> *Ambitious November with the humors of the year,*
> *With a particular zeal for every slab,*
> *Staining the uncomfortable angels that rot*
> *On the slabs, a wing chipped here, an arm there:*
> *The brute curiosity of an angel's stare*
> *Turns you, like them, to stone,*
> *Transforms the heaving air*
> *Till plunged to a heavier world below*
> *You shift your sea-space blindly*
> *Heaving, turning like the blind crab.*

There is rhymed with *year* (to many persons, perhaps, only a half-rhyme), and I hoped the reader would unconsciously assume that he need not expect further use of that sound for some time. So when the line, "The brute curiosity of an angel's stare," comes a moment later, rhyming with *year-there,* I hoped that the violence of image would be further reinforced by the repetition of a sound that was no longer expected. I wanted the shock to be heavy; so I felt that I could not afford to hurry the reader away from it until he had received it in full. The next two lines carry on the image at a lower intensity: the rhyme, "Transforms the heaving *air,"* prolongs the moment of attention upon that passage, while at the same time it ought to begin dissipating the shock, both by the introduction of a new image and by reduction of the "meaning" to a pattern of sound, the ere-rhymes. I calculated that the third use of that sound (stare) would be a surprise, the fourth (air) a monotony. I purposely made the end words of the third from last and last lines—*below* and *crab*—delayed rhymes for *row* and *slab,* the last being an internal and half-dissonant rhyme for the sake of bewilderment and incompleteness, qualities by which the man at the gate is at the moment possessed.

This is elementary but I cannot vouch for its success. As the dramatic situation of the poem is the tension that I have already described, so the rhythm is an attempt at a series of "modulations" back and forth between a formal regularity, for the heroic emotion, and a broken rhythm, with scattering imagery, for the failure of that emotion.

This is "imitative form," which Yvor Winters deems a vice worth castigation. I have pointed out that the passage, "You know who have waited by the wall," presents the heroic theme of "active faith"; it will be observed that the rhythm, increasingly after "You who have waited for the angry resolution," is almost perfectly regular iambic, with only a few initial substitutions and weak endings. The passage is meant to convey a plenary vision, the actual presence, of the exemplars of active faith: the man at the gate at that moment is nearer to realizing them than at any other in the poem; hence the formal rhythm. But the vision breaks down; the wind-leaves refrain supervenes; and the next passage, "Turn your eyes to the immoderate past," is the irony of the preceding realization. With the self-conscious historical sense he turns his eyes into the past. The next passage after this, beginning, "You hear the shout . . ." is the failure of the vision in both phases, the pure realization and the merely historical. He cannot "see" the heroic virtues; there is wind, rain, leaves. But there is sound; for a moment he deceives himself with it. It is the noise of the battles that he has evoked. Then comes the figure of the rising sun of those battles; he is "lost in that orient of the thick and fast," and he curses his own moment, "the setting sun." The "setting sun" I tried to use as a triple image, for the decline of the heroic age and for the actual scene of late afternoon, the latter being not only natural desolation but spiritual desolation as well. Again for a moment he thinks he hears the battle shout, but only for a moment; then the silence reaches him.

Corresponding to the disintegration of the vision just described, there has been a breaking down of the formal rhythm. The complete breakdown comes with the images of the "mummy" and the "hound bitch." (*Hound* bitch because the hound is a hunter, participant of a formal ritual.) The failure of the vision throws the man back upon himself, but upon himself he cannot bring to bear the force of sustained imagination. He sees himself in random images (random to him, deliberate with the author) of something lower than he ought to be: the human image is only that of preserved death; but if he is alive he is an old hunter, dying. The passages about the mummy and the bitch are deliberately brief—slight rhythmic stretches. (These are the only verses I have written for which I thought of the movement first, then cast about for the symbols.)

I believe the term "modulation" denotes in music the uninterrupted shift from one key to another: I do not know the term for change of rhythm without change of measure. I wish to describe a similar change in verse rhythm; it may be convenient to think of it as modulation of a certain kind. At the end of the passage that I have been discussing the final words are "Hears the wind only." The phrase closes the first main division of the poem. I have loosely called the longer passages strophes, and if I were hardy enough to impose the classical organization of the lyric ode upon a baroque poem, I should say that these words bring to an end the Strophe, after which must come the next main division, or Antistrophe, which was often employed to answer the matter set forth in the Strophe or to present it from another point of view. And that is precisely the significance of the next main division, beginning: "Now that the salt of their blood. . . ." But I wanted this second division of the poem to arise out of the collapse of the first. It is plain that it would not have suited my purpose to round off the first section with some sort of formal rhythm; so I ended it with an unfinished line. The next division must therefore begin by finishing that line, not merely in meter but with an integral rhythm. I will quote the passage:

> *The hound bitch*
> *Toothless and dying, in a musty cellar*
> Hears the wind only.
>
> Now that the salt of their blood
> *Stiffens the saltier oblivion of the sea,*
> *Seals the malignant purity of the flood. . . .*

The caesura, after *only,* is thus at the middle of the third foot. (I do not give a full stress to *wind,* but attribute a

"hovering stress" to *wind* and the first syllable of *only*.)
The reader expects the foot to be completed by the stress
on the next word, *Now,* as in a sense it is; but the phrase,
"Now that the salt of their blood," is also the beginning
of a new movement; it is two "dactyls" continuing more
broadly the falling rhythm that has prevailed. But with
the finishing off of the line with *blood,* the mounting
rhythm is restored; the whole line from *Hears* to *blood*
is actually an iambic pentameter with liberal inversions
and substitutions that were expected to create a counter-
rhythm within the line. From the caesura on, the rhythm
is new; but it has—or was expected to have—an organic
relation to the preceding rhythm; and it signals the rise
of a new statement of the theme.

I have gone into this passage in detail—I might have
chosen another—not because I think it is successful, but
because I labored with it; if it is a failure, or even an un-
interesting success, it ought to offer as much technical
instruction to other persons at it would were it both successful and interesting. But a word more: the broader
movement introduced by the new rhythm was meant to
correspond, as a sort of Antistrophe, to the earlier formal
movement beginning, "You know who have waited by the
wall." It is a new formal movement with new feeling and
new imagery. The heroic but precarious illusion of the
earlier movement has broken down into the personal symbols of the mummy and the hound; the pathetic fallacy
of the leaves as charging soldiers and the conventional
"buried Caesar" theme have become rotten leaves and
dead bodies wasting in the earth, to return after long
erosion to the sea. In the midst of this naturalism, what
shall the man say? What shall all humanity say in the
presence of decay? The two themes, then, have been struggling for mastery; the structure of the poem thus exhibits
the development of two formal passages that contrast the
two themes. The two formal passages break down, the
first shading into the second ("Now that the salt of their
blood . . ."), the second one concluding with the figure
of the jaguar, which is presented in a distracted rhythm
left suspended from a weak ending—the word *victim*.

This figure of the jaguar is the only explicit rendering of the Narcissus motif in the poem, but instead of a youth gazing into a pool, a predatory beast stares at a jungle stream, and leaps to devour himself.

The next passage begins:

> *What shall we say who have knowledge*
> *Carried to the heart?*

This is Pascal's war between heart and head, between *finesse* and *géométrie*. Should the reader care to think of these lines as the gathering up of the two themes, now fused, into a final statement, I should see no objection to calling it the Epode. But upon the meaning of the lines from here to the end there is no need for further commentary. I have talked about the structure of the poem, not its quality. One can no more find the quality of one's own verse than one can find its value, and to try to find either is like looking into a glass for the effect that one's face has upon other persons.

If anybody ever wished to know anything about this poem that he could not interpret for himself, I suspect that he is still in the dark. I cannot believe that I have illuminated the difficulties that some readers have found in the style. But then I cannot, have never been able to, see any difficulties of that order. The poem has been much revised. I still think there is much to be said for the original *barter* instead of *yield* in the second line, and for *Novembers* instead of *November* in line fifteen. The revisions were not undertaken for the convenience of the reader but for the poem's own clarity, so that, word, phrase, line, passage, the poem might at worst come near its best expression.

Editor's Note

Yeats and His Symbols first appeared in *The Kenyon Review*, Summer 1939. Slightly revised for its publication here. Reprinted by permission of the author and of *The Kenyon Review*.

John Crowe Ransom was born in Pulaski, Tennessee, in 1888, and educated at Vanderbilt and Oxford (as a Rhodes scholar). He has taught at Vanderbilt and Kenyon, was an editor of *The Fugitive,* and has edited *The Kenyon Review* since its founding in 1939. Ransom's books of verse are represented in *Selected Poems* (1945); his criticism in *God Without Thunder* (1930), *The World's Body* (1938), *The New Criticism* (1941); and both in *Poems and Essays* (1955).

TEN

John Crowe Ransom

Yeats and His Symbols

Before I become involved in some local studies in the
poetry of Yeats, and some theory which it suggests, I had
better record my general tribute to the poet. I concur as
instantly as any other critic in the judgment that he had
by nature the finest poetic gift in our time, and by technical discipline one of the subtlest and surest instruments
in the history of English poetry. This is to see the poet at
his best, but the condition is frequent in his later work.
He was a great poet—if there are readers who cannot bear
to have the ultimate adjective withheld.

He might have failed on the whole, as he did in many
poems, if he had not been driven by a powerful sense of
vocation. And, particularly, he might have become a sort
of Villiers de L'Isle-Adam, or Rimbaud. He was a symbolic poet and might have become a Symbolist one—
though there has never quite been one in English poetry,
and Blake, who may be thought to have come near to it,
was different in an obvious way, while Mr. Eliot is different
in another way.

I do not mean disrespect to religion, but quite the
contrary, if I schematize the religious impulse in its bold
aesthetic phase as being simply the best instance of the
poetic impulse. Since I have said that Yeats wrote great
poetry, I need not surrender the adjective before remarking that the great style as we have had it in English is
the style that works upon the great theme, and this theme
is the metaphysical. I had almost called it the supernatural; but that term has become trite and inhibiting to
perception. I mean the world which is over or under the

natural world, but sustaining and explaining it, not violating it; the world shared by poetry and religion. Yeats was born into a barren or unreligious age, and lived to see it become a naturalistic or irreligious one. That was the background against which he had to exercise his gift of poetry which, like that of Shakespeare and Donne and Milton, was a gift for splendid metaphysical imagery. His importance for us now is that over the facile excitements of swarms of naturalistic poets—the tame villatic fowl we had come to—he has saved our poetic tradition in its dignity.

So far as I know, Mr. Edmund Wilson was the first to offer significant comments on Yeats, though I think they were inadequate, and Mr. Blackmur later has treated Yeats with the best general sense of his achievement. Criticism of Yeats in the light of the whole of his testament, now that it is finished, would be ideally done if Mr. Wilson and Mr. Blackmur could do it in collaboration. Mr. Wilson would be continually objecting to the vulnerable poems on the ground that intellectual authority did not attach to their metaphysical symbols, and that in using them Yeats was too much like an irresponsible French Symbolist. Mr. Blackmur's service would be to insist that at any rate the symbols were grasped and held to with fierce sincerity; and he would also be able to argue that at many times the symbols were entirely suitable and defensible. Mr. Wilson's part would be negative but important, since in an age of naturalism the poet is properly subjected to the rule of reason. Mr. Blackmur, granting everything that deserved to be granted, would not be deterred from his perception of a magnificence that could not ultimately be diverted, and finally of poems that were objectively and simply magnificent.

Fifteen or eighteen years ago I was saying, and everybody was saying, for it was easy to say: There can be no more poetry on the order of its famous triumphs until we come again upon a time when an elaborate Myth will be accepted universally, so that the poet may work within a religious frame which is conventional, and therefore universal: having at least that kind of objectivity. The saying declared our own difficulties though it echoed Matthew Arnold. Yeats has disproved it. We have no common religion but we have not stopped being religious. There is no one religion but none of the old religions has quite died, for we still respond to its symbols. Yeats did not found a religion though it appears from his prose that he tinkered with a system for private use. In his public poetry he was a tireless religious eclectic and improviser of religious imagery, and this strategy, which was perhaps the only possible strategy, succeeded. There must have been a few ages in which unofficial poetry has kept religion alive if not flourishing during the weakness or the collapse of the establishments. After all, Yeats' accomplishment in this respect is of the same kind as Shakespeare's, though it is far less diffuse, it is more compacted, and willed.

The religious system that was most available was the one he scarcely used. Roman Catholicism, flourishing outwardly at least, was all round him in his Ireland. But, for one thing, it was not congenial with his ethical feelings; and what must have been more forbidding, and is more significant with respect to the difficulties of poets generally, its imagery had gone rather stale. So many generations of poets had explored its handsome framework that now the late poets found themselves anticipated; it was too hard to obtain fresh perceptions within it. I suppose this stage may come for any religion, with its exclusive range of images.

I will try a simple argument without properly citing the supporting evidences; I know I shall be over-simplifying it. While the public religion is crystallizing, and just afterwards, the poets are probably glad to serve it by elaborating the images of its persons and events. The sacred story is told over and over, and always, as long as real poets are telling it, with fresh invention. This would be a very direct kind of religious poetry; and here we have *Paradise Lost,* which in design is not subtle at all. Milton, always the virtuoso, saw fit to work within the vast but simple range of the ingenuous Du Bartas, not that of the advanced religious lyric poets then current in his England,

and to hark back to the first principles of religious poetry; to the direct attack. This means merely I suppose, that he was intending a heroic poem. But eventually, and all the sooner after a Milton, this sort of thing will have gone as far as the poets can take it, and then they will abandon it.

The next stage in the religion, still speaking of its use for poets, would be the stage of poetic symbols. The poetry here is strategically and structurally more interesting. The poets come down to earth, and they import into their secular or human recitals the powerful symbols which refer to the metaphysical features of the public religion. The symbols keep the natural and the supernatural systems in relation. It is in this stage of more personal religious poetry that we find most of the 17th Century religious poets. But we should recall to ourselves just what sort of poetic device is the symbol, and why it is potent. It is a compendium of imagery, not content with the immediate image evoked by the word, but starting the imagination back upon the realization of the image in its special religious history; and it does not work, it lapses from being a poetic device into being an ordinary tag of identification, if it does not really evoke the image that originated it; it fails all the more if it does not have an image to evoke.

A proper symbol would refer to the authoritative context of a public religion. With the French Symbolists began, I suppose, the habit of faking the symbol; the word would look as if it ought to have had a brilliant history within some system of metaphysical images, but one was embarrassed to know just what it could have been. I remember my distaste of years ago with some of Maeterlinck's writing (he must have represented a softer side of the school) where the mere repetition of the word, otherwise a senseless proceeding, invited the reader to import a symbolic meaning into it, when no symbolic meaning came to mind. No amount of repetition will substitute for a history in creating a symbol; and that is just the trouble I find with Miss Gertrude Stein's heavily weighted nonsense prose. We think something must be

signified by the little phrases which bear such an emphasis
of repetition; but we conclude after a certain time that the
thing is an amiable imposture, and that nothing special is
being signified. The symbol needs its public genealogy.

I do not mean to slander the dead Symbolists whose
example accounts for so much that has been brilliant in
English poetry since. Tentatively I venture that they felt
the force of both of the twin considerations: first, that
delicate minds will always relish something better than
the stock religious images that serve the obtuse and vulgar, and will have to set up a kind of unformalized
religion of their own; second, that in the late days of
a religion the stock images are not really images but bare
terms of reference. At any rate our impression of Symbolist effects is of symbols uncertain enough to have been
taken as either religious or secular, according to the
authors' convenience. The imagery cannot be objectified.
It is arbitrary if it works at all, and by the standards of
public discourse it is obscure. The obscurity to which we
find ourselves attributing this kind of history is probably
the bigger and nobler portion of all that famous obscurity
of the moderns. It may be deplorable but it is essential
to the pseudo-religious effect, for if unequivocal terms are
substituted the depth of this poetry, with the possibility
of religious feeling, is drained away.

It must at any rate be said that powerful symbols, like
lovely airs, are not immune to wear. With increased
familiarity comes the instant "identification" of the thing
symbolized, on the part of the economical intellect, and
no evocation of imagery. For poetry the religion has lost
its standing. (We need not conclude that religion at this
stage has finished its highly compounded program.)
There has not been for a long time in English a systematic
poetry using Christian symbols on a large scale. That was
the condition under which Yeats as a poet renounced
Christianity.

The best exception I find is the poem, "A Prayer for
My Son." If the son is a small child, no religion will
answer to the occasion like Christianity, and Yeats' recourse to it is spontaneous. He begins:

> *Bid a strong ghost stand at the head*
> *That my Michael may sleep sound,*
> *Nor cry, nor turn in the bed*
> *Till his morning meal come round.*

By a strong ghost he means one with "sword in fist," for the father's premonition is that actual murder seeks out his son, who is destined to great deeds. Therefore he addresses his prayer to Christ, who has known precisely that situation:

> *Though You can fashion everything*
> *From nothing every day, and teach*
> *The morning stars to sing,*
> *You have lacked articulate speech*
> *To tell your simplest want, and known,*
> *Wailing upon a woman's knee,*
> *All of that worst ignominy*
> *Of flesh and bone.*

And now the account of Yeats will be worse than negative; I have to advert to a creative effort long sustained and all but wasted. He tried with all his might to establish his poetry within the frame of the Ossianic or Irish mythology. It occupied many of his early years, and produced nothing, I believe, that is worthy of his ultimate stature as a poet. But that is a hazard of vocation; at any rate it painfully educates the poet both in technique and in strategy.

The ethical paganism of this religion suited Yeats as a preference over Christian mortification of the flesh; yet it did not have for him the solid structure of an eligible religion. The rehearsal of the legends is of something remote and romantic. Actually Yeats and his friends with all their persuasion did not restore to modern Ireland her Gaelic myth; perhaps because Ireland had been too fully subjugated to the sterner and more intellectual European tradition. Its tense remains the past. It does not yield a present, for symbols do not come out of it to apply to the situations of life. We can see why Yeats, when he has kept these old-Irish poems in his successive editions, has accompanied them with an apology for his youth.

The remainder of the symbolic poetry, so far as the origin of the symbols is concerned, might be lumped together as eclectic. Its religious ancestry goes back to nearly every source with which European tradition is familiar.

It may derive from Greek religion, whether the public one or that of the secret cults; for Yeats was a studious man, and always conceived the way of philosophy to be the way of religion. More commonly it derives from the contemporary occult schools; Rosicrucian, Cabalistic, Hermetic, or all together. The occultists are themselves eclectics, with a hospitality to symbols so promiscuous that they are always forgetting the boundaries of intellectual responsibility. The other modern poet who has Yeats' range of symbols is Mr. Eliot. But there is a great difference in their strategies. Mr. Eliot attaches the occult symbols like captives to his Christian chariot, and it gives a fresh and interesting status to his Christianity. (Changing the figure, it is as if he were the doctor infusing strange blood into a decadent organism, and reviving it for another while. The figure is precisely as reasonable as his poetic strategy.) The important achievement for Mr. Eliot lies of course in his really recovering to the Christian symbols some of their original energy as images. Yeats is both more and less orthodox than Mr. Eliot; more orthodox in his intellectual technique, working with one set of symbols at a time; less, in that he does not at all feel bound to take the Christian symbols as his base.

Yeats never—rarely if we look through the whole body of the collected poems, never if we look at that segment of them which seems destined to stand—never requires much editorial gloss to explain a symbol because it is the property of an occult sodality or because it is private to himself alone. (In this again he contrasts with Mr. Eliot.) The symbol is objective and easy, or else it is actually developed a little way so that the "impartial spectator" who reads (and who stands in our mind for the test of the poem's objectivity) can go on and obtain a sufficiently clear and exciting image to answer to it. There is an interesting point of biography here which it would be a service in some historian to clear up. Much of the prose of Yeats is far more difficult than any of the verse, being crowded with obscure and unaided symbols. It is as if his scruple in the poetry were his sense of a professional responsibility, while his prose is for his own consumption. Florid Neo-Platonism, theosophy, even a little astrology, for his privacy, but in his poetry only symbols fit for the public currency.

But it is certain that there is a religiousness which is not based on instruction in systematic religion, and that poets will have at least that sort of religiousness if they are not enervated (as by a naturalistic climate), and that Yeats has many poems which come out of this religiousness; these too may be considered under the general head of eclectic. For what is technically called "natural religion" might better be called "poetic religion." Natural religion also consists in having metaphysical images, and carrying them to the natural world. The images are spontaneous and genuine, but they must be valid almost at first sight if they are to carry persuasion. They cannot expect to be entertained as the result of a discipline that has already instructed the public in them as in the images of a dogmatic system; nor can one of them singly imply a whole historical system of images that is intellectually coherent. They are inferior in force to the properly symbolic images; and I mean such pretty improvisations as

> But look, the morn, in russet mantle clad,
> Walks o'er the dew of yon high eastward hill.

Yeats' unofficial religious images are more significant than this, just as Donne's are, and the reason is the same for both poets: they are educated in the official images, so that they have a superior skill in improvising. I owe this point principally to Mr. Blackmur. He argues to the effect that religious discipline is the making of a fine poet even if he is to throw away every specific image in whose use he has been instructed. It is such a good argument that it deserves to be repeated. It might be extended to cover this principle: that in an age of naturalism the aesthetic hunger obtains many satisfactions, though they may be furtive ones, from images that still echo the old official systems which the revolution has run out of business, and so the age is still living on the remainder works of a capital which it has stopped from further productive employment.

And now I must illustrate the eclectic symbolism from the text.

A famous and startling poem is of course "The Second Coming":

> Turning and turning in the widening gyre
> The falcon cannot hear the falconer;
> Things fall apart; the centre cannot hold;
> Mere anarchy is loosed upon the world,
> The blood-dimmed tide is loosed, and everywhere
> The ceremony of innocence is drowned;
> The best lack all conviction, while the worst
> Are full of passionate intensity.
>
> Surely some revelation is at hand;
> Surely the Second Coming is at hand.
> The Second Coming! Hardly are those words out
> When a vast image out of Spiritus Mundi
> Troubles my sight: somewhere in sands of the desert
> A shape with lion body and the head of a man,
> A gaze blank and pitiless as the sun,
> Is moving its slow thighs, while all about it
> Reel shadows of the indignant desert birds.
> The darkness drops again; but now I know
> That twenty centuries of stony sleep
> Were vexed to nightmare by a rocking cradle,
> And what rough beast, its hour come round at last,
> Slouches towards Bethlehem to be born?

The first part of this poem would consist with any sort of religiosity. It is not a naturalistic passage, to any public experienced in reading poetry; for either the falcon and falconer are symbolic, or else they are a boldly new and cosmic image; and there are the images of the centripetal force of the world turning to centrifugal, of anarchy being loosed upon it (by evil forces or by destiny), and of the blood-dimmed tide, which may have an occult meaning or may be a metaphysical image of war. The last two lines sound most naturalistic, and they might be undistinguished elsewhere, but here they are the climax and we have to dwell upon them, because it is a metaphysical context which advances to their summary truth; and the more we dwell upon them, the more adequate they become.

The second part sounds Christian in the beginning, but develops an image whose source is not Scripture but Spiritus Mundi, and which concerns something like an Egyptian Sphinx, and the passing of Christ in his favor. The language is worthy of the matter. The matter is valid enough if it is reasonable to say: Twenty centuries have passed, and the ideal they professed has come to perfect ineptitude and impotence; a new millennium will dawn, and we cannot tell what ideal it will obey; very likely, a monstrous ideal of abstract animal power. Even in this substitute form it is not a pure intellectual speculation, but is fringed with metaphysical imagery; and in the poem itself the obvious content is that imagery in distinctness.

Upon an even more famous poem, "Sailing to Byzantium," I have read Mr. Blackmur and Mr. Cleanth Brooks. But I think the high-powered exegesis of the symbols which is possible for the scholar is not really needed for a very deep lay satisfaction in the poem. I omit the first stanza for the sake of space:

> An aged man is but a paltry thing,
> A tattered coat upon a stick, unless
> Soul clap its hands and sing, and louder sing
> For every tatter in its mortal dress,
> Nor is there singing school but studying
> Monuments of its own magnificence;
> And therefore I have sailed the seas and come
> To the holy city of Byzantium.

> *O sages standing in God's holy fire*
> *As in the gold mosaic of a wall,*
> *Come from the holy fire, perne in a gyre,*
> *And be the singing-masters of my soul.*
> *Consume my heart away; sick with desire*
> *And fastened to a dying animal*
> *It knows not what it is; and gather me*
> *Into the artifice of eternity.*
>
> *Once out of nature I shall never take*
> *My bodily form from any natural thing,*
> *But such a form as Grecian goldsmiths make*
> *Of hammered gold and gold enamelling*
> *To keep a drowsy Emperor awake;*
> *Or set upon a golden bough to sing*
> *To lords and ladies of Byzantium*
> *Of what is past, or passing, or to come.*

In this poem the old poet, electing the body for his next incarnation, chooses to inhabit an artificial Byzantine bird that will sing; then he will not have to feel his living body decay as he does now, and have to pray to be delivered of it. The prayer is addressed to holy sages who dwell I do not know where; it does not seem to matter where, for they appear qualified to receive the prayer, and it is a correct and elevated prayer. The poem offers a certain version of Pythagorean philosophy, but that is not too steep for me, and the version is a human and charming one.

In these two poems the images are as recondite as Yeats usually permits them to be. If we will put together the fact of his eclecticism, or the catholicity of his symbols, and the fact of his care to see that the symbols are practicable and actually set in motion their intended imagery, we will conclude that he had an excellent understanding of how to use and how not to abuse his symbols; that his religiousness was wholly intelligent. But he has many passages commenting upon his practice. In "Nineteen Hundred and Nineteen" he says, for example:

> *Some moralist or mythological poet*
> *Compares the solitary soul to a swan:*
> *I am satisfied with that,*
> *Satisfied if a troubled mirror show it,*
> *Before that brief gleam of its life be gone,*
> *An image of its state;*
> *The wings half spread for flight,*
> *The breast thrust out in pride*
> *Whether to play, or to ride*
> *Those winds that clamour of approaching night.*

And in "The Tower" he asserts that he like all men has (as we would say) created his gods in his own image; but he does not reprobate himself for doing it; it is the commonest necessity, and as an old man he must now declare it plainly to the proud young men—not the animalists and naturalists—whom he wishes to inherit him:

> *And I declare my faith:*
> *I mock Plotinus' thought*
> *And cry in Plato's teeth,*
> *Death and life were not*
> *Till man made up the whole,*
> *Made lock, stock and barrel*
> *Out of his bitter soul,*
> *Aye, sun and moon and star, all,*
> *And further add to that*
> *That, being dead, we rise,*
> *Dream and so create*
> *Translunar Paradise.*
> *I have prepared my peace*
> *With learned Italian things*
> *And the proud stones of Greece,*
> *Poet's imaginings*
> *And memories of love,*
> *Memories of the words of women,*
> *All those things whereof*
> *Man makes a superhuman*
> *Mirror-resembling dream.*

These terms can be made to do in deriving the epistemology of religion; they are a little bit on the soft and "romantic" side, but philosophy will support them. Concluding this poem, he indicates that as he grows old the "superhuman dream" dispossesses in reality the concerns of the body:

> *Now shall I make my soul,*
> *Compelling it to study*
> *In a learned school*
> *Till the wreck of body,*
> *Slow decay of blood,*
> *Testy delirium*
> *Or dull decrepitude*
> *Or what worse evil come—*
> *The death of friends, or death*
> *Of every brilliant eye*
> *That made a catch in the breath—*
> *Seem but the clouds of the sky*
> *When the horizon fades;*
> *Or a bird's sleepy cry*
> *Among the deepening shades.*

In Yeats there is no element of that seeking for special favors from Heaven, that expectation of being relieved of the incidence of the ordinary physical laws, which makes degenerate religions, or religions in the hands of degenerate priests, positively vicious. The body of his poetry breathes a tragic sense. His gods are true gods rather than easy ones. And to a veteran and accomplished religionist like Yeats a purely secular moment, into which the forms of gods do not enter, is likely to be a context dignified by the sense that gods are immanent within it, and may appear at any instant; it is like the prelude to a specifically religious experience. A score of poems could show this. But I will stop with his "Prayer for My Daughter." It might as well be entitled, "Wish for My Daughter," since it is addressed to no particular deities and has no official religious symbolism. The blessings desired are qualified by great modesty and fastidiousness as the father reasons on their serviceability to the woman in her world; and the poem concludes:

And may her bridegroom bring her to a house
Where all's accustomed, ceremonious;
For arrogance and hatred are the wares
Peddled in the thoroughfares.
How but in custom and in ceremony
Are innocence and beauty born?
Ceremony's a name for the rich horn,
And custom for the spreading laurel tree.

The abbreviated quotation as I have it does not suggest what is the fact, that ceremony and custom are climactic for the poem in being identified here with the horn of plenty and the laurel tree, which have had attention earlier. The horn and laurel tree have been treated by a cunning creative imagination, till they virtually, before our eyes, are promoted to something like the status of religious symbols.

Editor's Note

On *Rereading Balzac: The Artist as Scapegoat* first appeared in *The Kenyon Review,* Summer 1940. With a postscript written for this volume. Reprinted by permission of the author and of *The Kenyon Review.*

William Troy was born in Chicago, Illinois, in 1903, and educated at Yale, Columbia, Grenoble, and the Sorbonne. He has taught at the University of New Hampshire, New York University, Bennington College, and the New School for Social Research, and in 1955–6 was a visiting professor at the universities of Bordeaux and Rennes. Examples of Troy's literary criticism are available in: *Literary Opinion in America,* edited by Morton Dauwen Zabel (1937, 1951), *The Partisan Reader,* edited by William Phillips and Philip Rahv (1946), *James Joyce: Two Decades of Criticism,* edited by Seon Givens (1948), and *F. Scott Fitzgerald: The Man and His Work,* edited by Alfred Kazin (1951).

ELEVEN

William Troy

On Rereading Balzac:
The Artist as Scapegoat

Balzac is little read nowadays; he is remembered as one of the more unkempt geniuses of an unkempt century. As a psychologist he is not to be compared with his contemporary Stendhal, nor as a craftsman with his successor Flaubert. He is rather to be held up to the young as a monumental example of the consequences of indiscipline. The highest compliment likely to be paid him is that he was one of the first and most "strenuous" critics of bourgeois society. Karl Marx admitted to having learned much of his knowledge and his theory of that society from the *Comédie Humaine.* This is in a straight line with Brunetière's judgment, in his famous Centenary Address at Tours in 1899, that Balzac would gain in value and importance with the passage of the years because his works were essentially "scientific documents."

Yet an open minded rereading of Balzac can only leave us with the feeling that neither of these judgments does justice to the real quality and nature of his achievement. True, his psychological analysis lacks the concentrated brilliance of Stendhal at his best. But, then, it comes out of an incomparably broader grasp of the complexities of the situation. Balzac is continually trying to get more into the picture than Stendhal was capable even of imagining. (His own criticism of the author of *Le Rouge et le Noir* is that he was completely lacking in the moral sense.) And the same defense may be made in any comparison with his two immediate successors: his obsession with fact did not cause his emotions to seek relief either in the sulphurous pessimism of Flaubert on the one hand or in the blowsy optimism of Zola on the other. The view of life on which he operated was equally realistic with theirs; but it was a realism that had more in common with that of the Church than with that of 19th Century science. If we look at all closely into the view of life on which he was most of the time working we must decide that it was the tragic: the human will, taken either in the individual or in society as a whole, is the principle of evil. It is a force for destruction that it is the better part of wisdom to recognize from the beginning.

To refer to Balzac as if he were a tragic poet is of course to throw a certain amount of confusion into those who have become accustomed to Brunetière's estimate of the work. But it is to keep well in mind Balzac's own plan of the *Comédie Humaine*, according to which the first part, the *Études de Moeurs*, was to be devoted to a comprehensive treatment of every one of the social *effects* of French national life in the early 19th Century, while the second part, the *Études Philosophiques*, was going to deal with its more abstract and generalized *causes*. A third part, the *Études Analytiques*, which was to deal with its *principles*, was never completed. "Then, after I have made the poesy, the demonstration of a whole system," he writes, "I will write the Science of it in an 'Essay on Human Forces.'" Although a word like "demonstration" has a rather bad sound here, it is clear that he is making a sharp distinction between "poesy" and "Science"; that the *Comédie* is to be taken as a vast symbolical edifice, rising in tiers from the twenty-four volumes of the first part to the fifteen of the second and the nine of the proposed third. Not only is this "poesy" but it is "poesy" on a Dantesque scale; and we hardly need the title to suggest that he was attempting nothing less than a parallel for his time of the synthesis represented in the *Divina Commedia*. And here also we may see how he intended that science was to enter the work.

It is evident that Balzac hoped to reconcile both the method and the discoveries of the science of his time with poetry. The building of effects by the massing of factual detail is the application to narrative of the quantitative method of science. The Balzacian world is on the surface an interlocking system of atoms separately collected and put together by the synthetic will. Part of our response to his work—as with painters like Meissonier and Delacroix—is expected to be an awareness of the amount of sheer labor that has gone into the execution. And in this sense its quantitative aspect may be said to be imponderably bound up with the total aesthetic effect. For Balzac's generation the immense world of fact opened up by science had something like the awe-inspiring fascination of Nature for the primitive mind; it made possible once again a poetry of size. But there is the more important sense in which all this elaborate and painstaking documentation is after all no more than the *vehicle* of what is an essentially imaginative reading of life. The celebrated description of the Pension Vauquer, for example, is as itemized as a bailiff's inventory. At the same time there is scarcely an article of furniture that is not symbolical of the theme and subject as a whole. Quasi-scientific documentation is simply an expansion of what is the "literal" level of communication in a poet like Dante. The great difference between Dante and Balzac, of course, is that where the first had his meanings already embodied and ordered in a set of traditional symbols the second has laboriously to reassemble into wholes meanings that have been fractured through the analytical exploits of the previous two centuries.

So much for method. More interesting to consider perhaps would be the ambitious attempt to identify the laws of science with the moral and metaphysical concepts of the older religious or poetic synthesis. To Louis Lambert "Will" and "Thought" were "living forces" capable of being measured and charted. Raphael, in *The Magic Skin*, refers to the human will as "a natural force, like steam." "The boldest physiologists," he writes in *César Birotteau*, "are frightened by the physical results of this moral phenomenon, which is, nevertheless, an inward blasting, and, like all electrical effects, capricious and strange in its methods." Is it too much to see here what would be the promise of a harmonization of the most advanced bio-chemistry, like that of Dr. Carrel, with the most advanced modern physics? The human "field of forces" is elsewhere defined: "Our brain is the matrix into which we transport all that our diverse organizations can absorb of ethereal matter—the common basis of several substances known under the improper names of electricity, heat, light, gal-vanic and magnetic fluid, etc.—and from which it issues in the form of thought." Like Poe in "Eureka," it is clear that Balzac had the dream of a fusion of all the branches of human knowledge. Instead of submitting to the scientific absolutism of his epoch like the naturalists or of retreating from it like the romantic sentimentalists, he sought to ab-sorb the scientific world-view into the larger vision of the mystic.

But these notes must confine themselves to the single consideration of what more than anything else reveals the fundamentally poetic pattern that lies beneath the vast farraginous mass of the *Comédie Humaine*. If Balzac possessed the tragic vision, as has been suggested, we should expect to find it expressed nowhere more forcibly than in the treatment of his hero. And here also we may see how sharply he is to be distinguished in depth and breadth of imagination from any of the members of the two important schools of fiction that grew out of him in France.

II

Balzac identifies himself with two quite different types of hero, corresponding to a division between his intellec-tual will and his imagination. Vautrin is the supreme ex-ample of the first type—a lineal descendant of Macheath through the Noble Brigand of German romantic drama and the Fatal Man of the Gothic novel. The other type is the Man of Sensibility of the eighteenth century now appearing under his true light as the artist himself suffer-ing at the hands of a vulgar and immoral society. In Lucien de Rubempré and Raphael de Valentin, Balzac has drawn this type so fully that one wonders why so many writers throughout the remainder of the century felt impelled to repeat the pattern. Although we have stated that the two types are distinct, they have a common historical origin, and even in Balzac they are continually melting into each other. For the Fatal Man was in the beginning a sensitive and even radiant soul. Feeling lies at the root of his rebellion against authority; and the intellectual will of a Satan, a Faust, or a Manfred can easily enough be interpreted in modern psychological terms as inverted love. The Fatal Man—with his aspect of fallen angel of light, his harrowed countenance, and his addiction to sadism—was an expression of the violent revenge that Feeling began to inflict upon Reason by the end of the 18th Century. He was the personification of an exasperated sentimentalism. If the man of refined moral and emotional impulses fared so badly in a world given over to a cynical skepticism in thought and an uninhibited selfishness in action, one solution for the superior individual was to outwit this world at its own game. The victim of life can always make the world his victim. Vautrin has not less feeling than Lucien or Raphael; his homosexual attachment to the young murderer whom he saves from the gallows is evidence of his capacity for suffering. It is simply that feeling in his case has been diverted into a monomaniac anti-social passion.

In Vautrin, Balzac exhausts imaginatively that contempt for the hypocrisy and corruption of Restoration society which might very easily, in a man of his extraordinary vigor and detachment, have been converted into action. There is a sense of course in which all the personages of the *Comédie* are autobiographical. Every one of them, from pathetic little Birotteau to the rapacious de Nucingens, is a projection of the same terrific will that their creator is working off in his writing. When one of them looks down from the Butte Montmartre and swears to bring the whole city to his feet, it is Balzac himself supplying another image of his own determination to submit the whole of French life to his pen. But Vautrin is the will-to-power as pure reason; he is motivated not so much by material

interests as by simple pride of intellect. And this is the un-
pardonable sin—the sin of Lucifer. When we first encounter him, in *Père Goriot,* he is the evil mentor of Rastignac,
whom he is assisting in plotting a match with a rich so-
ciety-woman. The plot fails, and he is unmasked as the
notorious Jacques Collin, former galley-slave, long wanted
by the police. In *Splendor and Misery of Courtesans* he
appears in the robes of an important Spanish ecclesiastic
whom he has murdered, and whose credentials that he
has stolen will open to him all the doors of the Court
and the Government. On the road to Paris he picks up
poor Lucien de Rubempré, and the thought occurs to him
to make him his creature. In the Machiavellian oration
that he delivers on the vices and follies of high society,
on how much the young poet must sacrifice if he would
be a success in it, it is the very voice of Balzac himself
that we seem to hear; it is like the plot of one of his
novels. And it is then that we are made aware of the
parallel between the artist and the criminal, between
the "detached" observer of society and its detached enemy.
Not only are both outside the pale but both are professionally given to the spinning of enormous plots. Vautrin
is simply the artist functioning in the realm of action, the
Fatal Man transported from the pages of fiction into
actual life.

In *The Last Transformation of Vautrin,* which was
probably the first gangster novel ever written, there is
hardly any difference between the viewpoint of the author
and his hero. Now we are introduced right inside the
prison-yard of St. Lazare and into the secret of that vast
organization which Vautrin has built up and over which
he rules like a dictator. Later, upon his escape, this organization will enable him to pass through the police-nets
of Paris as through a sieve. For this underworld confed-
eration is represented not as a section or portion, a specific
area of infection, of the body of society as a whole. It is
rather a counter-society, with its own laws, customs, and
loyalties, and with what may be described as only a *func-
tional* relationship to "good" or official society. It exists
by virtue of the failure of the latter to maintain at all

times a proper equilibrium between its practical interests and its avowed moral or ethical attitudes. The rôle of a Vautrin, the man of superior intellect unimpeded by such self-deceptions, is to serve as a constant threat and menace to the universal fiction, to keep the writing on the wall always fresh and terrifying. For this reason the attitude of society toward the criminal is always ambivalent— divided between fear and respect: fear, lest its own motives be brought into the light through open prosecution; respect, in that he realizes with a brutal finality instincts which it can express only through the impure medium of its ritual. This is demonstrated in the altogether cynical manner in which Vautrin's long-drawn-out feud with society is brought to a close. His system of espionage and counter-espionage has reduced so many of its best elements to his mercy that there is no solution but to make him chief of the secret police of Paris.

Vautrin corresponds, as has been said, to what must have been in Balzac the temptation of the intellectual will. Confronted with the teeming world of Restoration society, with a world altogether without values of any kind, that temptation must have been great indeed. Out of the mentality reflected in Vautrin and in that other great master of masquerade Stendhal, was to develop the whole movement of thought that culminates in Stirner and Nietzsche. And out of these power-philosophers in turn were to be spawned in the 20th Century those exponents of power-politics whose success in "calling the bluff" of the more genteel *quartiers* of Europe is one of the most remarkable phenomena of the moment. But Balzac preferred art to action; he sought power elsewhere than in the Tuileries or in St. Lazare. And while he admits the perennial threat, even necessity at certain times, of a Vautrin he discovers his fullest image in his other type of hero—the victim not so much of society as of life.

III

The simplest interpretation of the de Rubempré cycle is to discover in it another study of the manner in which

bourgeois society treats the artist. In *Lost Illusions* Lucien
is the poet as unspoiled child of nature, an innocent sen-
timentalist composing bad imitations of De Musset and
Lamartine for the local blue-stockings. But already his
head is turned by flattery and he is willing to cast aside
the image of idyllic domestic life presented by his friend
and brother-in-law Séchard. *A Great Man of the Provinces
in Paris* takes him to the capital in the equipage of Madame de Langeais, who soon abandons him, through a brief
period of self-imposed asceticism in the Latin Quarter, to
a rapid ascent and even more rapid descent in the vast
ant-hill of Parisian journalism. No more devastating picture of the perennial corruption of the newspaper and
publishing world has ever been drawn than in this section.
And there is no depravity of this world that Lucien is not
made to taste before he loses his fortune, his reputation,
and his mistress. The section closes with two agonizing
scenes: one in which he is forced to write a rollicking
drinking-song to pay the expenses of his mistress' funeral;
another in which he has to accept from her maid money
that she has earned through prostitution. His first great
assault on the city has ended in a descent into the abyss
—like Joseph's in the land of Egypt. The second is made
possible only by a complete sacrifice of what remains of
his soul to the devil. When Vautrin picks him up on the
road to Paris he has just succeeded in ruining his brother-
in-law; he has suffered the mockery of being fêted by his
fellow-townsmen; and he is altogether penniless. Nothing
remains but absolute capitulation to the forces that have
already twice betrayed him. Throughout the first part of
Splendor and Misery of Courtesans he seems relatively
happy in the luxurious establishment that Vautrin has set
up for him and his new mistress, the fabulous Esther
Gobseck, in an obscure corner of Paris. But he is soon
caught like a fly in the ever more complicated web of
intrigue that his proctor has spun in his feud with society.
In the end the de Nucingens triumph; and this most
Arabian of all Balzac's modern Arabian Nights Tales
closes with Esther's murder, Vautrin's return to prison,
and Lucien's suicide.

Such a long summary is offered to make clear the point that guilt is not shifted from the artist to society—as in the treatment of the subject by the Naturalists, for example. Lucien is betrayed by the weakness of his own nature. Essentially a noble soul in the most sentimental tradition, he has been undone by his need for fame, luxury, and social position. For these things he has sacrificed love, whose symbols are his family, the friends of the Latin Quarter period, and poetry. Society is involved in the drama, however, in one very important respect and in a manner quite different from the way in which it is ordinarily involved in tragedy. Even in *Antigone,* in which the claims of society are held in uncertain balance with more ancient pieties, society stands for order—an objective and authoritative norm by which individual conduct may be measured. But the society that Balzac describes is itself given over to the unregenerate expression of "Will"; it is simply an aggregation of predatory individuals. It is in no sense better than the individual. This is to admit that society is to blame for Lucien's situation to the extent that it offered him no values other than its own value of success at any price. It is no more than his own career written large—without, as yet, the tragic culmination. Or, to reverse this description, Lucien rehearses in his career the immemorial struggle between will and reason, matter and form, of which his society is unconscious because it has not yet been brought to tragic knowledge. He is the scapegoat of his society. He is the scapegoat not only in the degenerated modern sense of the term but in the original religious sense of someone who takes on himself the guilt of existence, who undergoes the agony of matter whenever it assumes form.

But before developing this idea it may be well to look at an even more transparent rendition of the same theme. The Rubempré cycle belongs to the *Études de Moeurs;* the symbolical pattern must be reconstructed out of the welter of detail into which it is analyzed. In *The Magic Skin,* which belongs to the *Études Philosophiques,* the symbols are reduced to the brittle abstractions of allegory. Raphael is another young provincial writer (he has ac-

tually composed a "Treatise on the Will") who has come
to Paris only to make the classic gesture by the Seine.
On the way to self-destruction he stops in at an old anti-
quarian's shop, where history heaped up in the floor upon
floor of *objets d'art* is made to seem to him "like a witches'
sabbath worthy of the Brocken and Doctor Faust." "He
saw the conquest of Alexander on a cameo, the massacres
of Pizarro in a matchlock arquebuse . . ." The effect is
to alter his mood from despair to an intense yearning for
life, and he accepts the offer of the Magic Skin. Possession of it guarantees the immediate realization of every
desire—with the terrible proviso that thereby so much is
cut off from the term of life. At once Raphael is sur-
rounded by wealth, fame, and admiring friends. But soon
the sense that with the Skin his life is shrinking with the
gratification of every wish makes him live in a state of
desperate anguish. Previously he had laid unsuccessful
siege to a very beautiful but strangely "cold and disinterested" society woman named Fédora. But now he experiences no feeling at the sight of her in an opera-box.
For a while there is promise of salvation through his
marriage with the poor hotel-keeper's daughter who had
befriended him in his worst poverty. But his love for
Pauline is not the "true love" that she bears for him; it
is still too much infected with lust; and the Skin shrinks
to the size of an oak-leaf. Resort to science does not help
him, for his malady is "on the dividing-line between word
and deed, matter and spirit." And at the end of two
months he dies in Pauline's arms.

This fable scarcely needs interpretation: the Skin is of
course the substance of its being which Balzac's society,
like Raphael, was using up through the "material explo-
sions" of the will. The beautiful and sterile Fédora is
finally personified as "Society." Balzac is working out what
we have seen was his abiding obsession—the identity of
material and spiritual forces in both the individual and
the social organism. As one of the physicians in the book
sums it up, "The fraction of the great All which by some
higher will works within us the phenomenon called *life*,
is formulated in a distinct manner in each human being,

making him apparently a finite being, but at one point co-existent with the Infinite."

This may also be taken as a statement of the manner in which the sensitive artist-type is related to society and both to the universe: each is a repetition of the same tension between the drive outward toward expansion and destruction and the drive inward toward conservation and order. Insofar as they are the concrete representations of this tension both Lucien and Raphael may be said to fulfill, as has been suggested, the rôle that in more primitive and more religious societies is assigned to the scapegoat. For it is the function of the scapegoat to hold up to the group a vivid and incontrovertible image of its own inner conflict—which is between what we have called its "interests" and its "pretensions"—and by the relief that is provided to make possible a new equilibrium. It is a device by which the Many are restored to the One through a temporary dissolution of the One. And if the artist-type is selected by Balzac to enact this rôle it is because no other type, in a society given over to the uninhibited expression of the individual will, retained as much sense of the moral and ethical values that had attached to the older religious and poetic synthesis. The Rastignacs, the de Nucingens, and the rest of their crew lacked even the consciousness of guilt; they were simply the mechanical products of will; and they could not, therefore, qualify as tragic characters. It is their capacity for suffering that make Lucien and Raphael eligible for the rôle. "Whoever suffers in body or soul, or lacks power and money, is a Pariah in society," Raphael concludes. And it is, finally, because he is made to suffer most of all in soul—that is, as a man—that the artist-type in Balzac appears to us as the nearest equivalent that we have for the dismembered god or hero of more unified cultures. He is the nearest that we have to a symbol of unity.

Balzac's view is, in the last analysis, the religious—despite the fact that his defense of the Catholic religion is pragmatic and insincere. It is religious not only in the sense of being profoundly and at all times moral—which distinguishes him from almost everyone else in his age but Baudelaire—but in plunging us back to the most fundamental problems in metaphysics. And since the religious view must always come to rest in its treatment of love, the reconciliation of the Many with the One, the great sprawling mass of the *Comédie Humaine* may be said to seek its center in the idea of a perfect and disinterested love. The Skin does not shrink when Raphael wishes to be loved by Pauline; for the difference between the desire for love, which is a state of pure being, and the possession of the object of love, which is an act, is absolute. Love in Balzac is that state of contemplation in which the individual is temporarily relieved of the solicitations of the will and therefore put into communication with the order of the universe. It is the mystic vision of the Whole. Like Blake, whom he so closely resembles, Balzac was forced to invent his own mythology—out of the materials of history, however, rather than out of hallucination. And, as is the case in Blake, the strain is so great that we cannot be sure that he is in perfect control. In *Louis Lambert,* the most philosophical of his narratives, the hero's successful attempt to synthesize all knowledge is accompanied by a perfect love-affair and marriage. But the vision has apparently been too much for him; he lapses into a condition of inarticulate madness. There is an ambiguity in this tale which can only raise questions regarding the degree of faith that Balzac actually did manage to summon to the possibility of mystical experience in his age. But these are questions that would carry us far outside the scope of this paper.

Postscript 1955

This piece was written in July, 1939, on the eve of a world conflict largely precipitated by two specimens of the artist *manqué* turned man of action, whose methods in undermining the whole European political structure were essentially those of Vautrin in his feud with the Paris police system. Both Hitler and Mussolini in their beginnings also wallowed in the same morbid sense of victimage that Balzac traces in his more sympathetic character Lucien de Rubempré. Shortly after the publication of this essay there appeared in France a brilliant monograph by Albert Béguin significantly entitled *Balzac Visionnaire*, which develops more fully the view of Balzac as seer and mystic here presented.

Editor's Note

The Rise of Theatricals: The Indian Background first appeared in *The Roots of American Culture* (1942) by Constance Rourke, edited with a preface by Van Wyck Brooks. Copyright, 1942, by Harcourt, Brace and Company, Inc.

Constance Rourke was born in Cleveland, Ohio, in 1885, and educated at Vassar and the Sorbonne. She taught at Vassar and worked on the Index of American Design. Miss Rourke died in 1941, leaving the unfinished manuscript of a three-volume *History of American Culture,* of which this essay is a fragment. Her books exploring aspects of the American folk tradition include *Trumpets of Jubilee* (1927), *Troupers of the Gold Coast* (1928), *American Humor* (1931), *Davy Crockett* (1934), *Audubon* (1936), and *Charles Sheeler* (1938).

TWELVE

Constance Rourke

The Rise of Theatricals:
The Indian Background

Hardly had Columbus brought back to Europe tidings of his first voyage when a fanciful woodcut was made in Augsburg showing a cluster of Indians wearing feather headdresses and decked with precious stones. Portions of a human being were hung on a limb in preparation for a feast.

Nearly a century later John White, the governor of Roanoke, made a series of exquisite water-color drawings in which he noted flora and fauna of the new continent with some of the aboriginal inhabitants. Engraved by de Bry, they passed into a considerable European currency.

Early in the seventeenth century small figures in wood called "black boys" were placed outside apothecaries' shops in London to advertise tobacco: they were the first of a long lineage of shop-signs continuing to this day in the last of the cigar-store Indians, now shabbily and obscurely. With tobacco and later cigars in an outstretched hand they symbolized the fact that the white men had first received the assuaging gift from the Indian.

The symbolic, the fanciful invaded many of the colonial writings on the Indian; yet John Smith, Bradford, Thomas Morton and many others studiously sought to record their experiences and their knowledge of the Indian in terms of fact. A great body of writing developed in all the colonies whose intent was historical. The stories of captivities experienced by white men and women alone made a small literature. In *The History of the American Indians* (1775),

James Adair advanced the theory that the Indians were
the lost tribes of Israel, but, in spite of this flight of the
imagination, which was to obtain widespread credence
and to be repeated and embroidered many times, the
book was a record, particularly as to the character and
customs of the Cherokees and the Chickasaws: even the
lofty hypothesis was formulated with a scientific purpose,
to account for the origins of the race. Some of these
records were practical; some were early ventures in anthropology. Adair was an Irish trader, a man of education,
instinctively a scholar, who poured into his book a genuine
passion for the wilderness. Few of these writings were
wholly detached. Some of them were harsh. A positive
freshness belongs to many of them, as if the momentous
drama being enacted between the two races in this morning of the new world were instinctively realized.

In most of these works dramatic episodes were outlined
in terms of character and dialogue with an interplay of
action between the Indians and the whites. This relationship found its most complete expression in the Indian
treaties, set down in amplitude as early as 1677. These
treaties were essentially plays—chronicle plays—recording
what was said in the parleys, including bits of action, the
exchanges of gifts, of wampum, the smoking of pipes, the
many ceremonials with dances, cries and choral songs.
Even the printed form of the treaties was dramatic: the
participants were listed like a cast of characters, and precise notations were made as to ceremonial action. Symbolic phrases were used to seal promises, even to raise
questions.

In the Iroquois treaties the very beautiful ceremonial
beginning "At the wood's edge" from the Iroquois book
of rites was invariably introduced. On one occasion
Takanunty, an Onondaga chief, courteously told Conrad
Weiser that the Six Nations could not go to Williamsburg
to meet the southern Indians to make a treaty "as there
is no road to that place. We never travel through bushes
to treaties of peace. It is too dangerous, and we have no
fire at Williamsburg. . . . Such a thing cannot be done in
a corner, it must be done by public fire." This contention

would have been accepted by leaders in all the Indian tribes because the fire and the road were established symbols, because ceremonials springing from deeply rooted communal experience must be preserved, because human dignity was a force that was widely understood.

Indian speech was characteristically grave and rhythmic, but it attained a sharp and witty realism in the discussion of rum, trappers, traders and white trickery. The Indian style of address was generally accepted and used by the white men, even to the sly introduction of humor, and the Indians imposed their own rituals of procedure.

The participants were proprietors, agents, interpreters: Thomas Penn—whose father William was frequently mentioned—Franklin, Croghan, Conrad Weiser, Peter Randolph. They included such sachems as the Oneida chief, Shikellamy, Teedyuscung, chief of the Delawares, the famous Onondaga orator Canasatego and Tamamend—Tammany. The Penobscots, the Tuscaroras, the Senecas, the Mohawks, all the most popular tribes were represented in these transactions and the chief came to them attended by a crowd of warriors, women, even children.

These treaties were formulated in most of the colonies, as far to the west as Fort Pitt.

"Forest diplomacy" in all ways was cast against wide horizons. The Indians—particularly the powerful Six Nations—held the balance of power between the English and the French; they played cunningly upon it: this circumstance made the great fulcrum upon which their successive actions turned. The early treaties are linked by this underlying theme, but they were also bound by a tragedy plainly revealed as tribe after tribe retreated westward.

Some fifty of these treaties are known to have been printed: their cycle has epic proportions as well as an epic theme. In the exact sense they are incomparable; nothing like them exists in our own literature or any other. Quite strictly they belong to practical letters; they were created for practical ends, yet these products of two races were poetry of a high order. In their own time they had a wide currency not only because of their political significance but for their rich episodes, their bold portraiture, their singular fragments of human history. Franklin, who published thirteen of them, had three hundred copies of the Lancaster Treaty of 1774 struck off for sale in England as a literary curiosity, and William Parks also printed this stately treaty—one of the finest and most dramatic of them all—for an audience in Virginia and Maryland concerned with literary as well as historical values.

The treaties have never been included within the sequence of our drama, yet they are in truth our first American plays. The first of them antedates by some eighty years Godfrey's *The Prince of Parthia,* usually considered the first American play, a poetic drama that seems narrow, stilted and remote by comparison with any one of the treaties—a piece of philosophical elegance by a would-be *littérateur.* That the treaties could be matched in poetic or imaginative values by individual effort in their own time was hardly to be expected: they were traditional, communal, they expressed values that had long been accumulated. They were part of an evolving sequence that was to endure long past the period of the Revolution. Yet they had a powerful expressive influence upon the drama: *Ponteach,* the first American play on a native subject, used a theme related to theirs with something of their ritual. Though the language lacks the poetic Indian concentration, some of the typical symbolism of the treaties recurs in the play. Robert Rogers, its author, was in no sense literary though he could write a good straightforward prose. He was a frontiersman, a great strapping giant with a bold humor, a genius for organization and a dream of empire. He was also an unscrupulous Indian trader, a merciless destroyer of Indians. In *Ponteach,* Rogers seemed to set down episodes from his own ruthless career, yet with bitter satire. Rascally traders set the story in motion. The white governors are Sharp, Gripe and Catchum; the commanders of the fort are Cockum and Frisk. All these people lie, cheat, fill the Indians with cheap rum, and are so short-sighted, so greedily concerned with the wealth of the forest—fur—that they plunge themselves as well as the Indians into disaster. Ponteach, on the other hand, is a noble figure: he was the

Ottawa chief who figured largely in the French and Indian War. Rogers had known Ponteach at Detroit when he led his rangers there at the end of the campaign, and, though the nobility of the chief's character has been questioned by a few contemporary historians, on the whole the portrait in the play has been accepted pretty much as Rogers drew it. Parkman and others have followed its outline.

Why Rogers lampooned his own character and exploits in the play is an enigma that will probably remain insoluble. He is said to have written it during a brief visit to London in 1776, and his authorship has been denied, though without the indication of another source. From his stories, his journals, from a few copies of the treaties a literary carpenter might have put the play together, turning the tables on Rogers by its satire; but he is usually accepted as the author, and the play established a dramatic pattern that was long to endure, that was clearly our own. Strange as was the satire on the white men in *Ponteach,* this was only part of a whole reversal of attitudes which might have been expected. As the title signifies, the Ottawa chief is the hero; his character is exalted. The interaction between the whites and the Indians was precisely that often sketched by the Indians in the treaties in protest. The Indians had somehow imposed their own view on this first imaginative embodiment of the two races. The noble savage emerged; and strangely enough this concept fitted a body of philosophical thought emerging in Europe. This was the concept long since embedded in Montaigne's little essay on "Cannibals." It had been abstractly assumed by Vico and had been powerfully outlined by Rousseau in the *Discours* some fifteen years before *Ponteach* appeared. The frontiersman Rogers would hardly have read any of these works, either in London or New England, though there is some evidence that the *Discours* reached Salem, at least, not long after its publication. In any event this concept was materialized at full length in the play, probably for the first time, certainly for the first time in the new world. In it were embodied not only the concept of the noble savage—the child of nature

—but also Rousseau's ideas as to the damaging effect of
civilization, in portrayal of the white trappers, traders and
officers. None of this was in philosophical terms, but the
meaning was unmistakable.

This effort at perspective and judgment was a bold
achievement when relationships between the Indians and
the whites were still unresolved and even bitter. Something
headlong appears in it, and the resulting portraiture of the
Indians belonged to fantasy: it was an ideal, another
eidolon. But the mood which was to be sustained in many
similar portrayals was wholly different from that with
which the Yankee had been drawn or the sketchy back-
woodsman and Negro. The American self-portraits—as in
a genuine sense they were—showed a shrewd realism, a
pawky humor, an entire lack of flattery or illusion.
Ponteach was drawn almost tenderly, without any attempt
at realism—even the lively touches with which the Indian
chiefs often embellished references to themselves in the
treaties were missing. The underlying American attitude
was persistent, surviving the clash of events, the lapse of
years, accompanying downright warfare with the Indians.

In 1774, the Mingo chief Logan, who had long considered himself a friend of the whites, found his family
slaughtered in the Yellow Creek Massacre. His bitterness
was unbounded. Later he sent a terse communication to
Lord Dunmore through whom it was published in the
Virginia Gazette. It "flew," as Jefferson said, "through all
the papers of the continent and through the magazines
and other publications of Great Britain: and those who
were boys at that time will attest that the speech of Logan
used to be given them as a school exercise for repetition."
Young American orators were indeed to practice and
rehearse its inflections for years, with the tragic climax:
"This called on me for revenge. I have sought it. I have
killed many, I have fully glutted my vengeance. For my
country I rejoice at the beams of peace. But do not
harbor the thought that mine is the joy of fear. Logan
never felt fear. He will not turn his heel to save his life.
Who is there to mourn for Logan? Not one."

Jefferson's inclusion of the speech in his *Notes on Vir-*

ginia gave rise to the theory that he was its author, but he had only offered it as testimony in what had become a *cause célèbre,* that created by Raynal's remarks on the degeneration of natural life in America. The speech was offered as proof to the contrary, for its noble qualities. He explicitly denied that he had written it, but he undoubtedly extended its currency. Some seventy years after it was sent to Lord Dunmore, the speech was enshrined by McGuffey in his Fifth Reader, again with the declaration that Jefferson had written it. As a boy of Shadwell, Jefferson had listened to the oratory of the great Cherokee warrior Ontassere: his knowledge of the Indian manner of address and of Indian ceremonials was ample. Few themes were more frequently touched upon in his writings than Indian customs, history, wars, language, treaties, councils, government. No doubt he could have written such a speech as that of Logan, but his participation in the imaginative tradition of the tribes was far broader and more significant. As President he continued the great cycle of the treaties, speaking for the government where in earlier periods diverse groups of white men had spoken for the colonies, and preserving in perfection the ancient rituals, the established symbols, the broad dramatic form. Today Jefferson's Indian addresses are far too little known; but with the Indian replies and the climactic treaties they too merge into the history of the American drama.

In their own time these treaties and the circumstances that surround them were widely known. When the Seneca chiefs came to Washington for their conferences, their portraits were drawn in noble profile by the French artist St. Memin, whose work in this manner was having a widespread vogue. The spirit was clearly that of commemoration: with all the ceremonial gravity, the outcome for the great tribes was tragic retreat. A few individuals such as the Moravian missionaries Heckewelder and Zeisberger were seeking to frame a mode of existence between the two races, and Jefferson had this purpose in view, but the elegiac mood prevailed. Freneau's verses on Indian themes were in this vein. In *The Contrast,* Tyler somewhat irrelevantly introduced a Cherokee lament, which he may or may not have written: this plaintive song of Indian submission to fate had an enormous vogue, was printed as a broadside, found its way into the songsters, and had an independent existence down the century in many an out-of-the-way village.

All the arts were engaged by this theme, but its widest expression was to be found in the drama or the theater. Beginning with *Ponteach,* the effort to portray the Indian character in flowery idealized fashion was consistent, emerging in the broad historical pantomimes that so engaged the American fancy in the years immediately following the Revolution. In *Tammany* the theme went off into boisterous masquerade, but this only proved it to be so familiar that it could be played with. In one fashion the whites had often masqueraded as Indians. That stirring pageant known as the Boston Tea Party, with New England citizens expressing their instinct for theater and drama as well as their rebellion, had been an instance: it may well be a question whether the participants enjoyed more dumping the tea in the harbor or masquerading in warpaint and feathers with brandished tomahawks. On every frontier the whites had adopted Indian dress, had used Indian weapons, had quickly learned to scalp their enemies, indeed often scalped the Indians to obtain bounties. Even as *Tammany* was being produced in New York, it was being noted regretfully in the New England village of Marietta on the Ohio that some young men had come back from a foray into the wilderness with the scalp of only one Indian.

Paradoxically, even as these Indian themes were being developed on the stage and elsewhere, savagery between the two races was reaching a new intensity. The Battle of Fallen Timbers on the Maumee in 1794 had seemed a decisive defeat for the Indians in the newly expanding West; but their struggle continued underground. Tecumseh and his twin brother Tenskwatawa—sometimes called Elkswatawa—of the Shawnees became engaged in a far-reaching conspiracy that was political, intellectual, legalistic, religious, even philosophical. By shrewd reasoning

Tecumseh argued that the Indian treaties relating to the Ohio country should be declared void, since the undoubted fact of Indian communal ownership had not been recognized in their formulation. By no means all the tribes sharing the Indian lands had given their consent to the transfer. Tecumseh, who must be ranked as a statesman, was a powerful orator. He was no less effective in quiet counsels around the fire at night; he moved, a tireless shadow, from tribe to tribe over wide reaches of the western territory. Tenskwatawa was able to stir in his listeners a mystic sense of unity, the remembrance of ancient loyalties: he possessed and practiced the gifts of the revivalist. The two brothers became engaged in the clash of empire as had the earlier tribes: now rather than the French it was the British who seemed a source of strength. Tecumseh was encouraged to believe that an Indian buffer state might be created in the West which would restore to the tribes their ancient lands, their dignity, their power. Harrison, recognizing Tecumseh's genius for leadership, maneuvered his brother into defeat at Tippecanoe. Tecumseh fell at the Battle of the Thames. Their vast program had carried them into the War of 1812. Tenskwatawa, broken in power, moved west, across the Mississippi. But the struggle was not over. The Creeks, who had been pushed from their hunting grounds in Tennessee, had joined with the British to the south. Jackson's treaty-making with the defeated Creeks had a barbaric splendor. The chieftains were received with the customary dignity, but the outcome was familiar. This was the last of the great ceremonial treaties, though others retained the framework of the past. In spite of the fact that the tribes were considered nations treating in equality with the United States, in spite of earnest diplomatic assurances, pressure upon the tribes continued. Their lands were continually being seized on flimsy pretexts by speculators. They were soon to begin their exodus into the West along what they called "the trail of tears."

It was during the period between the two wars for national independence that the Indian was fully enshrined on the stage with outlines that were to endure, as if the triumphant ghost of the race imposed itself upon the conquerors in spite of the continued struggle and defeat. The drawing continued to be bold, tender, elegiac; the mournful backward glance was persistent. The story of Pocahontas and John Smith was told with music in an "operatic melodrama," *The Indian Princess,* by J. N. Barker, which became vastly popular, and was one of the first American plays to be produced in London. The Pocahontas story was to be repeated again and again. For a brief time these portrayals of the Indian on the stage ceased after the War of 1812, as if the fantasy had been shattered, but they were resumed at least by 1823 with a play based on the life of Logan. The stream of Indian plays had again begun in earnest, some of them having to do with Washington's journey to the Ohio country before the Revolution. The Pocahontas story took on a fresh existence. By this time Cooper had written *The Last of the Mohicans.* The Indian theme was prominent in both the novel and the play in the immediately ensuing years, but it may be noted that this theme had first arisen broadly in the drama and the theater or in related forms and was sustained in these before it was taken over in the more discursive writing of the novel. The direct graphic display of the theater seemed instinctively chosen by the new Americans as their own rather than the slower, sometimes richer approaches of the long narrative.

These Indian plays were naive, even primitive, they had an engaging simplicity of outline, but they were cleaving out salient American preoccupations within the popular forum of the theater. The persistence of the theme may be construed as representing a troubled collective conscience, an effort to obliterate a wrong by handsome tributes. In some measure it seemed a part of the wish to establish a past which so comically—as Irving noted in another connection in his preface to the *Knickerbocker History*—often went back to the dawn of civilization. Yet it was clearly related to the philosophical idea first fully formulated by Rousseau, the persuasive concept of "the child of nature," the related idea that nature was good. Suggested by *Ponteach,* this underlying idea was continued in a patriotic play of 1776, *The Fall of British Tyranny,* in which Tammany with other Indians were briefly sketched, to music. From his throne in "the crotch of a tree," Tammany dispensed justice and insisted upon liberty, expressing a philosophy close to that of Rousseau—

> *In freedom's bright cause Tammany pled with applause*
> *And reasoned most justly from nature.*

In his preface to *The Indian Princess,* Barker alludes to Rousseau. Sentiment was undoubtedly interwoven with this philosophical idea as was a sheer liking for the underlying stories. Nowhere in the Indian plays was nature apprehended as the Indian had apprehended it, with a deep animism, with lovely trenchant metaphors, yet the new Americans had sought to keep something of this poetry when they retained many of the Indian place-names, beautiful in sound and suggestion.

The names of Indian villages were often kept, even when the original inhabitants had been ruthlessly expelled. Nature in the plays was airy and flowery and remote. Hardly a touch of the earthy American landscape appeared there. Nature was drawn as the Indian characters were drawn, as fantasy, as belonging to the realm of untethered ideas. A kind of lilt ran through the plays even when their outcome was tragic: they were light, even a little merry, and the tragedy rarely ran deep.

The Indian plays remained the means by which this philosophy of nature was most clearly expressed on the stage, yet it was by no means confined to them, but found expression in such plays as *The Child of Feeling* and *Nature and Philosophy,* and infused a new exaltation of rural life in *The Forest Rose,* an opera first produced in 1825 and a perennial success, in which the philosophy of nature was somehow flung around the spare figure of Yankee Jonathan. The Yankee—and perhaps more generally the American—seemed to be reaching the conclusion that he too was "a child of nature." Irony may be discovered in the fact that these ideas were first materialized in a play that came out of New England, *Ponteach,* and that they were being repeated in relation to the Yankee character.

Editor's Note

A *Rage of Goodness:* THE IDIOT *of Dostoevsky* first appeared in *Accent,* Autumn 1942. Reprinted by permission of *Accent* and of the author.

Richard P. Blackmur was born in Springfield, Massachusetts, in 1904. He has lived in Boston and in Maine, has been an editor of *Hound and Horn,* and has taught at Princeton since 1940, with interludes as a member of the Institute for Advanced Study and a year abroad on a grant from the Rockefeller Foundation. Blackmur has published three books of verse: *From Jordan's Delight* (1937), *The Second World* (1942), and *The Good European and Other Poems* (1947). Of his four volumes of criticism, the first two are partially included in the latter two, *Language as Gesture* (1952) and *The Lion and the Honeycomb* (1955).

THIRTEEN

R. P. Blackmur

A Rage of Goodness:
The Idiot *of Dostoevsky*

We have here, almost plumb in the middle of Dostoevsky's work, a novel which in its major intention tried to dramatize God's gift of the good and perfect individual man beating down the proud evil of all human society by his mere example. The rest of his great work may, with a little stretching, be described as quite the opposite, as the attempt to dramatize the substantial goodness in human society beating down the obsessed pride, either carnal or intellectual, of evil individuals—or of individuals who, if not evil, were in their confusion dominated and driven by evil. We think of Raskolnikov and Svidrigailov, of Stravrogin, of Ivan and Dimitri Karamazov and how all of them are driven to find goodness in the lacerated, the injured, the insulted, the humiliated—in the sink and sewage of human society. Here, in *The Idiot,* we have Myshkin, a hero of another kind, whose heroism consists almost altogether in his lack of it: a hero who makes no effort to show himself and what he feels: that is to say, a positive hero, a hero who is already there, and who has therefore nothing to do, a complete image, idol, or ikon, before whom others, as they are drawn to him, must in the end abase and humiliate themselves. That Myshkin, the positive hero is himself engulfed in the process, and indeed destroyed beyond human redemption, is a natural and necessary result. The fault of the positive hero is the most fatal of all faults, that he has none. He has no being, no existence, apart from the vision of those who believe

in him. He is ideal only, an insight or aspiration divorced
from the human soil out of which he sprung. You cannot
uproot goodness and have it live any more than you can
altogether eradicate evil.

This is not how Dostoevsky meant, intellectually, for
the history of Myshkin to come out, but it is how, imaginatively, it had to come out. The conception of goodness out
of which he worked offered no other possible solution; and
his conception of goodness was lodged actually, like his
conception of evil, in the image of its own double: which
is to say, its own ruin. He was mistaken in thinking that
the idea of pure goodness could be dramatized so as to
dominate the kind of good and evil men and women he
could create; but his imagination went beyond the mistake of his intellect and overwhelmed it. Thus we have
a double, perhaps a triple, drama in the finished book.
There is the drama of Dostoevsky's own conscious attempt to create his positive hero. There is the dramatic
fable of the good man in an evil society. And there is,
as it were creating itself underneath and absorbing the
others, the drama, the immitigable and inexhaustible
drama, of the good man who, in submitting to evil, is
doomed not only to become evil but to enact evil without
losing a jot of his goodness. No wonder, thinking of
Myshkin, Dostoevsky thought that submissiveness was "the
most fearful force that can exist in the world."

Let us explore the three dramas and the relations between them, uniting them first, as they are united in the
book, by some consideration of the title. I do not know
how Dostoevsky came to call his book *The Idiot,* but I
do know that playing with any of the other obvious titles
only increases the inevitability of his choice. The book tried
of course for the title that all Dostoevsky's books tried for,
The Life of the Great Sinner, but it had too little scope,
as even *The Brothers Karamazov* had too little scope. Yet
the flavor of that alternative should be kept in mind as the
activating flavor of consciousness almost all Dostoevsky's
characters come to in their moments of crisis: they regard
themselves as living the lives of great sinners. A more
likely title might have been The Epileptic, for the moment

of vision and the scream that plunges the vision into intolerable darkness is in the recurrent heartbeat of the book as it is the recurrent clarifying *and* mutilating fate of Myshkin himself. Epilepsy is Le Grand Mal in the simple medicine of the past, as we should say that his goodness is Myshkin's Great Ill; for indeed the two are in the final drama of the book united. But such a play on words would have furnished an under-title at best, a quicksand of a title in which the book would have sunk two-thirds out of sight. *The Idiot* has advantages that none of the alternatives possess, and has besides a certain necessity *vis à vis* the *good* man in action—again, and always, having reference to Dostoevsky's deliberate idea of goodness. The word *idiot* is luckily the same in English as in Russian, with much the same history and much the same meanings. Fundamentally it means a private person or a layman, and by development a person who does not know what he is talking about, a fool in word or action, though with no sense that either word or action lack significance or responsiveness. It is the name we give the sense of incapability, of impotence, that attends some of our deepest responses. We all of us feel a sense of kinship with idiocy which in moments of peril we actually sometimes recognize, as when we say of a man in great terror that he was a chattering idiot, and know exactly what he felt like. Or again we use the word to measure the limits of intellect, as when we say of a problem that is beyond us that it has reduced us to idiocy. Beyond that, or on a good level rather than a bad level, we ally idiocy with kinds of generous or unthinking folly, as when we call a man an idiot for giving either his money or his mind away without thought for himself, and in calling him an idiot mean to praise him for what we would ourselves do were we less selfish. Still higher in our levels of meaning, or still deeper in our instincts, we often believe that acts of folly, of rash courage, win through at least as often as acts of thoughtfulness. In fact, the ancient beliefs that fools and madmen bear the wisdom and prophecies of the gods, have not at all died out with the gods but have survived them. We believe, for example, that he who

speaks without thinking may at least speak what he feels
or even what he "really" thinks. Similarly, as any prac-
ticing spiritualist and many surrealist poets will tell you,
idiocy, or the dive beneath the syntactical mind, is the
only available credible vehicle for second sight and intuition and feeling. All these levels of meaning return us
to the idea of the idiot as the lay or private substitute for
God who is blighted in the attempt to do God's work.
That is the role of the idiot as Myshkin, and that is the
fate of Myshkin as idiot.

So much for the advantages of *The Idiot* as title; they
rise from long and vital associations and flow naturally
through the symbolic reaches of the reader's mind. But
there was a necessity in the title, too. Only by making
his positive hero an idiot in the eyes of the other characters (and in some degree in the eyes of the reader) could
Dostoevsky envisage, that is, give face to his goodness.
Only so could he make credible in a created figure the
kind of goodness that Myshkin exemplified. You cannot
make a man talk or think like God, because your reasoning powers are clearly inadequate: they will miss the point
and involve you in all sorts of inadvertent blasphemy.
This is not from lack of knowledge of God, or even from
lack of skill in that knowledge; it is due rather to the
nature of the medium in which that knowledge comes to
you: the medium of feeling, direct perception, intuition: a
medium which unites itself with the whole sensibility
which it expresses. You become a submissive, a receptive
agent; you feel God as goodness within you and within
what you suffer, and the love you might otherwise (in the
absence of God) build with pride, becomes pity which
builds within you at the expense of every possible humiliation of spirit and every possible ignominy of mind and
body. It is only the idiot Christ, the mind reduced to
childish directness of perception—the perception of goodness through the means of pity—that the individual man
can reach. That is, the man who is to be the purely good
man, must divest himself not only of the love of created
things but must also divest himself of those attributes
which he has created in himself and by which he com-

petes with God. He must get down to instinct, which God gave him, and which reason only impairs. Idiocy is the condition of the great divestment; for in idiocy instinct is set to operating with the least possible impairment by reason; or at any rate idiocy is the condition which we are most likely to accept as the limit at which, as it is approached, instinct works best, and at which, as it is reached, it is obliterated. Idiocy, then, is the very condition of dramatic necessity for the novelist who would, like Dostoevsky, attempt to dramatize instinctive goodness and pity as the essence of Christianity.

How far Dostoevsky would have accepted this argument is doubtful; he would most likely have objected that it reasons too much, and insisted that what he had in mind goes without saying; yet it is only by following some such argument that his figure of Myshkin becomes dramatically credible within the limit of Dostoevsky's declared intention. To support my argument I would cite the following items from the book itself. There is, first, the story Myshkin tells in Part I of the persecuted Swiss girl Marie, who thought of herself as a great sinner but who had been actually only greatly humiliated—by her mother, by her church, by her community. Myshkin, taking pity on her, "corrupted"—that was the community's name for it—corrupted the children of the village into attending her through her mortal illness. Thus she died happy, saved by pity. The children seemed to her "like birds beating their wings against her window and calling to her every morning, 'Nous t'aimons, Marie.'" Myshkin goes on to relate how after this, Schneider, the doctor who had been caring for his idiocy, told him that he was a chlid. He told me, says Myshkin, "that I was a complete child myself, altogether a child; that it was only in face and figure that I was like a grown-up person, but that in development, in soul, in character, and, perhaps, in intelligence, I was not grown up, and that so should I remain, if I lived to be sixty." Myshkin says he laughed very much, but added that in one thing Schneider was right. "I don't like being with grown-up people . . . Whatever they say to me, however kind they are to me, I always feel somehow oppressed with them, and I am awfully glad when I can get away to my companions; and my companions have always been children, not because I am a child myself, but simply because I always was attracted by children."

Secondly, there is the anecdote Myshkin tells Rogozhin about the woman who crossed herself at her smiling six-weeks old baby, and who when he asked her what she did answered him: " 'God has just such gladness every time he sees from heaven that a sinner is praying to him with all his heart, as a mother has when she sees the first smile on her baby's face.' That," Myshkin went on, "was what the woman said to me almost in those words, this deep, subtle, truly religious thought—a thought in which all the essence of Christianity finds expression; that is the whole conception of God as our Father and of God's gladness in man, like a father's in his own child—the fundamental idea of Christ." It is not for nothing that directly after this Rogozhin exchanges his gold cross for Myshkin's tin cross and takes him to his mother—herself an idiot, understanding nothing of what was said—to be blessed. Only an idiot can bless an idiot.

Thirdly, there is Myshkin's outburst against Catholicism just before he breaks the Chinese vase at the Epanchins' party, an outburst which is about as near as Myshkin the idiot or Dostoevsky the author can come to an intellectual expression of what is meant by fundamental Christianity. What his outburst amounts to is a plea for revolt against intellectual authority, against grown-up pride of all sorts, and an insistence on the meekness of the child, the submissiveness of the idiot. "O, we need to have resistance at once, at once! Our Christ whom we have kept and they have never known must shine forth and vanquish the West." The depth to which Dostoevsky believed this is attested by the epileptic fit into which Myshkin falls immediately after his declaration. The moment before a fit was for Myshkin the highest clarity man could reach and was worth all the rest of life; and this particular moment does indeed reflect the central illumination of Christian meekness in about as passionate language as Dostoevsky was capable of. Nor should we complain that a plea for meekness, for submissiveness, for non-resistance to evil in the physical sense, should be expressed in violent and intolerant terms. There is no fanaticism so violent as that of humility cornered, humility humiliated by outward oppression. Christ ended in bloodshed, no less violent in that it was his own; and no Christ was more violent than the meek and childlike Christ Dostoevsky saw—in life visibly, in himself incipiently, and in the created figure of Myshkin the idiot potentially.

It is because of that violence, perhaps, that Dostoevsky is sometimes thought of as a Russian version of the Pauline Christian. Certainly Paul and Dostoevsky shared a violent eloquence; certainly both insisted on the charity of understanding as a prerequisite to salvation—both making their insistence in such violent and fanatic tones as to obscure their argument in the vehemence of its expression. Both in short were Protestants. But I think their similarity ended there. It is true that the ideas of Paul might have developed into those of Dostoevsky, but it would not have been the Paul that we know. For us Paul united spirit and intellect, whereas Dostoevsky united spirit and feeling. Pauline Christianity—western Christianity—imposes an order on human society capable of making room for the disorder of human lives. Dostoevsky's Christianity works rather the other way around, and would limit the possible order of human society to its capacity to submit to the disorder, as it must seem, of feeling and instinct and intuition. It is thus that Dostoevsky identifies Roman Catholicism with socialism, and sometimes with liberalism generally; he saw that it ought to have been so identified as a matter of logic. And it is thus that he identified Russian Orthodoxy, and its emphasis on suffering as the *condition* of salvation rather than, as in western Christianity, merely incidental to it, with the extreme conservative form of the state of the Tsars. For him, in his extreme moments, a society must needs seem to totter with corruption in order to prepare for the ordeal of salvation. He needed confusion and dismay and general gross unnecessary suffering, and not only in the heart where these things always are, but in the society around him; he needed them as a forcing bed in which his insights became images. As both a novelist and a prophet must, Dostoevsky took what he needed, insisting it was all there was.

We must say that for him there was nothing else; but we cannot say it was Pauline; it was too single a theft for Paul. Paul was a dualist in the lasting sense, or at any rate up through the dual mystery of the resurrection of the dead; for he saw always opposed man's higher and lower natures, spirit and flesh, god and devil, the heavenly order and the worldly order. If you think that Dostoevsky saw these opposites also, you have not clearly looked into the soul of the idiot.

The idiot is the living image, not of Pauline, but of primitive Christianity, the Christianity of a world ignominiously on its knees, knowing only that the next moment the face is in the mud. Dostoevsky's dualism—his doubles of the self-willed and the meek, of the intellectually proud and the spiritually humble—is only the dramatic prelude to a monistic collapse into an undifferentiated groveling humiliation. Thus the two Christian fables he was never tired of rehearsing were the fable of Christ and Mary Magdalen (in *The Idiot* the story of Myshkin and Marie) and that of the childlikeness of Christ, which is the general fable of Myshkin as it is of Alyosha in *The Brothers Karamazov*. For Dostoevsky as for Yeats Christianity "brought a fabulous, formless darkness in." It is not that Dostoevsky saw men and women in action with the oneness of the Essenes; he saw and felt them in sufficient variety; but that he tried to bring them back to that oneness, and tried especially so in *The Idiot*.

The trial was made by exposing a series of characters— Nastasya, Rogozhin, Ippolit, Aglaia, Ganya, Keller, Radomsky, Lebedyev, and General Ivolgin—to the fearful force of Myshkin's submissiveness and to the creative force of his instinctive judgment or intuition: his reaction as he felt them press upon his submissiveness: their reaction as they feel the goodness of his presence and beyond it. All these characters are haunted by their other selves, which Myshkin brings into action, for good or for evil, for pride or for humility, as the case may be. This Myshkin is able to do because he alone is without a ghost. His submissiveness brings *him* nothing, because he is already there; yet to the others it brings everything. He exists to drag out of them, to absorb, their other selves, to perfect them, so to speak, by mutilation and deprivation.

We shall see in particular how these matters proceed with the different characters; but we have first to set up some sort of images for the submissiveness and the instinct that Myshkin uses to go along with the images of Christianity out of which they sprung. The submissiveness in Myshkin may be characterized as having the attractive force of the abyss; it is a version of that gulf which Pascal, as Baudelaire's poem says, always carried within him. It is the abyss of insensibility for which acute sensibility always hankers; it is the haunting possibility. But, not only a gulf of emptiness, it is also a dreadful reservoir; there is something positive to be got from it: precisely the sickening fall into salvation, that fall in which one leaves everything behind except the self, in which one arrives, still falling, in the vertigo of paradise. Who would know better than an epileptic what that fall was like? Epilepsy is not only the Great Ill, it is also the Falling Sickness; and the great scream of the fit is wrung out of the victim at the moment of falling. It was to the possibility of that scream, as much as anything, that Myshkin's friends reacted, as it was more than anything to that scream that Myshkin himself submitted and which he also invoked as a matter of course.

He invoked it, because it set him free. Like Ivan Karamazov, Myshkin was one of those to whom all things were permitted, and indeed Myshkin is in the writing of his drama much more like Ivan the damned than like Alyosha whose goodness he superficially resembles. If we think of Ivan and Myshkin together we shall see that the permitted pride of the one and the permitted instinct of the other come to much the same thing, intolerable suffering and humiliation, ending for both in the obliteration of sensibility. The man who acts out of pride and the man who acts out of instinct are equally driven and deprived creatures to the extent that they act purely. The damnation of the one is equivalent to the blessedness of the other, at least in this world. Each is beyond the possibility of balance or sanity, and each therefore comes to humiliation. There is another consideration, too, which but perfects the equivalence of pride and instinct. Both the wholly proud man and the wholly instinctive man are adequate only to those situations which are prepared for, patterned, and petrified: situations to which one needs to make no adjustment, which one does not need to reason about. How can one *not* see either instinct or pride except as brought to confusion? The great naturalist Fabre gives an account somewhat as follows of an experiment with the Pine Processionary caterpillar. Noticing that like many caterpillars this species followed the silken track laid down by the leader in the procession, and returned over it to their nest after feeding, he induced a short train of them to venture upon the rim of a round bowl, and when all were upon the rim cut their backward track. Not till many hours of steady marching had passed did the leader by accident leave the endless rim of mounting humiliation. Which was it, the obstinacy of pride or of instinct, that led them so fruitlessly to exhaust themselves? Had it been men rather than caterpillars we should conclude for pride, but that is only because we have a terror of distrusting instinct. The advantage of imagination—and I mean the artist's imagination—is that it is quite oblivious to such fears, quite superior to such temptations, and will conclude for images of both in so far as either is capable of being imagined—that is, dramatized—for all they are worth in the vast immediate field of the actual.

What Dostoevsky thought as a man is of only preliminary importance, but what he enacted as an artist is of great importance. What he thought was only the conventional machinery by which he put his imagination to work in a given direction. What he thought initiates movement and establishes connections on a social level. Both the thought and the plot will commonly operate as heresies; they will exaggerate the force of insight and intrigue in order to put the mass of imagination—what actually happens to the characters in the novel in motion. Thus the opposition of pride and instinct will seem to us a dramatic dodge, a device by which we get at, say, the relations between the instinctive man Myshkin and the proud man Rogozhin, or between Myshkin and the two women Nastasya and Aglaia. We still value the insight precisely as we value the device, by how much it frames those relationships, and in the end by the degree in which the imaginative experience of those relationships replace the insights. Because of the profound inadequacy of the imagination before the actual—it is only a version of the actual—the replacement will never be complete, which is why the machinery must be used in the first place in any art more complicated than the lyric cry, but if successful it will move in the direction of completeness.

Very much the same rule applies to Dostoevsky's substitute for the classic devices of tragic catharsis which he could not use since they involve the notion of a stable and completely human society. I mean his emphasis on humiliation as the necessary preface and absolute condition of humility, an emphasis which involves the conviction of a society with a drive towards collapse whether into the arms of God or the embrace of the devil, a society held together only by violence, with an operative discipline—to use Dostoevsky's own words—of laceration, insult, and injury, alleviated only by the individual humanitarian gesture. Whether looked at spiritually or politically, as an idea of society I cannot think of anything more repulsive; it is fascist society *in extremis*. To me such humiliation is not the prelude to humility, it either precludes it, or extinguishes it, or reduces it so far in the human scale that it is the desperate virtue of idiots or of the damned. We have seen recently M. Laval commending such humiliation to the people of France as humility before the facts; and we can say that Hitler has no doubt provided many people with the temptation to be true to the Dostoevsky type of character. It is for that reason, if for no other, that however repulsive we may find Dostoevsky's "humiliation-humility" sequence as an ethical idea, we must yet concede that it is an excellent focus for dramatizing at the highest possible tension a common and profound aspect of the human scene. If you believe that great sin must come before great salvation, that great extinction must precede great creation, then you will be exemplary as a dramatist if you insist on humiliation as the means of humility.

But you will most likely come on such heresy, as Dostoevsky did, by accident, and like him you will overcome your heresy to the degree that your power of imagination is more faithful than your power of thought to the actuality of life. It is imagination, not intellect, that is the charity of the understanding. That is one point at which we can use Dostoevsky's language. It is the intellect that sins and the imagination, by creating the sin, by making it actual, that redeems. Pushing the notion one degree further, we can say that so far as the arts are concerned the movements of intellect are accidental and intermittent and in their attempts to solve our problems cause most of our conflicts, whereas the imagination, so to speak, is the will of things and continuous, so that it is able to absorb the problems of the intellect by showing their counterparts in action. With the intellect we agree or disagree; the imagination either rouses our dissent in part or exacts our complete assent; in other words, the intellect of the man often sets the imagination of the artist to work at a job very much like purgation.

So it was with Dostoevsky and *The Idiot*. He made eight plans for the novel before he came on the idea that finally put him to work. These plans survive in the Dostoevsky Archives at Moscow and are described in Ernest Simmons' admirable study of Dostoevsky. It is upon his study that I here depend. At its inception the story was to have been of a family drama based upon a court trial. The three principal characters were to have been the Idiot, Mignon, and the Heroine, all of whom were violent characters given to extreme and passionate actions. The two women bear some resemblance to Nastasya and Aglaia in the finished book, but the original Idiot has nothing in common with Myshkin but the experience of epilepsy.

He is rather a Byronic hero, self-willed and criminal, sensual and extravagant, egoistic and proud: a pure type along the lines of Svidrigailov and Stavrogin. He is called Idiot principally because he is strange. On this basis Dostoevsky invented various combinations of characters and various romantic intrigues which would bring them into relation. "Situations involving murder, suicide, rape, incest, and diabolical hatred," says Mr. Simmons, "give a vivid impression of the confused drama of violent passions that agitated his brain as he sought for the artistic constants that would bring order into the chaos that he had created." What he principally lacked was a governing idea, something both general enough to make a large novel and specific enough to give the largeness focus. His first ideas were all too general: a struggle of love with hate; or, endless pride and endless hate; or again, endless idealism with endless sensualism. And so on. The one constant he had was the image of the character who finally became Nastasya, and the one near-constant was the theme of the radical generation, the young reformers, nihilists, socialists whom he feared and distrusted, and this theme was more a preoccupation and a hindrance than an active obsessive theme, and so remains in his finished novel. In the third plan there is a single phrase about the Idiot which belongs to the finished character: "He ends with a heavenly deed." Then in the fourth plan a new character begins to emerge, a meek, simple, and charming person, but nothing is done with him and he disappears. In the fifth plan the Idiot is still possible to identify with Rogozhin, but there is a description of a character named Ganya who has a Christian nature and in whom feeling predominates and whom he wants to be the most powerful figure in the novel. In the sixth plan this character becomes identified with the Idiot of the earlier plans. He differs from Myshkin, however, in being a Double, like Raskolnikov or Ivan or Dimitri Karamazov: he is both submissive *and* brutal; he has "The dualism of a profound nature." Dostoevsky has now, as Mr. Simmons observes, merely "to push the development one step further to arrive at the image of Myshkin—The

Meek opposite of the Self-Willed type." In the seventh
plan he is made a Prince and associated with children:
Myshkin is in sight. In the eighth plan the whole work is
brought into relation to this new conception of the Idiot
as the simple-minded Christian. "Dostoevsky plunges into
the details . . . as though he were feeling the greatest
satisfaction in ridding his imagination of the former
proud, vengeful, and passionate Idiot." The beginning of
the first draft was unsatisfactory and he "threw it all to
the devil." Beginning once more he wrote the whole novel,
with many interruptions, in the space of about a year,
which as it runs about a quarter of a million words was
fast work.

Despite the trouble he had in getting under way, in
arriving at a means of composition, at a governing idea
to transform into imagination, the idea of the Idiot
Myshkin, once it came, set him free to work out what
he claimed was an old ideal—as different from a more
operative idea—for a great theme. The following passages
are extracted from a letter which he wrote to his niece
Sofya Ivanova, after the first part of the novel had been
finished. They will serve as text both for Dostoevsky's
intended relations to the rest of the novel and for what
he was actually, as a novelist, compelled to do with his
material. After describing how difficult a job it is for a
novelist to tackle the ideal good man, he goes on: "There
is only one positively good man in the world—Christ,
. . . I recall that of the good figures in Christian literature, the most perfect is Don Quixote. But he is good
only because at the same time he is ridiculous. Dickens'
Pickwick (an infinitely weaker conception than Don
Quixote, but nevertheless immense) is also ridiculous and
succeeds by virtue of this fact. One feels compassion for
the ridiculous man who does not know his own worth as
a good man, and consequently sympathy is invoked in
the reader. This awakening of compassion is the secret of
humour. Jean Valjean is also a powerful attempt, but he
arouses sympathy by his horrible misfortune and society's
injustice to him. In my novel there is nothing of this

sort, positively nothing, and hence I am terribly afraid that I shall be entirely unsuccessful."

It should be emphasized that this was written after the first part, only, had been finished. The author is right so far. Myshkin is introduced with a description that makes him look like the typical Christ in the art of the Eastern Church: as "above the average height, with very fair thick hair, with sunken cheeks and a thin, pointed, almost white beard. His eyes were large, blue, and dreamy; there was something gentle, though heavy-looking in their expression." Mr. Simmons, after quoting this passage, adds that "in the manuscript notes his name is frequently coupled with that of Christ, and in one place he is called 'Prince Christ.' " For the rest, all through the first book, Myshkin is very kindly dealt with, laughed at a little only because he is strange, called an idiot only now and then to get the reader used to it, but generally arousing a mixture of admiration and compassion and respect. His unusual powers of direct instinctive perception are recognized at the Epanchins', at the Ivolgins', and at Nastasya's party. His opinions are asked, his judgment sought, and he is even required to decide Nastasya's marriage for her. As for himself he sees into the centres of people without managing to understand much of their outsides. He becomes attracted deeply, but in a mysteriously limited way, to the two proud and beautiful young women, Nastasya and Aglaia. By a combination of his judgment and his character and his feeling of attraction—by his deep but limited seeing—he precipitates the lives of most of the people with whom he comes in contact into new and intolerable forms—forms for which perhaps the goodness in them was ready but for which their living complexes of good and evil were not ready at all. The speed of this part of the novel is great; it is tight-woven and wide of scope, both with regard to the theme of Myshkin and with regard to the affairs of the Epanchins, the Ivolgins, and Totsky. It reaches a preliminary climax or crisis when with the fire of the roubles Nastasya goes off with Rogozhin, leaving Ganya in a swoon, the company shocked, and Myshkin deeply dismayed, but not at all troubled by what he has so evidently done. It is almost as if Dostoevsky had composed a dramatic fable of the alternative obedience and rebellion of these people to the sudden felt presence of their own conscience, with Myshkin, the simple, the innocent, acting the part of conscience.

The second part, after the first five chapters which proceed in a direct line and to which we shall return as the most powerfully composed single segment of the book, begins to show confusion of novelistic purpose, a mixture of themes, unexplained and unprepared for, incredible actions, and a more than occasional prolixity and positive redundancy of treatment, all of which last till at the very end Dostoevsky once again seized hold of his Idiot-Christ theme with complete imaginative power. It would seem as if Dostoevsky had partly relied on discarded bits of his earlier plans, partly let his pen run where it would in the hope of something turning up, and partly perhaps surrendered himself before the importunate assault of his mere ideas. The affair of the blackmailing nihilists, for example, is superfluous to the book, is dealt with at too much length as a side issue, runs off into Dostoevsky's emotional-intellectual dialectic against atheism and socialism, springs an incredible surprise (in Ganya's knowledge and proof of the falsity of the claim), and is saved, if it is saved, only by the outbursting character of Mrs. Epanchin or perhaps a little by the symbolic character of "Pavlishtchev's son" Burdowsky. There is something intriguing about a man who claims to be a bastard only to be proved legitimate; and it is surprising that Dostoevsky does not again return to the theme of the false bastard in connection with the main theme of Myshkin.

As a result of this confused and even bewildering treatment, the sound and clear things tend to lose some of their native force. I think particularly of Aglaia reading Pushkin's poem "The Poor Knight" with the initials transposed to make those of Nastasya—which is the last place in the book where Myshkin is seen as arousing laughter. Or again, there is the affair of Ippolit's attempted suicide which instead of being given the freed, independent treatment it deserved, was by a false economy fastened onto the tail of the blackmailing scenes. You have to think back, to feel back, later, to see what the scene ought to have meant at the time of its delivery.

The explanation of these confusions is predominately to be found, I think, in the intrusion of Dostoevsky's *ideas* upon his story. The middle areas of the book lose sight of the image of the Idiot in a maze of undramatized notions about the Russian soul, the east, the west, atheism, socialism, drunkenness, and so on, plus casual, almost spontaneous efforts to introduce complications of plot and character which might relieve the main theme from going where it is now clear that it must go—towards the collapse, focussed in the figure of Myshkin, of the ideal of positive good. There could be no clearer example than this of a great sensibility violated by an idea, no sharper case of a theme being surrendered by the author to a mere thesis, and then wrenched back by violence to safety.

Whether Dostoevsky—whether any novelist—could have done otherwise with a theme so intractable because initially so alien, is doubtful. We can defend him (or label his intentions, which is a form of defense) in two ways. It might have occurred to him that a major part of the material of character and event and intrigue in the central portion of his book had of necessity to be fortuitous. It is possible to hold that many of the items handled could as well have been others, and are themselves, and justified as themselves, all the more for their air of expressing mere casual possibilities. It is because they are immediate possibilities, perhaps, that they do their work; their fortuitousness is what makes them fatal—as, for example, General Ivolgin's probable theft of money from Lebedyev. They are the right objects for the Idiot Myshkin to affect precisely because they are unpredictable and superfluous. Myshkin is one of those who must have every sort of grist, the unexpected even more than the expected.

Again, there is a kind of rightness to the disordered apparitions of undigested material which becomes apparent if we think of the book as a fable, a sermon, a parable of

the good man in an evil world. The good man will by his
presence call forth exclamations and cries of both good
and evil, as in all of us our conscience, when we think
of it, creates qualms of ill deeds not otherwise remembered. We may say that Dostoevsky did not so much
sympathize with disorder; he felt the roots of it, in himself and others, both clutching and pushing. Thus his
primitive Christianity, his ideal of submissiveness, was always on the point of disclosing itself as a matrix of disorder. The man of instinct, of feeling, is always nearest
to the underlying dark disorder of things, just as the man
of pride, of intellect, always is found, at his focal moments, creating disorder in the name of the order that
turned him loose.

But, having once acknowledged the morass of form in
the middle parts of the book, let us proceed to acknowledge some of the things that emerge from the morass,
and especially those things that emerge in relation to the
theme of the Idiot Christ at large in the actual world.
Taking the smaller things first, one of the ablest things
Dostoevsky does is to show the immediate effect that
Myshkin has on the footman at the Epanchins'; he allows
Myshkin to smoke, to break artificial rules, and he listens
to what he has to say. Similarly with Keller, where the
process takes a little longer. Keller is the hard-drinking,
bellicose ruffian, with a chip on his shoulder, not to be
taken in by anybody; yet as soon as he has a chance to
see what Myshkin is like, he becomes a good egg, even a
good friend, and offers to second him in a duel. Totsky
and General Epanchin, being men of the world, make
allowances for Myshkin; they understand that there must
be such people. Mrs. Epanchin, a sensible, direct, warm-
hearted woman, knows Myshkin is a fool and a great
causer of trouble, not at all a safe man to have around,
but she not only puts up with him and forgives him, she
finds that she must seek him out. Lebedyev, the drunken
buffoon and vainglorious sponge, deeply enjoys being seen
through by Myshkin, even enjoys bringing each fresh
rascality out in the open. Radomsky, more a man of intellect but good-hearted and on the right side, cannot help

trying to confess himself to Myshkin, and goes out of his way and without reason to corroborate to him his father's thefts of public money and ensuing suicide. General Ivolgin, the constitutional liar and idler, similarly resorts to Myshkin with almost perfect candor because he feels that Myshkin alone knows that he is essentially an "honest" man. Kolya, too, the precocious child, the very one who ought to have stood aloof because he saw so much, and with so little reason, makes himself a follower of Myshkin. None of these persons loses anything to Myshkin; neither do they gain anything materially. They are the "ordinary" people who make up the world, and they have the same deep but slightly uneasy and superficially indifferent regard for Myshkin that such persons have towards their own conscience; and indeed that is what Myshkin is for them, an easy, objective form of conscience, to whom they can appeal without harm.

On a somewhat different level come Ganya Ivolgin and Ippolit Terentyev. Ganya is the man of vanity and ambition, but without pride; Ippolit is the man of overweening pride and intellect, but almost without vanity. To each, in a different way, Myshkin brings doom. His mere presence destroys first the possibility of Ganya's marriage to Nastasya, and second, indirectly, he prevents the possibility of his marriage to Aglaia. Further, he is present at, and is partial cause of, Ganya's supreme humiliation over the affair of the fire of roubles. Yet Ganya becomes Myshkin's man, and where he might have played Iago with cause, shows no slightest trace of jealousy after the beginning. As to Ippolit, Myshkin crushes, though by *tour de force* and not even eloquently, his Nihilism and makes a good deal of a fool of him in public, yet it is to him, and in his house, that he brings his death. Perhaps Dostoevsky arranged this in order to furnish a contrast to Myshkin of a kind not offered either by the girls or by Rogozhin. Ippolit is the man already maimed, diseased, lacerated by life, and as a consequence has rebelled against God. Redemption is not in his line; he is the Poor Knight Don Quixote *manqué,* mutilated even; and there is nothing he can rebel against except the God who has

condemned him. He is a kind of sink of personality on
the point of turning into a fount. To whom can he bring
his rebellion, on whom can he pour forth his fountain,
except Myshkin, the lay Christ of the God whom he
wishes to deny? Myshkin was responsible for the material
failure of Ganya; and he is morally responsible for Ippolit's realization of the doom that is upon him. Again he
acts as conscience—this time not as the friendly conscience, but as the insuppressible and insupportable conscience.

With Rogozhin that is the role he had always played,
but with him it was the role of a full person and not that
of a mere fabulous figure. It is in relation to Rogozhin,
even more than in relation to Nastasya and Aglaia, that
Myshkin comes alive, moves, has his being, and suffers.
This may be because, in the history of the eight plans for
the book, he is a split part or double of Rogozhin; if so,
that is an accident in the creative task but it is the central
fact in the created product. If we turn to chapters three,
four, and five of the second part, which begin with the
conversation between the two men about the nature of
their respective loves for Nastasya—Rogozhin's being hate
and Myshkin's pity—and end with Myshkin's saving epileptic fit just as Rogozhin is about to stab him, we shall
see what Dostoevsky was really capable of as a poetic
novelist dealing with the desperate theme of the good man
in action. One way of defining the effect of these chapters
would be to say that it did not matter what theme
Dostoevsky was dealing with, for the theme, whatever it is,
disappears into the texture of the images of insight and
wrestling contest in which they are delivered. They are
made things; the poet is operating as *maker,* and operating
inviolably. The atmosphere, which is the air in which the
scenes actually breathe and not backdrops laid on, was
first set when, that morning, Myshkin had seen "those
eyes" staring at him on the crowded platform of the railway station. He was sure enough in a half-conscious way
that they must have been Rogozhin's eyes, but they
seemed also like his own eyes, and he kept the memory
of them boring within him all day, while he searched for

Nastasya, for Kolya, and for Rogozhin himself. It is as if
he has been himself hunted and cornered when finally he
comes to Rogozhin's house; he is full of extraordinary
and inexplicable emotion and knows the house by instinct,
by its largeness, its gloominess, its frigid, inhospitable,
and hidden air. At the street level there is a money-
changer's shop owned by a member of the sect of Skoptsy
—one of those who practice self-mutilation for religious
purposes. The gloom of the house and the presence of the
Skoptsy are brought in again and again through the
following scenes; darkness and self-mutilation become virtually parts of the psychological image of the whole
scene. They make the right background for both men, for
both surely mutilate themselves spiritually in the darkness
of their own souls, Rogozhin out of passion and Myshkin
out of goodness. In this dark place they understand each
other. "When I am with you," says Myshkin, "you believe
me, but when I am away, you leave off believing me at
once and begin suspecting me." To which Rogozhin re-
sponds, "I believe your voice when I am with you. I understand, of course, we can't be put on the same level, you
and I." In this dark place they understand also what must
happen, that Nastasya, though she loves Myshkin, will
eventually marry Rogozhin in order to be murdered by
him, and that she will do so because of Myshkin. This
prophecy is enforced by the seven-inch horn-handled
knife, a new and unused knife, which Myshkin picks up
unconsciously off the table, and which Rogozhin seizes
from him. To complete the symbolic significance of the
scene, there is next introduced Holbein's picture of the
dead Christ, of which Rogozhin has a copy hanging
among portraits of bishops and landowners. It is the one
picture Rogozhin likes to look at. "At that picture!" cried
Myshkin. "Why that picture might make some people
lose their faith." Some two hundred pages further on in
the book the full meaning of the picture is made plain in
Ippolit's description of it. It lacks the spiritual beauty
found in most portraits of Christ, he says. "It's the face
of man *only just* taken from the cross—that is to say,
still bearing traces of warmth and life. . . . It is simply

nature, and the corpse of a man, whoever he might be, must really look like that after such suffering." The portrait is a temptation for Rogozhin, a doubt for Myshkin, and a symbol for the reader. Although it is a judgment, focused in Rogozhin's eyes, upon Myshkin as the idiot Christ. And for Myshkin, in his turn, after he has changed crosses with Rogozhin, been blessed by his idiot mother, been refused the embrace of brotherhood, and left the house, Rogozhin becomes, in terms of "those eyes," of the knife, and of the picture, first the pursuing demon, and lastly an accuser and a judge. When Myshkin discovers him at Nastasya's house, he exclaims, "With what eyes shall I look upon that man for the rest of my life!" The self-knowledge is not, however, perfected until Myshkin's epileptic fit supervenes upon Rogozhin's attempt at murder, and it endures only for the single moment in which his soul is "flooded with *inner* light," and which is terminated by the "first sound of the fearful scream which broke of itself from its breast." In that scream, says Dostoevsky, "everything human seems obliterated and it is impossible, or very difficult, for an observer to realize and admit that it is the man himself screaming. It seems as though it were someone else screaming from within the man."

So beautifully composed, so intensely felt, are these chapters at all three levels of meaning—the intellectual, the narrative, and the imaginative—and so united on the imaginative or symbolic level, that one feels Dostoevsky has created enough mass in momentum to carry through to a fitting end even his difficult and desperate theme of the ideal man; and so far as the novel *is* completed, it is the imaginative energy of these chapters that supplies the momentum. But unfortunately Dostoevsky had conceived his drama in terms of Myshkin's further relationship with Nastasya and Aglaia, for which he was unable to provide images deep enough and grasping enough to *deliver* the combination of idea and act as drama. Nastasya is carefully and imaginatively built up off-stage so that when she appears she is actual enough, and Aglaia is observed and made to act on-stage sufficiently to make her actual as a person; both women are created full of possibilities; and the reader is ready to believe not only that anything may happen, but that the right and justifying things *will* happen inevitably, out of the momentum of the characters. Yet at the crisis they are forced, and being forced they are not so much incredible as inadequate. Both women rage too much, and rage vainly, because Dostoevsky has not provided a focus for their rage in the *created* character of Myshkin, and, at the same time, because he has provided too much focus in his *idea* of that character. The inadequacy is Myshkin's, not the women's; he has nothing within him capable of satisfying the passionate desires which dominate both Nastasya and Aglaia in their feeling for him. Whether Dostoevsky deliberately omitted all sexual being from Myshkin's nature, or whether he simply was by his own nature incapable of deep sexual experience and so could not envisage it either in Nastasya and Aglaia or in Myshkin except as an idea, it was that lack, that incompleteness as a man in Myshkin, which brought on the downfall of the women, and transformed what ought to have been the tragic triumph of the good man into his reduction to complete idiocy. You cannot transmute what does not exist; you can only rage at your disability and end in ignominy and humiliation. Thus in Dostoevsky the mighty attempt to create always becomes involved in sin or ignominy and ends in humiliation and obliteration. The deprivation of his nature like the privations of his life led him to envisage emotions as released either as an ecstasy of rage or as a rage of ecstasy. The emotions do not express the people, they take them over. There is always, in the great creations of Dostoevsky, "someone else screaming from within the man." In *The Idiot* it is the rage of goodness.

Editor's Note

Symbolic Action in a Poem by Keats first appeared in *Accent,* Autumn 1943. Reprinted with permission of the publishers from *A Grammar of Motives,* by Kenneth Burke. Copyright, 1945, by Prentice-Hall, Inc., 70 Fifth Avenue, New York 11, New York.

Kenneth Burke was born in Pittsburgh, Pennsylvania, in 1897, and educated at Ohio State and Columbia. He has been an editor of *The Dial* and a member of the Institute of Advanced Study, and has taught at Bennington College since 1943. Burke's books include several translations from the German, two works of fiction, a book of verse, and six volumes of criticism, taking "criticism" in its widest sense: *Counter-Statement* (1931, revised edition 1953), *Permanence and Change* (1935, revised edition 1954), *Attitudes toward History* (1937), *The Philosophy of Literary Form* (1941), *A Grammar of Motives,* and *A Rhetoric of Motives* (1950).

FOURTEEN

Kenneth Burke

Symbolic Action in a Poem by Keats

We are here set to analyze the "Ode on a Grecian Urn" as a viaticum that leads, by a series of transformations, into the oracle, "Beauty is truth, truth beauty." We shall analyze the Ode "dramatistically," in terms of symbolic action.

To consider language as a means of *information* or *knowledge* is to consider it epistemologically, semantically, in terms of "science." To consider it as a mode of *action* is to consider it in terms of "poetry." For a poem is an act, the symbolic act of the poet who made it—an act of such a nature that, in surviving as a structure or object, it enables us as readers to re-enact it.

"Truth" being the essential word of knowledge (science) and "beauty" being the essential word of art or poetry, we might substitute accordingly. The oracle would then assert, "Poetry is science, science poetry." It would be particularly exhilarating to proclaim them one if there were a strong suspicion that they were at odds (as the assertion that "God's in his heaven, all's right with the world" is really a *counter*-assertion to doubts about God's existence and suspicions that much is wrong). It was the dialectical opposition between the "aesthetic" and the "practical," with "poetry" on one side and utility (business and applied science) on the other that was being ecstatically denied. The *relief* in this denial was grounded in the romantic philosophy itself, a philosophy which gave strong recognition to precisely the *contrast* between "beauty" and "truth."

Perhaps we might put it this way: If the oracle were to

have been uttered in the first stanza of the poem rather
than the last, its phrasing proper to that place would have
been: "Beauty is *not* truth, truth *not* beauty." The five
stanzas of successive transformation were necessary for the
romantic philosophy of a romantic poet to transcend itself
(raising its romanticism to a new order, or new dimension). An abolishing of romanticism through romanticism!
(To transcend romanticism through romanticism is, when
all is over, to restore in one way what is removed in another.)

But to the poem, step by step through the five stanzas.

As a "way in," we begin with the sweeping periodic
sentence that, before the stanza is over, has swiftly but
imperceptibly been transmuted in quality from the periodic
to the breathless, a cross between interrogation and exclamation:

> *Thou still unravish'd bride of quietness,*
> > *Thou foster-child of silence and slow time,*
> *Sylvan historian, who canst thus express*
> > *A flowery tale more sweetly than our rhyme:*
> *What leaf-fring'd legend haunts about thy shape*
> > *Of deities or mortals, or of both,*
> > > *In Tempe or the dales of Arcady?*
> *What men or gods are these? What maidens loth?*
> > *What mad pursuit? What struggle to escape?*
> > > *What pipes and timbrels? What wild ecstasy?*

Even the last quick outcries retain somewhat the quality
of the periodic structure with which the stanza began. The
final line introduces the subject of "pipes and timbrels,"
which is developed and then surpassed in Stanza II:

> *Heard melodies are sweet, but those unheard*
> > *Are sweeter; therefore, ye soft pipes, play on;*
> *Not to the sensual ear, but, more endear'd,*
> > *Pipe to the spirit ditties of no tone:*
> *Fair youth, beneath the trees, thou canst not leave*
> > *Thy song, nor ever can those trees be bare;*
> > > *Bold Lover, never, never canst thou kiss,*
> *Though winning near the goal—yet, do not grieve;*

> *She cannot fade, though thou hast not thy bliss,*
> *Forever wilt thou love, and she be fair!*

If we had only the first stanza of this Ode, and were speculating upon it from the standpoint of motivation, we could detect there tentative indications of two motivational levels. For the lines express a doubt whether the figures on the urn are "deities or mortals"—and the motives of gods are of a different order from the motives of men. This bare hint of such a possibility emerges with something of certainty in the second stanza's development of the "pipes and timbrels" theme. For we explicitly consider a contrast between body and mind (in the contrast between "heard melodies," addressed "to the sensual ear," and "ditties of no tone," addressed "to the spirit").

Also, of course, the notion of inaudible sound brings us into the region of the mystic oxymoron (the term in rhetoric for "the figure in which an epithet of a contrary significance is added to a word: e.g., *cruel kindness; laborious idleness*"). And it clearly suggests a concern with the level of motives-behind-motives, as with the paradox of the prime mover that is itself at rest, being the unmoved ground of all motion and action. Here the poet whose sounds are the richest in our language is meditating upon *absolute* sound, the *essence* of sound, which would be soundless as the prime mover is motionless, or as the "principle" of sweetness would not be sweet, having transcended sweetness, or as the sub-atomic particles of the sun are each, in their isolate purity, said to be devoid of temperature.

Contrast Keats's unheard melodies with those of Shelley:

> *Music, when soft voices die,*
> *Vibrates in the memory—*
> *Odours, when sweet violets sicken,*
> *Live within the sense they quicken.*
>
> *Rose leaves, when the rose is dead,*
> *Are heaped for the beloved's bed;*
> *And so thy thoughts, when thou art gone,*
> *Love itself shall slumber on.*

Here the futuristic Shelley is anticipating retrospection; he is looking forward to looking back. The form of thought is naturalistic and temporalistic in terms of *past* and *future*. But the form of thought in Keats is mystical, in terms of an *eternal present*. The Ode is striving to move beyond the region of becoming into the realm of *being*. (This is another way of saying that we are here concerned with two levels of motivation.)

In the last four lines of the second stanza, the state of immediacy is conveyed by a development peculiarly Keatsian. I refer not simply to translation into terms of the erotic, but rather to a quality of *suspension* in the erotic imagery, defining an eternal prolongation of the state just prior to fulfilment—not exactly arrested ecstasy, but rather an arrested pre-ecstasy.[1]

Suppose that we had but this one poem by Keats, and knew nothing of its author or its period, so that we could treat it only in itself, as a series of internal transformations to be studied in their development from a certain point, and without reference to any motives outside the Ode. Under such conditions, I think, we should require no further observations to characterize (from the standpoint of symbolic action) the main argument in the second stanza. We might go on to make an infinity of observations about the details of the stanza; but as regards major deployments we should deem it enough to note that the theme of "pipes and timbrels" is developed by the use of mystic oxymoron, and then surpassed (or given a development-atop-the-development) by the stressing of erotic imagery (that had been ambiguously adumbrated in the references to "maidens loth" and "mad pursuit" of Stanza I). And we could note the quality of *incipience* in this imagery, its state of arrest not at fulfilment, but at the point just prior to fulfilment.

Add, now, our knowledge of the poem's place as an enactment in a particular cultural scene, and we likewise

[1] Mr. G. Wilson Knight, in *The Starlit Dome*, refers to "that recurring tendency in Keats to image a poised form, a stillness suggesting motion, what might be called a 'tiptoe' effect."

note in this second stanza a variant of the identification between death and sexual love that was so typical of 19th-century romanticism and was to attain its musical monument in the Wagnerian *Liebestod*. On a purely dialectical basis, to die in love would be to be born to love (the lovers dying as individual identities that they might be transformed into a common identity). Adding historical factors, one can note the part that capitalist individualism plays in sharpening this consummation (since a property structure that heightens the sense of individual identity would thus make it more imperiously a "death" for the individual to take on the new identity made by a union of two). We can thus see why the love-death equation would be particularly representative of a romanticism that was the reflex of business.

Fortunately, the relation between private property and the love-death equation is attested on unimpeachable authority, concerning the effect of consumption and consummation in a "mutual flame":

> *So between them love did shine,*
> *That the turtle saw his right*
> *Flaming in the phoenix' sight;*
> *Either was the other's mine.*

> *Property was thus appall'd,*
> *That the self was not the same;*
> *Single nature's double name*
> *Neither two nor one was called.*

The addition of fire to the equation, with its pun on sexual burning, moves us from purely dialectical considerations into psychological ones. In the lines of Shakespeare, fire is the third term, the ground term for the other two (the synthesis that ends the lovers' roles as thesis and antithesis). Less obviously, the same movement from the purely dialectical to the psychological is implicit in any imagery of a *dying* or a *falling* in common, which when woven with sexual imagery signalizes a "transcendent" sexual consummation. The figure appears in a lover's compliment when Keats writes to Fanny Brawne, thus:

I never knew before, what such a love as you have
made me feel, was; I did not believe in it; my Fancy
was afraid of it lest it should burn me up. But if you
will fully love me, though there may be some fire,
'twill not be more than we can bear when moistened
and bedewed with pleasures.

Our primary concern is to follow the transformations of
the poem itself. But to understand its full nature as a
symbolic act, we should use whatever knowledge is available. In the case of Keats, not only do we know the place
of this poem in his work and its time, but also we have
material to guide our speculations as regards correlations
between poem and poet. I grant that such speculations
interfere with the symmetry of criticism as a game.
(Criticism as a game is best to watch, I guess, when one
confines himself to the single unit, and reports on its
movements like a radio commentator broadcasting the
blow-by-blow description of a prizefight.) But linguistic
analysis has opened up new possibilities in the correlating
of producer and product—and these concerns have such
important bearing upon matters of culture and conduct in
general that no sheer conventions or ideals of criticism
should be allowed to interfere with their development.

From what we know of Keats's illness, with the peculiar
inclination to erotic imaginings that accompany its fever
(as with the writings of D. H. Lawrence) we can glimpse
a particular bodily motive expanding and intensifying the
lyric state in Keats's case. Whatever the intense *activity*
of his thoughts, there was the material *pathos* of his physical condition. Whatever transformations of mind or body
he experienced, his illness was there as a kind of constitutional substrate, whereby all aspects of the illness would
be imbued with their derivation from a common ground
(the phthisic fever thus being at one with the phthisic
chill, for whatever the clear contrast between fever and
chill, they are but modes of the same illness, the common
underlying substance).

The correlation between the state of agitation in the

poems and the physical condition of the poet is made quite clear in the poignant letters Keats wrote during his last illness. In 1819 he complains that he is "scarcely content to write the best verses for the fever they leave behind." And he continues: "I want to compose without this fever." But a few months later he confesses, "I am recommended not even to read poetry, much less write it." Or: "I must say that for 6 Months before I was taken ill I` had not passed a tranquil day. Either that gloom overspre[a]d me or I was suffering under some passionate feeling, or if I turn'd to versify that exacerbated the poison of either sensation." Keats was "like a sick eagle looking at the sky," as he wrote of his mortality in a kindred poem, "On Seeing the Elgin Marbles."

But though the poet's body was a *patient,* the poet's mind was an *agent.* Thus, as a practitioner of poetry, he could *use* his fever, even perhaps encouraging, though not deliberately, esthetic habits that, in making for the perfection of his lines, would exact payment in the ravages of his body (somewhat as Hart Crane could write poetry only by modes of living that made for the cessation of his poetry and so led to his dissolution).

Speaking of agents, patients, and action here, we might pause to glance back over the centuries thus: in the Aristotelian grammar of motives, action has its reciprocal in passion, hence *passion* is the property of a *patient.* But by the Christian paradox (which made the martyr's action identical with his passion, as the accounts of the martyrs were called both Acts and Passionals), *patience* is the property of a moral *agent.* And this Christian view, as secularized in the philosophy of romanticism, with its stress upon creativeness, leads us to the possibility of a bodily suffering redeemed by a poetic act.

In the third stanza, the central stanza of the Ode (hence properly the fulcrum of its swing) we see the two motives, the action and the passion, in the process of being separated. The possibility raised in the first stanza (which was dubious whether the level of motives was to be human or divine), and developed in the second stanza (which contrasts the "sensual" and the "spirit"), becomes definitive in Stanza III:

> *Ah, happy, happy boughs! that cannot shed*
> *Your leaves, nor ever bid the Spring adieu;*
> *And, happy melodist, unwearied,*
> *For ever piping songs for ever new;*
> *More happy love! more happy, happy love!*
> *For ever warm and still to be enjoy'd,*
> *For ever panting, and for ever young;*
> *All breathing human passion far above,*
> *That leaves a heart high-sorrowful and cloy'd,*
> *A burning forehead, and a parching tongue.*

The poem as a whole makes permanent, or fixes in a state of arrest, a peculiar agitation. But within this fixity, by the nature of poetry as a progressive medium, there must be development. Hence, the agitation that is maintained throughout (as a mood absolutized so that it fills the entire universe of discourse) will at the same time undergo internal transformations. In the third stanza, these are manifested as a clear division into two distinct and contrasted realms. There is a transcendental fever, which is felicitous, divinely above "all breathing human passion." And this "leaves" the other level, the level of earthly fever, "a burning forehead and a parching tongue." From the bodily fever, which is a passion, and malign, there has split off a spiritual activity, a wholly benign aspect of the total agitation.

Clearly, a movement has been finished. The poem must, if it is well-formed, take a new direction, growing out of and surpassing the curve that has by now been clearly established by the successive stages from "Is there the possibility of two motivational levels?" through "there are two motivational levels" to "the 'active' motivational level 'leaves' the 'passive' level."

Prophesying, with the inestimable advantage that goes with having looked ahead, what should we expect the new direction to be? First, let us survey the situation. Originally, before the two strands of the fever had been definitely drawn apart, the bodily passion could serve as the scene or ground of the spiritual action. But at the end of the third stanza, we abandon the level of bodily passion. The action is "far above" the passion, it "leaves" the fever. What then would this transcendent act require, to complete it?

It would require a scene of the same quality as itself. An act and a scene belong together. The nature of the one must be a fit with the nature of the other. (I like to call this the "scene-act ratio," or "dramatic ratio.") Hence, the act having now transcended its bodily setting, it will require, as its new setting, a transcendent scene. Hence, prophesying *post eventum*, we should ask that, in Stanza IV, the poem *embody* the transcendental act by endowing it with an appropriate scene.

The scene-act ratio involves a law of dramatic consistency whereby the quality of the act shares the quality of the scene in which it is enacted (the synecdochic relation of container and thing contained). Its grandest variant was in supernatural cosmogonies wherein mankind took on the attributes of gods by acting in cosmic scenes that were themselves imbued with the presence of godhead.[2]

Or we may discern the logic of the scene-act ratio behind the old controversy as to whether "God willed the good because it is good," or "the good is good because God willed it." This strictly theological controversy had political implications. But our primary concern here is with the *dramatistic* aspects of this controversy. For you will note that the whole issue centers in the problem of the *grounds* of God's creative act.

Since, from the purely dramatic point of view, every act requires a scene in which it takes place, we may note that one of the doctrines (that "God willed the good because it is good") is more symmetrical than the other. For by it, God's initial act of creation is itself given a ground, or

[2] In an article by Leo Spitzer, "*Milieu and Ambiance:* An Essay in Historical Semantics" (September and December 1942 numbers of *Philosophy and Phenomenological Research*), one will find a wealth of material that can be read as illustrative of "dramatic ratio."

scene (the objective existence of goodness, which was so real that God himself did not simply make it up, but acted in conformity with its nature when willing it to be the law of his creation). In the scholastic formulas taken over from Aristotle, God was defined as "pure act" (though this pure act was in turn the ultimate ground or *scene* of human acting and willing). And from the standpoint of purely dramatic symmetry, it would be desirable to have some kind of "scene" even for God. This requirement is met, we are suggesting, in the doctrine that "God willed the good *because* it is good." For this word, "because," in assigning a reason for God's willing, gives us in principle a kind of scene, as we may discern in the pun of our word, "ground," itself, which indeterminately applies to either "place" or "cause."

If even theology thus responded to the pressure for dramatic symmetry by endowing God, as the transcendent act, with a transcendent scene of like quality, we should certainly expect to find analogous tactics in this Ode. For as we have noted that the romantic passion is the secular equivalent of the Christian passion, so we may recall Coleridge's notion that poetic action itself is a "dim analogue of Creation." Keats in his way confronting the same dramatistic requirement that the theologians confronted in theirs, when he has arrived at his transcendent act at the end of Stanza III (that is, when the benign fever has split away from the malign bodily counterpart, as a divorcing of spiritual action from sensual passion), he is ready in the next stanza for the imagining of a scene that would correspond in quality to the quality of the action as so transformed. His fourth stanza will concretize, or "materialize," the act, by dwelling upon its appropriate ground.

> *Who are these coming to the sacrifice?*
> *To what green altar, O mysterious priest,*
> *Lead'st thou that heifer lowing at the skies,*
> *And all her silken flanks with garlands drest?*
> *What little town, by river or sea shore,*
> *Or mountain built with peaceful citadel,*
> *Is emptied of this folk, this pious morn?*

> *And, little town, thy streets for evermore*
> *Will silent be; and not a soul to tell*
> *Why thou art desolate, can e'er return.*

It is a vision, as you prefer, of "death" or of "immortality." "Immortality," we might say, is the "good" word for "death," and must necessarily be conceived in terms of death (the necessity that Donne touches upon when he writes, ". . . but thinke that I / Am, by being dead, immortall"). This is why, when discussing the second stanza, I felt justified in speaking of the variations of the love-death equation, though the poem spoke not of love and *death,* but of love *for ever.* We have a deathy-deathless scene as the corresponding ground of our transcendent act. The Urn itself, as with the scene upon it, is not merely an immortal act in our present mortal scene; it was originally an immortal act in a mortal scene quite different. The imagery, of sacrifice, piety, silence, desolation, is that of communication with the immortal or the dead.[3]

Incidentally, we might note that the return to the use of rhetorical questions in the fourth stanza serves well, on a purely technical level, to keep our contact with the mood of the opening stanza, a music that now but vibrates in the memory. Indeed, one even gets the impression that the form of the rhetorical question had never been aban-

---

[3] In imagery there is no negation, or disjunction. Logically, we can say, "this or that," "this, *not* that." In imagery we can but say "this and that," "this *with* that," "this-that," etc. Thus, imagistically considered, a commandment cannot be simply a proscription, but is also latently a provocation (a state of affairs that figures in the kind of stylistic scrupulosity and/or curiosity to which Gide's heroes have been particularly sensitive, as "thou shalt not . . ." becomes imaginatively transformed into "what would happen if . . ."). In the light of what we have said about the deathiness of immortality, and the relation between the erotic and the thought of a "dying," perhaps we might be justified in reading the last line of the great "Bright Star!" sonnet as naming states not simply alternative but also synonymous:

> *And so live ever—or else swoon to death.*

This use of the love-death equation is as startlingly paralleled in a letter to Fanny Brawne:

> I have two luxuries to brood over in my walks, your loveliness and the hour of my death. O that I could take possession of them both in the same moment.

doned; that the poet's questings had been couched as questions throughout. This is tonal felicity at its best, and something much like unheard tonal felicity. For the actual persistence of the rhetorical questions through these stanzas would have been wearisome, whereas their return now gives us an inaudible variation, by making us feel that the exclamations in the second and third stanzas had been questions, as the questions in the first stanza had been exclamations.

But though a lyric greatly profits by so strong a sense of continuousness, or perpetuity, I am trying to stress the fact that in the fourth stanza we *come upon* something. Indeed, this fourth stanza is related to the three foregoing stanzas quite as the sestet is related to the octave in Keats's sonnet, "On First Looking Into Chapman's Homer":

> *Much have I travell'd in the realms of gold,*
> *And many goodly states and kingdoms seen;*
> *Round many western islands have I been*
> *Which bards in fealty to Apollo hold.*
> *Oft of one wide expanse had I been told*
> *That deep-brow'd Homer ruled as his demesne;*
> *Yet did I never breathe its pure serene*
> *Till I heard Chapman speak out loud and bold;*
>
> *Then felt I like some watcher of the skies*
> *When a new planet swims into his ken;*
> *Or like stout Cortez when with eagle eyes*
> *He stared at the Pacific—and all his men*
> *Look'd at each other with a wild surmise—*
> *Silent, upon a peak in Darien.*

I am suggesting that, just as the sestet in this sonnet, *comes upon a scene,* so it is with the fourth stanza of the Ode. In both likewise we end on the theme of silence; and is not the Ode's reference to the thing that "not a soul can tell" quite the same in quality as the sonnet's reference to a "wild surmise"?

Thus, with the Urn as viaticum (or rather, with the *poem* as viaticum, and *in the name* of the Urn), having

symbolically enacted a kind of act that transcends our
mortality, we round out the process by coming to dwell
upon the transcendental ground of this act. The dead
world of ancient Greece, as immortalized on an Urn surviving from that period, is the vessel of this deathy-
deathless ambiguity. And we have gone dialectically from
the "human" to the "divine" and thence to the "ground
of the divine" (here tracing in poetic imagery the kind of
"dramatistic" course we have considered, on the purely
conceptual plane, in the theological speculations about the
"grounds" for God's creative act). Necessarily, there must
be certain inadequacies in the conception of this ground,
precisely because of the fact that immortality can only be
conceived in terms of death. Hence the reference to the
"desolate" in a scene otherwise possessing the benignity
of the eternal.

The imagery of pious sacrifice, besides its fitness for
such thoughts of departure as when the spiritual act splits
from the sensual pathos, suggests also a bond of communication between the levels (because of its immortal character in a mortal scene). And finally, the poem, in the name
of the Urn, or under the aegis of the Urn, is such a bond.
For we readers, by re-enacting it in the reading, use it as
a viaticum to transport us into the quality of the scene
which it depicts on its face (the scene containing as a
fixity what the poem as act extends into a process). The
scene *on* the Urn is really the scene *behind* the Urn; the
Urn is literally the ground of this scene, but transcend-
entally the scene is the ground of the Urn. The Urn contains the scene out of which it arose.

We turn now to the closing stanza:

> *O Attic shape! Fair attitude! with brede*
>   *Of marble men and maidens overwrought,*
> *With forest branches and the trodden weed;*
>   *Thou, silent form, dost tease us out of thought*
> *As doth eternity: Cold Pastoral!*
>   *When old age shall this generation waste,*
>   *Thou shalt remain, in midst of other woe*

> *Than ours, a friend to man, to whom thou say'st,*
> *'Beauty is truth, truth beauty,'—that is all*
> *Ye know on earth, and all ye need to know.*

In the third stanza we were at a moment of heat, emphatically sharing an imagery of loves "panting" and "for ever warm" that was, in the transcendental order, companionate to "a burning forehead, and a parching tongue" in the order of the passions. But in the last stanza, as signalized in the marmorean utterance, "Cold Pastoral!" we have gone from transcendental fever to transcendental chill. Perhaps, were we to complete our exegesis, we should need reference to some physical step from phthisic fever to phthisic chill, that we might detect here a final correlation between bodily passion and mental action. In any event we may note that, the mental action having departed from the bodily passion, the change from fever to chill is not a sufferance. For, as only the *benign* aspects of the fever had been left after the split, so it is a wholly benign chill on which the poem ends.[4]

I wonder whether anyone can read the reference to "brede of marble men and maidens overwrought" without thinking of "breed" for "brede" and "excited" for "overwrought." (Both expressions would thus merge notions of sexuality and craftsmanship, the erotic and the poetic.) As for the designating of the Urn as an "Attitude," it fits in admirably with our stress upon symbolic action. For an attitude is an arrested, or incipient *act*—not just an *object*, or *thing*.

Yeats, in *A Vision*, speaks of "the diagrams in Law's *Boehme*, where one lifts a paper to discover both the human entrails and the starry heavens." This equating of the deeply without and the deeply within (as also with Kant's famous remark) might well be remembered when we think of the sky that the "watcher" saw in Keats's

[4] In a letter to Fanny Brawne, Keats touches upon the fever-chill contrast in a passage that also touches upon the love-death equation, though here the chill figures in an untransfigured state:

> I fear that I am too prudent for a dying kind of Lover. Yet, there is a great difference between going off in warm blood like Romeo; and making one's exit like a frog in a frost.

sonnet. It is an internal sky, attained through meditations induced by the reading of a book. And so the oracle, whereby truth and beauty are proclaimed as one, would seem to derive from a profound inwardness.

Otherwise, without these introductory mysteries, "truth" and "beauty" were at odds. For whereas "beauty" had its fulfilment in romantic poetry, "truth" was coming to have its fulfilment in science, technological accuracy, accountancy, statistics, actuarial tables, and the like. Hence, without benefit of the rites which one enacts in a sympathetic reading of the Ode (rites that remove the discussion to a different level), the enjoyment of "beauty" would involve an esthetic kind of awareness radically in conflict with the kind of awareness deriving from the practical "truth." And as regards the tactics of the poem, this conflict would seem to be solved by "estheticizing" the true rather than by "verifying" the beautiful.

Earlier in our essay, we suggested reading "poetry" for "beauty" and "science" for "truth," with the oracle deriving its *liberating* quality from the fact that it is uttered at a time when the poem has taken us to a level where earthy contradictions do not operate. But we might also, in purely conceptual terms, attain a level where "poetry" and "science" cease to be at odds; namely: by translating the two terms into the "grammar" that lies behind them. That is: we could generalize the term "poetry" by widening it to the point where we could substitute for it the term "act." And we could widen "science" to the point where we could substitute "scene." Thus we have:

"beauty"	equals	"poetry"	equals	"act"
"truth"	equals	"science"	equals	"scene"

We would equate "beauty" with "act," because it is not merely a decorative thing, but an assertion, an affirmative, a creation, hence in the fullest sense an act. And we would equate "truth" or "science" with the "scenic" because science is a knowledge of *what is*—and *all that is* comprises the over-all universal *scene*. Our corresponding transcendence, then, got by "translation" into purely grammatical terms, would be: "Act is scene, scene act." We have got to this point by a kind of purely conceptual transformation that would correspond, I think, to the transformations of imagery leading to the oracle in the Ode.

"Act is scene, scene act." Unfortunately, I must break the symmetry a little. For poetry, as conceived in idealism (romanticism) could not quite be equated with *act,* but rather with *attitude.* For idealistic philosophies, with their stress upon the subjective, place primary stress upon the *agent* (the individual, the ego, the will, etc.). It was medieval scholasticism that placed primary stress upon the *act.* And in the Ode the Urn (which is the vessel or representative of poetry) is called an "attitude," which is not outright an act, but an incipient or arrested act, a *state of mind,* the property of an *agent.* Keats, in calling the Urn an attitude, is *personifying* it. Or we might use the italicizing resources of dialectic by saying that for Keats, beauty (poetry) was not so much "the *act* of an agent" as it was "the act of an *agent.*"

Perhaps we can re-enforce this interpretation by examining kindred strategies in Yeats whose poetry similarly derives from idealistic, romantic sources. Indeed, as we have noted elsewhere,[5] Yeats's vision of immortality in his Byzantium poems but carries one step further the Keatsian identification with the Grecian Urn:

> *Once out of nature I shall never take*
> *My bodily form from any natural thing,*
> *But such a form as Grecian goldsmiths make*
> *Of hammered gold and gold enamelling . . .*

Here certainly the poet envisions immortality as "esthetically" as Keats. For he will have immortality as a golden bird, a fabricated thing, a work of Grecian goldsmiths. Here we go in the same direction as the "overwrought" Urn, but farther along in that direction.

The ending of Yeats's poem, "Among School Children," helps us to make still clearer the idealistic stress upon agent:

[5] "On Motivation in Yeats" (*The Southern Review,* Winter 1942).

> Labour is blossoming or dancing where
> The body is not bruised to pleasure soul,
> Nor beauty torn out of its own despair,
> Nor blear-eyed wisdom out of midnight oil.
> O chestnut tree, great rooted blossomer,
> Are you the leaf, the blossom or the bole?
> O body swayed to music, O brightening glance,
> How can we know the dancer from the dance?

Here the chestnut tree (as personified agent) is the ground of unity or continuity for all its scenic manifestations; and with the agent (dancer) is merged the act (dance). True, we seem to have here a commingling of act, scene, and agent, all three. Yet it is the *agent* that is "foremost among the equals." Both Yeats and Keats, of course, were much more "dramatistic" in their thinking than romantic poets generally, who usually center their efforts upon the translation of *scene* into terms of *agent* (as the materialistic science that was the dialectical counterpart of romantic idealism preferred conversely to translate *agent* into terms of *scene,* or in other words, to treat "consciousness" in terms of "matter," the "mental" in terms of the "physical," "people" in terms of "environment").

To review briefly: The poem begins with an ambiguous fever which in the course of the further development is "separated out," splitting into a bodily fever and a spiritual counterpart. The bodily passion is the malign aspect of the fever, the mental action its benign aspect. In the course of the development, the malign passion is transcended and the benign active partner, the intellectual exhilaration, takes over. At the beginning, where the two aspects were ambiguously one, the bodily passion would be the "scene" of the mental action (the "objective symptoms" of the body would be paralleled by the "subjective symptoms" of the mind, the bodily state thus being the other or ground of the mental state). But as the two become separated out, the mental action transcends the bodily passion. It becomes an act in its own right, making discoveries and assertions not grounded in the bodily passion. And this quality of action, in transcending the merely physical symptoms of the fever, would thus require a different ground or scene, one more suited in quality to the quality of the transcendent act.

The transcendent act is concretized, or "materialized," in the vision of the "immortal" scene, the reference in Stanza IV to the original scene of the Urn, the "heavenly" scene of a dead, or immortal, Greece (the scene in which the Urn was originally enacted and which is also fixed on its face). To indicate the internality of this vision, we referred to a passage in Yeats relating the "depths" of the sky without to the depths of the mind within; and we showed a similar pattern in Keats's account of the vision that followed his reading of Chapman's Homer. We suggested that the poet is here coming upon a new internal sky, through identification with the Urn as act, the same sky that he came upon through identification with the enactments of Chapman's translation.

This transcendent scene is the level at which the earthly laws of contradiction no longer prevail. Hence, in the terms of this scene, he can proclaim the unity of truth and beauty (of science and art), a proclamation which he needs to make precisely because here was the basic split responsible for the romantic agitation (in both poetic and philosophic idealism). That is, it was gratifying to have the oracle proclaim the unity of poetry and science because the values of technology and business were causing them to be at odds. And from the perspective of a "higher level" (the perspective of a dead or immortal scene transcending the world of temporal contradictions) the split could be proclaimed once more a unity.

At this point, at this stage of exaltation, the fever has been replaced by chill. But the bodily passion has completely dropped out of account. All is now mental action. Hence, the chill (as in the ecstatic exclamation, "Cold Pastoral!") is proclaimed only in its benign aspect.

We may contrast this discussion with explanations such as a materialist of the Kretschmer school might offer. I refer to accounts of motivation that might treat disease as cause and poem as effect. In such accounts, the disease would not be "passive," but wholly active; and what we have called the mental action would be wholly passive, hardly more than an epiphenomenon, a mere symptom of the disease quite as are the fever and the chill themselves. Such accounts would give us no conception of the essential matter here, the intense linguistic activity.*

* Editor's Note: For completeness, Burke writes in 1955, this essay should be supplemented by the discussion of the Ode on pp. 204 and 317 of *A Rhetoric of Motives*, and the final footnote to his essay "Mysticism as a Solution to the Poet's Dilemma," in *Spiritual Problems in Contemporary Literature*, edited by Stanley Romaine Hopper.

Editor's Note

George Herbert first appeared in *Scrutiny*, Volume XII, No. 3 (1944), and was reprinted in *Explorations* (London 1946, New York 1947) by L. C. Knights. Used here with the permission of the author and of the American publisher, George W. Stewart.

Lionel Charles Knights was born in Grantham, Lincolnshire, England, in 1906, and educated at Cambridge. He was a member of the editorial board of *Scrutiny* from 1932 to its demise in 1953, has taught at the universities of Manchester and Sheffield, and is now Winterstoke Professor of English at Bristol University. In addition to *Explorations*, Knights is the author of *Drama and Society in the Age of Jonson* (1937) and *Poetry, Politics and the English Tradition* (1954).

FIFTEEN

L. C. Knights

George Herbert

The poetry of George Herbert is so intimately bound up
with his beliefs as a Christian and his practice as a priest
of the Church of England that those who enjoy the poetry
without sharing the beliefs may well feel some presump-
tion in attempting to define the human, as distinguished
from the specifically Christian, value of his work. The
excuse for such an attempt can only be the conviction
that there is much more in Herbert's poetry for readers of
all kinds than is recognized in the common estimate. That
his appeal is a wide one is implicit in the accepted claim
that he is a poet and not simply a writer of devotional
verse; but I think I am right in saying that discussion of
him tends to take for granted that admirers are likely to
be drawn from a smaller circle than admirers of, say,
Donne or Marvell. Even Canon Hutchinson, whose superbly edited and annotated edition of the complete Works is
not likely to be superseded [1]—it would be difficult to
imagine a better qualified editor and introducer—even
Canon Hutchinson remarks that, "if to-day there is a less
general sympathy with Herbert's religion, the beauty and
sincerity of its expression are appreciated by those who do
not share it." True; but there is also much more than the
"expression" that we appreciate, as I shall try to show.
Herbert's poetry is an integral part of the great English
tradition.

[1] *The Works of George Herbert*, edited with a Commentary by
F. E. Hutchinson (Oxford University Press, 30s.). Canon Hutchinson's
essay on Herbert in *Seventeenth-Century Studies Presented to Sir
Herbert Grierson* should also be consulted.

It is, however, with expression, with form and manner, that appreciation must begin, and Dr. Hutchinson directs our attention to what are unquestionably the most important features of Herbert's style. "His craftsmanship is conspicuous. Almost any poem of his has its object well defined," he says. And again:

> Few English poets have been able to use the plain words of ordinary speech with a greater effect of simple dignity than Herbert. From Donne he had learnt the use of the conversational tone, which establishes an intimacy between poet and reader; and when his poems are read aloud, the emphasis falls easily on the natural order of the speaking idiom.

In other words, Herbert, like Donne, is a realist in literature. The first *Jordan* poem ("Who says that fictions only and false hair Become a verse?") is not only an expression of personal dedication, it is also, as the second poem of the same title is explicitly, a literary manifesto:

> *Is it no verse, except enchanted groves*
> *And sudden arbours shadow course-spunne lines?*
> *Must purling streams refresh a lovers loves?*
> *Must all be vail'd, while he that reades, divines,*
> * Catching the sense at two removes?*
>
> *Shepherds are honest people; let them sing:*
> *Riddle who list, for me, and pull for Prime. . . .*

The "pure, manly and unaffected" diction that Coleridge noted, the rhythm that, though musical, is close to the rhythm of living speech, the construction that almost always follows the evolution of thought and feeling, even in the most intricate of the stanza forms that he used in such variety—these elements of Herbert's style show his determination to make his verse sincere and direct, to avoid even the slightest degree of the distortion that occurs when a preconceived idea of "the poetical" takes charge of the matter. And the effort of craftsmanship involved was one with the moral effort to know himself, to bring his conflicts into the daylight and, so far as possible, to resolve them. It is in the wide application of Herbert's self-discovery that the value of his poetry lies; but before approaching the substance of his verse I should like to examine some aspects of his style that have had less attention than those so far glanced at. For the "definition of the object" that Dr. Hutchinson rightly puts in the forefront of Herbert's achievement as a poet is not simply a matter of surface purity and naturalness; it has depth and solidity, and we need to become conscious of the variety of resources brought to bear in the process—simple only in appearance—that the defining is.

It is here that literary criticism necessarily joins hands with "the sociology of literature," since what we are concerned with is the personal use of a more than personal idiom with its roots in tradition and the general life. To the critic no less than to the student of English civilization in the first half of the seventeenth century it is of considerable significance that Herbert, as man and artist, is not the product of one social class alone. An aristocrat by birth, and related to some of the more prominent figures at court, the protégé of James I, the friend of Donne and Bacon, he has also that ingrained sense of "common" English life which in so many representative figures of the time blends with and modifies the intellectual currents from the world of courtly refinement, learning and public affairs. His poetry has plainly an upper-class background. The Metaphysical subtlety and intellectual analysis that he learnt from Donne,[2] the skill in music—so pleasantly attested by Walton—that one senses even in his handling of the spoken word, the easy and unostentatious references

---

[2] Herbert's metaphysical wit has marked differences from Donne's as well as affinities with it. It tends in one direction towards humour, which is saved by its intellectual quality from anything like whimsicality. The following verse from *Vanitie* (i) shows his amused play of mind:

> The subtil Chymick can devest
> And strip the creature naked, till he finde
> The callow principles within their nest:
>   There he imparts to them his minde,
> Admitted to their bed-chamber, before
>   They appeare trim and drest
> To ordinarie suitours at the doore.

to science and learning, all imply a cultivated milieu.[3] And although the rightness of tone that keeps even his most intimate poetry free from sentimentality or over-insistence springs from deeply personal characteristics, it is also related to the well-bred ease of manner of "the gentleman." [4]

Turn, however, to that poem with the characteristic title, *The Quip,* and a different aspect of Herbert's genius, implying a different source of strength, is at once apparent.

> *The merrie world did on a day*
> *With his train-bands and mates agree*
> *To meet together, where I lay,*
> *And all in sport to geere at me.*
>
> *First, Beautie crept into a rose,*
> *Which when I pluckt not, Sir, said she,*
> *Tell me, I pray, Whose hands are those?*
> But thou shalt answer, Lord, for me.
>
> *Then Money came, and chinking still,*
> *What tune is this, poore man? said he:*
> *I heard in Musick you had skill.*
> But thou shalt answer, Lord, for me.
>
> *Then came brave Glorie puffing by*
> *In silks that whistled, who but he?*
> *He scarce allow'd me half an eie.*
> But thou shalt answer, Lord, for me. . . .

The personifications here have nothing in common either with Spenser's allegorical figures or with the capitalized abstractions of the eighteenth century: "Brave Glorie puffing by In silks that whistled" might have come straight from *The Pilgrim's Progress.* And Bunyan, as Dr. G. R. Owst has shown,[5] had behind him not only the rich folk-

[3] See in this connexion his fine poem, *The Pearl.*

[4] That Herbert's invariable courtesy is based on a genuine responsiveness to other people—that it is not simply "good manners"—is plain from the advice given in *The Church Porch,* e.g. stanzas 52–55. See also Letter XII in Dr. Hutchinson's edition, where Herbert discusses the needs of his orphan nieces.

[5] In *Literature and Pulpit in Medieval England.*

culture that produced the ballads, but also a long line of preachers in the vernacular. Again and again Herbert reminds us of the popular preacher addressing his audience —without a shade of condescension in doing so—in the homely manner that they themselves use. There is humour, mimicry and sarcasm, seen most clearly when the verses are read aloud with the inflexions they demand.

> *He doth not like this vertue, no;*
> *Give him his dirt to wallow in all night:*
> > *These Preachers make*
> > *His head to shoot and ake.*   (Miserie)

> Love God, and love your neighbour. Watch and pray.
> > Do as ye would be done unto.
> *O dark instructions; ev'n as dark as day!*
> > *Who can these Gordian knots undo?*   (Divinitie)

> > *To be in both worlds full*
> *Is more then God was, who was hungrie here.*
> *Wouldst thou his laws of fasting disanull?*
> > *Enact good cheer?*
> *Lay out thy joy, yet hope to save it?*
> *Wouldst thou both eat thy cake, and have it?*
> > > (The Size)

Herbert, we know, made a collection of "Outlandish [*sc.* foreign] Proverbs" for the community at Little Gidding, and although he does not often, as in the last quotation, incorporate a popular saying, many of his terse sentences have a proverbial ring.

Herbert's "popular" manner is, however, far more deeply grounded—and serves a more important purpose in his poetry—than these last examples might suggest.

> *Let forrain nations of their language boast,*
> *What fine varietie each tongue affords:*
> *I like our language, as our men and coast:*
> *Who cannot dresse it well, want wit, not words.*

This, from *The Sonne*, is explicit,—"I like our language": and one way of enforcing the judgment that he is in the great English tradition is to point out how surely he uses

the native idiom to give the effect of something immediately present, something going on under one's eyes. In the
colloquial expostulation of *Conscience* an over-active scru-
pulousness comes to life as it is rebuked:

> *Peace pratler, do not lowre:*
> *Not a fair look, but thou dost call it foul:*
> *Not a sweet dish, but thou dost call it sowre:*
> *Musick to thee doth howl.*
> *By listning to thy chatting fears*
> *I have both lost mine eyes and eares.*

The opening of *The Discharge* has a similar, almost dramatic, effect:

> *Busie enquiring heart, what wouldst thou know?*
> *Why dost thou prie,*
> *And turn, and leer, and with a licorous eye*
> *Look high and low:*
> *And in thy lookings stretch and grow?*

Even his simplest poems have a muscular force, an almost physical impact, as in the description of "the honest
man" (in *Constancie*):

> *Whom neither force nor fawning can*
> *Unpinne, or wrench from giving all their due.*

He uses alliteration and assonance in the native Elizabethan way, not, that is, as a poetic or musical device, but
as a means of controlling emphasis and movement so as
to obtain the maximum immediacy. To the examples already given may be added these lines from *The Flower:*

> *Many a spring I shoot up fair,*
> *Offring at heav'n, growing and groning thither,*

where the effect is, in Shakespearean fashion, to assimilate
the participles to each other, so that the groans seem an
intrinsic part of the growing. It is the artist's feeling for
all the resources of "our language" that gives to the
greater poems of spiritual conflict their disturbing immediacy.

Herbert's style, then, is "popular" as well as courtly and

Metaphysical, and his leaning towards the manner of common Elizabethan speech is further emphasized by his well-known liking for homely illustrations, analogies and metaphors. His poems contain plenty of learned allusions (especially, as was natural in that age, to astronomy), but he certainly "goes less far afield for his analogies than Donne and finds most that will serve his purpose from common life,"—from carpentry, gardening and everyday domestic activity: Redemption "spreads the plaister equal to the crime," after the refreshment of sleep, day will "give new wheels to our disorder'd clocks," and so on. But although this feature of Herbert's style is so commonly recognized that further illustration is unnecessary, its function is sometimes misinterpreted, as though Herbert's experience were somehow *limited* by his interest in the commonplace. Even Professor Grierson, after listing some of Herbert's comparisons, remarks:

> These are the "mean" similes which in Dr. Johnson's view were fatal to poetic effect even in Shakespeare. We have learned not to be so fastidious, yet when they are not purified by the passionate heat of the poet's dramatic imagination the effect is a little stuffy, for the analogies and symbols are more fanciful or traditional than natural and imaginative.

The last sentence, it is true, contains a qualifying clause, *"when* they are not purified by . . . imagination"; but since Professor Grierson goes on to describe Herbert as a "sincere and sensitive" rather than a "greatly imaginative" poet, some undue emphasis remains on the phrase "a little stuffy." [6]

The significance of Herbert's "homely" imagery—pointing as it does to some of the central preoccupations of his poetry—is something that we need to get clear. But before taking up this question—or, rather, as a way of taking it

[6] "But if not a greatly imaginative, Herbert is a sincere and sensitive poet, and an accomplished artist elaborating his argumentative strain or little allegories and conceits with felicitous completeness, and managing his variously patterned stanzas . . . with a finished and delicate harmony."—*Metaphysical Lyrics and Poems of the Seventeenth Century*, pp. xliii–xliv.

up—I should like to bring into focus another aspect of his imagery. As well as metaphor and simile Herbert uses symbols and allegory. Now whereas metaphor conveys its meaning directly from common experience, in symbolism there is usually an element of the arbitrary. *The Church-floore* is an obvious example:

> *Mark you the floore? that square & speckled stone,*
> *Which looks so firm and strong,*
> *Is* Patience.

But this arbitrary use of symbols is not characteristic of Herbert. Much more often his verse (like Bunyan's prose) gives life to his symbolic figures and allegorical situations, so that they appear as something immediately experienced, and carry their meaning with them. Even the highly emblematic poem, *Love Unknown*, has a matter-of-fact quality that makes it something more than a monument to a bygone taste. In *The Pilgrimage* the allegory is completely realized in terms of the actual.

> *I travell'd on, seeing the hill, where lay*
> *My expectation.*
> *A long it was and weary way.*
> *The gloomy cave of Desperation*
> *I left on th' one, and on the other side*
> *The rock of Pride.*
>
> *And so I came to Fancies medow strow'd*
> *With many a flower:*
> *Fain would I here have made abode,*
> *But I was quicken'd by my houre.*
> *So to Cares cops I came, and there got through*
> *With much ado.*
>
> *That led me to the wilde of Passion, which*
> *Some call the wold;*
> *A wasted place, but sometimes rich.*
> *Here I was robb'd of all my gold,*
> *Save one good Angell, which a friend had ti'd*
> *Close to my side.*

Mr. Empson, analysing the rich meaning of the third verse,[7] remarks that Herbert's manner is that of a traveller, "long afterwards, mentioning where he has been and what happened to him, as if only to pass the time." But the air of verisimilitude, the impression of a difficult journey actually undertaken, is not only an effect of the sober tone; it springs also from the sensitive and subtle movement. In reading the second verse we feel that we ourselves have been in "Cares cops" and scrambled out

—got through
With much ado—

as best we might. The fourth verse, making skilful use of the varied lengths of line and of the slight end-of-line pauses, reproduces the sensations of the traveller, as expectation—rather out of breath, but eager and confident— gives way abruptly to flat disappointment:

At length I got unto the gladsome hill,
Where lay my hope,
Where lay my heart; and climbing still,
When I had gain'd the brow and top,
A lake of brackish waters on the ground
Was all I found.

The allegorical form is of course a reminder that what we are concerned with is a graph of more than one kind of experience, but at no point in the poem are we simply interpreting an allegory; the bitter poignancy of the conclusion springs from deeply personal feelings that we have been made to share.

With that abash'd and struck with many a sting
Of swarming fears,
I fell, and cry'd, Alas my King!
Can both the way and end be tears?
Yet taking heart I rose, and then perceiv'd
I was deceiv'd:

[7] *Seven Types of Ambiguity*, pp. 163–165. Mr. Empson also has some excellent criticism of other poems by Herbert.

> *My hill was further: so I flung away,*
> > *Yet heard a crie*
> *Just as I went,* None goes that way
> And lives: *If that be all, said I,*
> *After so foul a journey death is fair,*
> > *And but a chair.*

This use of vivid allegory—tied down, as it were, to the actual and immediate—represents one aspect of Herbert's method. In poems such as *Vertue* and *Life* ("I made a posie, while the day ran by") we have the opposite and complementary process, where natural objects, without ceasing to be natural, have a rich symbolic meaning. In the lovely lines of *Vertue* the rose is no less a real rose, "angrie and brave," for being at the same time a symbol of life rooted in death. It is here that we see something of the significance of Herbert's consistent use of homely and familiar imagery. We may recall Coleridge's account of the genesis of the *Lyrical Ballads:* "Mr. Wordsworth was to propose to himself as his object to give the charm of novelty to things of every day, and to excite a feeling analogous to the supernatural, by awakening the mind's attention from the lethargy of custom, and directing it to the loveliness and wonder of the world before us." It is "the things of every day" that Herbert's poetry keeps consistently before us; but instead of invoking a rather adventitious "charm of novelty" or exciting "a feeling analogous to the supernatural" (one thinks of *Peter Bell*), he sees them in direct relation to a supernatural order in which he firmly believes. Thus in his poetry, just as the supernatural is apprehended in terms of the familiar, so common things—*whilst remaining common things,* clearly observed, and deeply felt—have a supernatural significance, and the familiar is perpetually new. "This is the skill, and doubtless the Holy Scripture intends thus much," he says, "when it condescends to the naming of a plough, a hatchett, a bushell, leaven, boyes piping and dancing; shewing that things of ordinary use are not only to serve in the way of drudgery, but to be washed and cleansed, and serve for lights even of Heavenly Truths." [8] Once more we are reminded of Bunyan, in whose blend of Biblical language and native idiom the august events of the Bible seem to be transacted in a familiar world, and the humble doings of every day are placed in a context that reveals how momentous they are.

II

Herbert's message to Nicholas Ferrar when, a few weeks before his death, he sent him the manuscript of *The Temple,* is well known.

> Sir, I pray deliver this little book to my dear brother Ferrar, and tell him he shall find in it a picture of the many spiritual conflicts that have passed betwixt God and my soul, before I could subject mine to the will of Jesus my Master; in whose service I have now found perfect freedom; desire him to read it: and then, if he can think it may turn to the advantage of any dejected poor soul, let it be made public; if not let him burn it; for I and it are less than the least of God's mercies.

Herbert's poetry was for him very largely a way of working out his conflicts. But it does not, like some religious poetry, simply *express* conflict; it is consciously and steadily directed towards resolution and integration. Dr. Hutchinson rightly describes the poems as "colloquies of the soul with God or self-communings which seek to bring order into that complex personality of his which he analyses so unsparingly."

This general account of conflict and resolution as the stuff of Herbert's poetry is, I believe, commonly accepted. But the conflict that gets most—indeed almost exclusive —attention is the struggle between the ambitious man of the world and the priest. Dr. Huchinson rightly insists that Herbert's conflict of mind was not simply about the priesthood, that his spiritual struggle "was over the more

[8] *A Priest to the Temple or, The Country Parson,* Chapter XXI.

general issue of his submission to the Divine will" (p. lxviii); but he elsewhere records the opinion that "his principal temptation, the 'one cunning bosome-sin' which is apt to break through all his fences, is ambition." [9] Now it would certainly be unwise to underestimate Herbert's worldly ambitions, or the severity of the struggle that took place in one "not exempt from passion and choler," who liked fine clothes and good company, before he could renounce his hopes of courtly preferment and, finally, become a country parson. But it seems to me that if we focus all our attention there, seeing the struggle simply as one between "ambition" and "renunciation," we ignore some even more fundamental aspects of Herbert's self-division and at the same time obscure the more general relevance of his experience. Most criticism of the poet tends to suggest that we are simply watching someone else's conflict—sympathetic, no doubt, but not intimately involved ourselves.

Behind the more obvious temptation of "success" was one more deeply rooted—a dejection of spirit that tended to make him regard his own life, the life he was actually leading, as worthless and unprofitable. Part of the cause was undoubtedly persistent ill-health. "For my self," he said, "I alwaies fear'd sickness more then death, because sickness hath made me unable to perform those Offices for which I came into the world, and must yet be kept in it" (p. 373); and this sense of the frustration of his best purposes through illness is expressed in *The Crosse* and other poems:

> *And then when after much delay,*
> *Much wrastling, many a combate, this deare end,*
> *So much desir'd, is giv'n, to take away*
>   *My power to serve thee; to unbend*
> *All my abilities, my designes confound,*
> *And lay my threatnings bleeding on the ground*

It is, however, difficult to resist the impression that his agues and consumption only intensified a more ingrained

[9] *Seventeenth-Century Studies Presented to Sir Herbert Grierson*, p. 154.

self-distrust. Commenting on some lines from *The Temper*
(i),

> —*O let me, when thy roof my soul hath hid,*
> *O let me roost and nestle there—*

Dr. Hutchinson remarks that "Herbert often shows a fear
of unlimited space and loves the shelter of an enclosure";
and his shrinking from the kind of experience that was
possible for him shows itself now in the frequently recorded moods of despondency, now in the desire for a
simpler and apparently more desirable form of existence:

My stock lies dead, and no increase
Doth my dull husbandrie improve. (Grace)

All things are busie; onely I
Neither bring hony with the bees,
Nor flowres to make that, nor the husbandrie
> *To water these.*

I am no link of thy great chain,
But all my companie is a weed. . . . (Employment [*i*])

Oh that I were an Orenge-tree,
> *That busie plant!*
Then should I ever laden be,
> *And never want*
Some fruit for him that dressed me. (Employment [*ii*])

Now this feeling of uselessness and self-distrust has two
further consequences: one is a preoccupation with time
and death,

> —*So we freeze on,*
> *Untill the grave increase our cold;* (Employment [*ii*])

the other is a sense that life, real life, is going on elsewhere, where he happens not to be himself. It was his
weakness, as well as his more positive qualities of "birth
and spirit," that made a career at court seem so intensely
desirable: "the town" was where other people lived active
and successful lives. Certainly, then, it was not a small
achievement to "behold the court with an impartial eye,

and see plainly that it is made up of fraud, and titles, and
flattery, and many other such empty, imaginary, painted
pleasures; pleasures that are so empty, as not to satisfy
when they are enjoyed." [1] But it was an even greater
achievement to rid himself of the torturing sense of frustration and impotence and to accept the validity of his
own experience. His poems come home to us because they
give new meanings to "acceptance."

The first condition of development was that the disturbing elements in experience should be honestly recognized;
and here we see the significance of Herbert's technical
achievement, of his realism, of his ability to make his
feelings immediately present. In the masterly verse of
Affliction (i) we have one of the most remarkable records
in the language of the achievement of maturity and of
the inevitable pains of the process. In the opening stanzas
movement and imagery combine to evoke the enchanted
world of early manhood, when to follow the immediate
dictates of the soul seems both duty and pleasure.

> *When first thou didst entice to thee my heart,*
> > *I thought the service brave:*
> *So many joyes I writ down for my part,*
> > *Besides what I might have*
> *Out of my stock of naturall delights,*
> *Augmented with thy gracious benefits.*

> *I looked on thy furniture so fine,*
> > *And made it fine to me:*
> *Thy glorious household-stuffe did me entwine,*
> > *And 'tice me unto thee.*
> *Such starres I counted mine: both heav'n and earth*
> *Payd me my wages in a world of mirth.*

> *What pleasures could I want, whose King I served,*
> > *Where joyes my fellows were?*
> *Thus argu'd into hopes, my thoughts reserved*
> > *No place for grief or fear.*
> *Therefore my sudden soul caught at the place,*
> *And made her youth and fierceness seek thy face.*

[1] Herbert to Woodnot, on the night of his induction to Bemerton:
recorded by Walton.

At first thou gav'st me milk and sweetnesses;
I had my wish and way:
My days were straw'd with flow'rs and happinesse;
There was no moneth but May.

But implicit in the description—as we see from "entice" and "entwine" [2] and the phrase, "argu'd into hopes"—is the admission that there *is* enchantment, an element of illusion in the "naturall delights," and we are not surprised when the triumphant fourth verse ends with the sudden bleak recognition of ills previously unperceived but inherent in the processes of life:

But with my yeares sorrow did twist and grow,
And made a partie unawares for wo.

The three central verses not merely describe the "woes"— sickness, the death of friends, disappointed hopes—they evoke with painful immediacy the feelings of the sufferer.

Sorrow was all my soul; I scarce beleeved,
Till grief did tell me roundly, that I lived.

With characteristic honesty Herbert admits the palliative of "Academick praise"—something that temporarily "dissolves" the mounting "rage"; but the current of feeling is now flowing in a direction completely opposite to that of the opening.

Whereas my birth and spirit rather took
The way that takes the town;
Thou didst betray me to a lingring book,
And wrap me in a gown.
I was entangled in the world of strife,
Before I had the power to change my life.

"Betray" and "entangle" make explicit a sense already present but not openly acknowledged in "entice" and "en-

---

[2] The earlier reading, in the Williams MS., is more explicit:

I looked on thy furniture so rich,
And made it rich to me:
Thy glorious houshold-stuffe did me bewitch
Into thy familie.

twine"; and instead of direct spontaneity—"I had my wish and way"—there is division and uncertainty:

> *I took thy sweetned pill, till I came where*
> *I could not go away, not persevere.*

In the eighth stanza the potentialities of emphasis latent in the spoken language are used to evoke the full sense of frustration and conflict:

> *Yet lest perchance I should too happie be*
> > *In my unhappinesse,*
> *Turning my purge to food, thou throwest me*
> > *Into more sicknesses.*
> *Thus doth thy power crosse-bias me, not making*
> *Thine own gift good, yet me from my wayes taking.*

Verse nine is quieter in tone, bringing into prominence an element in the whole complex attitude of the poet previously expressed only in the quiet control of the verse in which such turbulent feelings have been presented:

> *Now I am here, what thou wilt do with me*
> > *None of my books will show:*
> *I reade, and sigh, and wish I were a tree;*
> > *For sure then I should grow*
> *To fruit or shade: at least some bird would trust*
> *Her household to me, and I should be just.*

The opening lines of the last stanza can be read in two ways according as we bring into prominence the resigned or the rebellious tone:

> *Yet, though thou troublest me, I must be meek;*
> > *In weaknesse must be stout . . .*

But resignation and rebellion are alike half-measures, and it is here, where the feelings are so subtly poised, that the need for an absolute decision makes itself felt. Return for a moment to the eighth stanza. There the last line, with its strong alliterative emphasis, makes plain that the problem of the will (*"my* wayes") is the central theme of the poem. What we call happiness ("no moneth but May") is the result of events meeting our desires,—"I had my wish and way"; but the universe is not constructed on our plan, and when the will cannot bring itself to accept the cross-bias of existence frustration is inevitable. This common-place is something that everyone admits in a general way; to accept it fully, in terms of our own personal experience, is another matter. It is because Herbert has faced the issues so honestly and completely that the first alternative that presents itself in the moment of decision has only to be brought into focus to be seen as no real solution at all; and it is because its rejection has behind it the whole weight of the poem that the sudden reversal of feeling is so unforced, the undivided acceptance of the ending so inevitable.

> *Yet, though thou troublest me, I must be meek;*
> > *In weaknesse must be stout.*
> *Well, I will change the service, and go seek*
> > *Some other master out.*
> *Ah my deare God! though I am clean forgot,*
> *Let me not love thee, if I love thee not.*

In *The Collar* the same problem is approached from a slightly different angle.

> *I struck the board, and cry'd, No more.*
> > *I will abroad.*
> > *What? shall I ever sigh and pine?*
> *My lines and life are free; free as the rode,*
> > *Loose as the winde, as large as store. . . .*
>
> *But as I rav'd and grew more fierce and wilde*
> > *At every word,*
> *Me thoughts I heard one calling, Child!*
> > *And I reply'd,* My Lord.

At one time I felt that in this well-known ending—a similar sudden "return" to that of *Affliction* (i)—Herbert was evading the issue by simply throwing up the conflict and relapsing into the naïve simplicity of childhood. But of course I was wrong. The really childish behaviour is the storm of rage in which the tempestuous desires—superbly evoked in the free movement of the verse—are directed towards an undefined "freedom." What the poem enforces is that to be "loose as the wind" is to be as incoherent and purposeless; that freedom is to be found not in some undefined "abroad," but, in Ben Jonson's phrase, "here in my bosom, and at home."

The mature "acceptance" that one finds in Herbert's poetry has little in common with a mere disillusioned resignation. The effort towards it is positive in direction. Just as Herbert shows no fear of any imposed punishment for sin—of Hell—but only of the inevitable consequences of sin's "venome," [3] so the recurring stress of his poetry is on life. That "nothing performs the task of life" is the complaint of *Affliction* (iv);

> *O give me quicknesse, that I may with mirth*
>   *Praise thee brim-full*

is his prayer when "drooping and dull" (*Dulnesse*). And one reason why his religion appears so humane, in a century tending more and more to associate religion with fear and gloom, is that his God is a God of the living.

> *Wherefore be cheer'd, and praise him to the full*
> *Each day, each houre, each moment of the week,*
> *Who fain would have you be new, tender, quick.*
>   (Love Unknown)

It is because he actually did learn from experience to find life "at hand," [4] life realized in the commonplace details of every day, that so many of his "homely" metaphors have such freshness and are the opposite of "stuffy." But acceptance has a further, final meaning. It involves the recognition not only of one's limited sphere but (the paradox is only apparent) of one's own value. It is this that gives such wide significance to the poem, "Love bade me welcome: yet my soul drew back," placed deliberately at the end of the poems in "The Church":

---

[3] See the second verse of the poem, *Nature*, in which it is not, I think, fanciful to see some resemblance to the far more searching analysis of evil in *Macbeth*.

[4]   Poore man, thou searchest round
To finde out *death*, but missest *life* at hand. (*Vanitie* [i]).

> *You must sit down, sayes Love, and taste my meat:*
> *So I did sit and eat.*

The achieved attitude—"accepted and accepting"—marks the final release from anxiety.

With this release not only is significance restored to the present ("Onely the present is thy part and fee . . ." [5]), but death is robbed of its more extreme terrors. [6] The ending of the poem *Death* (which begins, "Death, thou wast once an uncouth hideous thing") is entirely unforced:

> *Therefore we can go die as sleep, and trust*
> *Half that we have*
> *Unto an honest faithfull grave;*
> *Making our pillows either down, or dust.*

The integration of attitude thus achieved lies behind the poetry of *Life* ("I made a posie while the day ran by"), and of the well-known *Vertue*—a poem that shows in a quite personal way the characteristically Metaphysical "reconciliation of opposites": the day has lost none of its freshness because its end is freely recognized as implicit in its beginning. But it is in *The Flower* that the sense of new life springing from the resolution of conflict is most beautifully expressed. [7]

> *How fresh, O Lord, how sweet and clean*
> *Are thy returns! ev'n as the flowers in spring;*
> *To which, besides their own demean,*
> *The late-past frosts tributes of pleasure bring.*
> *Grief melts away*
> *Like snow in May,*
> *As if there were no such cold thing.*

[5] The Discharge.

[6] I should like to refer to D. W. Harding's review of *Little Gidding* in *Scrutiny* (Spring, 1943): "For the man convinced of spiritual values life is a coherent pattern in which the ending has its due place and, because it is part of a pattern, itself leads into the beginning. An overstrong terror of death is often one expression of the fear of living, for death is one of the life-processes that seem too terrifying to be borne."

[7] I think it should be noticed that in the original order, apparently Herbert's own, *The Flower* is immediately preceded by *The Crosse*, another poem on the theme of acceptance, ending, "Thy will be done."

> *Who would have thought my shrivel'd heart*
> *Could have recover'd greenesse? It was gone*
> *Quite under ground; as flowers depart*
> *To see their mother-root, when they have blown;*
> *Where they together*
> *All the hard weather,*
> *Dead to the world, keep house unknown.*

He still feels the need for security, for a guaranteed permanence:

> *O that I once past changing were,*
> *Fast in thy Paradise, where no flower can wither.*

But in the poem as a whole even the fact that the good hours do not last, that they are bound to alternate with "frosts" and depression, is accepted without bitterness:

> *These are thy wonders, Lord of power,*
> *Killing and quickning. . . .*

As a result the renewed vitality, waited for without fret or fuss, has something of the naturalness and inevitability of the mounting sap. The sixth stanza takes up the spring imagery:

> *And now in age I bud again,*
> *After so many deaths I live and write;*
> *I once more smell the dew and rain,*
> *And relish versing: O my onely light,*
> *It cannot be*
> *That I am he*
> *On whom thy tempests fell all night.*

The sense of refreshment, conveyed in imagery of extraordinary sensuous delicacy, is as completely realized as the suffering expressed in the poems of conflict. And like the flower it comes from "under ground," from the deeper levels of the personality.

The account I have given of the positive direction of Herbert's poetry is not meant to imply that anything like a continuous development can be traced in the poems, few of which can be dated with any precision.[8] In any case, development—when it is of the whole man, not simply of a line of thought—rarely shows the smooth curve that biographers like to imagine. We do know, however, that his life at Bemerton was one of uncommon sweetness and serenity, expressing what Dr. Hutchinson calls "an achieved character of humility, tenderness, moral sensitiveness, and personal consecration, which he was very far from having attained or even envisaged when he was dazzled by the attractions of the great world." The poems in which the fluctuating stages of this progress are recorded are important human documents because they handle with honesty and insight questions that, in one form or another, we all have to meet if we wish to come to terms with life.

[8] A few seem to be early work, some contain references to the priesthood, and poems that appear in the Bodleian, but not in the Williams, Manuscript may be assumed to be later than the others: see Dr. Hutchinson's Introduction, pp. l–lvi, and pp. lxvii–lxix. It is worth remarking that *The Pilgrimage, Vertue, Life* and *The Flower* are among the poems found only in the Bodleian MS.

Editor's Note

The Guilty Vicarage: Notes on the Detective Story, by an Addict first appeared in Harper's, May 1948. Copyright, 1948, by Harper and Brothers. Reprinted by permission of the author.

Wystan Hugh Auden was born in York, England, in 1907, and educated at Christ Church College, Oxford. He taught school in England and worked in government film production. Since 1939 Auden has been a resident of the United States, teaching at a number of colleges and universities, and since 1946 he has been an American citizen. Auden has published three verse dramas in collaboration with Christopher Isherwood, and many volumes of verse, among them Collected Poems (1945), The Age of Anxiety (1948), Nones (1951), and The Shield of Achilles (1955). He has edited a number of anthologies, and is the author of one volume of criticism, The Enchafèd Flood (1950).

SIXTEEN

W. H. Auden

The Guilty Vicarage:
Notes on the Detective Story,
by an Addict

A Confession

FOR ME, as for many others, the reading of detective stories is an addiction like tobacco or alcohol. The symptoms of this are: Firstly, the intensity of the craving—if I have any work to do, I must be careful not to get hold of a detective story for, once I begin one, I cannot work or sleep till I have finished it. Secondly, its specificity—the story must conform to certain formulas (I find it very difficult, for example, to read one that is not set in rural England). And, thirdly, its immediacy. I forgot the story as soon as I have finished it, and have no wish to read it again. If, as sometimes happens, I start reading one and find after a few pages that I have read it before, I cannot go on.

Such reactions convince me that, in my case at least, detective stories have nothing to do with works of art. It is possible, however, that an analysis of the detective story, *i.e.,* of the kind of detective story I enjoy, may throw light, not only on its magical function, but also, by contrast, on the function of art.

Definition

THE vulgar definition, "a Whodunit," is correct. The basic formula is this: a murder occurs; many are suspected; all but one suspect, who is the murderer, are eliminated; the murderer is arrested or dies.

This definition excludes:

(1) studies of murderers whose guilt is known, *e.g.*, *Malice Aforethought*. There are borderline cases in which the murderer is known and there are no false suspects, but the proof is lacking, *e.g.*, many of the stories of Freeman Wills Crofts. Most of these are permissible.

(2) thrillers, spy stories, stories of master crooks, etc., when the identification of the criminal is subordinate to the defeat of his criminal designs.

The interest in the thriller is the ethical and eristic conflict between good and evil, between Us and Them. The interest in the study of a murderer is the observation, by the innocent many, of the sufferings of the guilty one. The interest in the detective story is the dialectic of innocence and guilt.

As in the Aristotelian description of tragedy, there is Concealment (the innocent seem guilty and the guilty seem innocent) and Manifestation (the real guilt is brought to consciousness). There is also peripeteia, in this case not a reversal of fortune but a double reversal from apparent guilt to innocence and from apparent innocence to guilt. The formula may be diagrammed as follows.

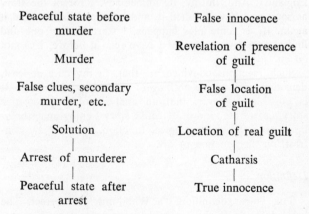

Peaceful state before murder	False innocence
Murder	Revelation of presence of guilt
False clues, secondary murder, etc.	False location of guilt
Solution	Location of real guilt
Arrest of murderer	Catharsis
Peaceful state after arrest	True innocence

In Greek tragedy the audience knows the truth; the actors do not, but discover or bring to pass the inevitable. In modern, *e.g.,* Elizabethan, tragedy the audience knows neither less nor more than the most knowing of the actors. In the detective story the audience does not know the truth at all; one of the actors—the murderer—does; and the detective, of his own free will, discovers and reveals what the murderer, of his own free will, tries to conceal.

Greek tragedy and the detective story have one characteristic in common, in which they both differ from modern tragedy, namely, the characters are not changed in or by their actions: in Greek tragedy because their actions are fated, in the detective story because the decisive event, the murder, has already occurred. Time and space therefore are simply the when and where of revealing either what has to happen or what has actually happened. In consequence, the detective story probably should, and usually does, obey the classical unities, whereas modern tragedy in which the characters develop with time can only do so by a technical tour de force; and the thriller, like the picaresque novel, even demands frequent changes of time and place.

Why Murder?

THERE are three classes of crime: (a) offenses against God and one's neighbor or neighbors; (b) offenses against God and society; (c) offenses against God. (All crimes, of course, are offenses against oneself.)

Murder is a member and the only member of Class B. The character common to all crimes in Class A is that it is possible, at least theoretically, either that restitution can be made to the injured party (*e.g.,* stolen goods can be returned), or that the injured party can forgive the criminal (*e.g.,* in the case of rape). Consequently, society as a whole is only indirectly involved; directly, its representatives (the police, etc.) act in the interests of the injured party.

Murder is unique in that it abolishes the party it in-
jures, so that society has to take the place of the victim
and on his behalf demand restitution or grant forgiveness;
it is the one crime in which society has a direct interest.

Many detective stories begin with a death that appears
to be suicide and is later discovered to have been murder.
Suicide is a crime belonging to Class C in which neither
the criminal's neighbors nor society has any interest, direct
or indirect. As long as a death is believed to be suicide,
even private curiosity is improper; as soon as it is proved
to be murder, public inquiry becomes a duty.

THE detective story has five elements—the milieu, the
victim, the murderer, the suspects, the detectives.

The Milieu (*Human*)

The detective story requires:

(1) A closed society so that the possibility of an outside murderer (and hence of the society being totally
innocent) is excluded; and a closely related society so
that all its members are potentially suspect (*cf.* the thriller,
which requires an open society in which any stranger may
be a friend or enemy in disguise).

Such conditions are met by: (a) the group of blood
relatives (the Christmas dinner in the country house);
(b) the closely knit geographical group (the old world
village); (c) the occupational group (the theatrical company); (d) the group isolated by the neutral place (the
Pullman car).

In this last type the concealment-manifestation formula
applies not only to the murder but also to the relations
between the members of the group who first appear to be
strangers to each other, but are later found to be related.

(2) It must appear to be an innocent society in a state
of grace, *i.e.,* a society where there is no need of the law,
no contradiction between the aesthetic individual and the
ethical universal, and where murder, therefore, is the un-

heard-of act which precipitates a crisis (for it reveals that some member has fallen and is no longer in a state of grace). The law becomes a reality and for a time all must live in its shadow, till the fallen one is identified. With his arrest, innocence is restored, and the law retires forever.

The characters in a detective story should, therefore, be eccentric (aesthetically interesting individuals) and good (instinctively ethical)—good, that is, either in appearance, later shown to be false, or in reality, first concealed by an appearance of bad.

It is a sound instinct that has made so many detective-story writers choose a college as a setting. The ruling passion of the ideal professor is the pursuit of knowledge for its own sake so that he is related to other human beings only indirectly through their common relation to the truth; and those passions, like lust and avarice and envy, which relate individuals directly and may lead to murder are, in his case, ideally excluded. If a murder occurs in a college, therefore, it is a sign that some colleague is not only a bad man but also a bad professor. Further, as the basic premise of academic life is that truth is universal and to be shared with all, the *gnosis* of a concrete crime and the *gnosis* of abstract ideas nicely parallel and parody each other.

(The even more ideal contradiction of a murder in a monastery is excluded by the fact that monks go regularly to confession and, while the murderer might well not confess his crime, the suspects who are innocent of murder but guilty of lesser sins cannot be supposed to conceal them without making the monastery absurd. Incidentally, is it an accident that the detective story has flourished most in predominantly Protestant countries?)

The detective story writer is also wise to choose a society with an elaborate ritual and to describe this in detail. A ritual is a sign of harmony between the aesthetic and the ethical in which body and mind, individual will and general laws, are not in conflict. The murderer uses his knowledge of the ritual to commit the crime and can be caught only by someone who acquires an equal or superior familiarity with it.

The Milieu (*Natural*)

IN THE detective story, as in its mirror image, the Quest for the Grail, maps (the ritual of space) and timetables (the ritual of time) are desirable. Nature should reflect its human inhabitants, *i.e.*, it should be the Great Good Place; for the more Eden-like it is, the greater the contradiction of murder. The country is preferable to the town, a well-to-do neighborhood (but not too well-to-do—or there will be a suspicion of ill-gotten gains) better than a slum. The corpse must shock not only because it is a corpse but also because, even for a corpse, it is shockingly out of place, as when a dog makes a mess on a drawing room carpet.

Mr. Raymond Chandler has written that he intends to take the body out of the vicarage garden and give murder back to those who are good at it. If he wishes to write detective stories, *i.e.*, stories where the reader's principal interest is to learn who did it, he could not be more mistaken; for in a society of professional criminals, the only possible motives for desiring to identify the murderer are blackmail or revenge, which both apply to individuals, not to the group as a whole, and can equally well inspire murder. Actually, whatever he may say, I think Mr. Chandler is interested in writing, not detective stories, but serious studies of a criminal milieu, the Great Wrong Place, and his powerful but extremely depressing books should be read and judged, not as escape literature, but as works of art.

The Victim

THE victim has to try to satisfy two contradictory requirements. He has to involve everyone in suspicion, which requires that he be a bad character; and he has to make everyone feel guilty, which requires that he be a good character. He cannot be a criminal because he could then be dealt with by the law and murder would be unnecessary. (Blackmail is the only exception.) The more general the temptation to murder he arouses, the better; *e.g.,* the desire for freedom is a better motive than money alone or sex alone. On the whole, the best victim is the negative Father or Mother Image.

If there is more than one murder, the subsequent victims should be more innocent than the initial victim, *i.e.,* the murderer should start with a real grievance and, as a consequence of righting it by illegitimate means, be forced to murder against his will where he has no grievance but his own guilt.

The Murderer

MURDER is negative creation, and every murderer is therefore the rebel who claims the right to be omnipotent. His pathos is his refusal to suffer. The problem for the writer is to conceal his demonic pride from the other characters and from the reader, since, if a person has this pride, it tends to appear in everything he says and does. To surprise the reader when the identity of the murderer is revealed, yet at the same time to convince him that everything he has previously been told about the murderer is consistent with his being a murderer, is the test of a good detective story.

As to the murderer's end, of the three alternatives—execution, suicide, and madness—the first is preferable; for if he commits suicide he refuses to repent, and if he goes mad he cannot repent, but if he does not repent society cannot forgive. Execution, on the other hand, is the act of atonement, by which the murderer is forgiven by society.

(*A suggestion for Mr. Chandler:* Among a group of efficient professional killers who murder for strictly professional reasons, there is one to whom, like Leopold and Loeb, murder is an *acte gratuite.* Presently murders begin to occur which have not been commissioned. The group is morally outraged and bewildered; it has to call in the police to detect the amateur murderer and rescue the professionals from a mutual suspicion which threatens to disrupt their organization and to injure their capacity to murder.)

The Suspects

THE detective-story society is a society consisting of apparently innocent individuals, *i.e.*, their aesthetic interest as individuals does not conflict with their ethical obligations to the universal. The murder is the act of disruption by which innocence is lost, and the individual and the law become opposed to each other. In the case of the murderer this opposition is completely real (till he is arrested and consents to be punished); in the case of the suspects it is mostly apparent.

But in order for the appearance to exist, there must be some element of reality; *e.g.*, it is unsatisfactory if the suspicion is caused by chance or the murderer's malice alone. The suspects must be guilty of something, because, now that the aesthetic and the ethical are in opposition, if they are completely innocent (obedient to the ethical) they lose their aesthetic interest and the reader will ignore them.

For suspects, the principal causes of guilt are:

(1) the wish or even the intention to murder;

(2) crimes of Class A or vices of Class C (*e.g.*, illicit amours) which the suspect is afraid or ashamed to reveal (see *Why Murder?*);

(3) a *hubris* of intellect which tries to solve the crime itself and despises the official police (assertion of the supremacy of the aesthetic over the ethical). If great enough, this *hubris* leads to its subject getting murdered;

(4) a *hubris* of innocence which refuses to co-operate with the investigation;

(5) a lack of faith in another loved suspect, which leads its subject to hide or confuse clues.

The Detective

COMPLETELY satisfactory detectives are extremely rare. Indeed, I only know of three: Sherlock Holmes (Conan Doyle), Inspector French (Freeman Wills Crofts), and Father Brown (Chesterton).

The job of the detective is to restore the state of grace in which the aesthetic and the ethical are as one. Since the murderer who caused their disjunction is the aesthetically defiant individual, his opponent, the detective, must be either the official representative of the ethical or the exceptional individual who is himself in a state of grace. If he is the former, he is a professional; if he is the latter, he is an amateur. In either case, the detective must be the total stranger who cannot possibly be involved in the crime; this excludes the local police and should, I think, exclude the detective who is a friend of one of the suspects. The professional detective has the advantage that, since he is not an individual but a representative of the ethical, he does not need a motive for investigating the crime; but for the same reason he has the disadvantage of being unable to overlook the minor ethical violations of the suspects, and therefore it is harder for him to gain their confidence.

Most amateur detectives, on the other hand, are failures either because they are priggish supermen, like Lord Peter Wimsey and Philo Vance, who have no motive for being detectives except caprice, or because, like the detectives of the hard-boiled school, they are motivated by avarice or ambition and might just as well be murderers.

The amateur detective genius may have weaknesses to give him aesthetic interest, but they must not be of a kind which outrage ethics. The most satisfactory weaknesses are the solitary oral vices of eating and drinking or childish boasting. In his sexual life, the detective must be either celibate or happily married.

Between the amateur detective and the professional policeman stands the criminal lawyer whose *telos* is, not to discover who is guilty, but to prove that his client is innocent. His ethical justification is that human law is ethically imperfect, *i.e.*, not an absolute manifestation of the universal and divine, and subject to chance aesthetic limitations, *e.g.*, the intelligence or stupidity of individual policemen and juries (in consequence of which an innocent man may sometimes be judged guilty).

To correct this imperfection, the decision is arrived at through an aesthetic combat, *i.e.*, the intellectual gifts of the defense versus those of the prosecution, just as in earlier days doubtful cases were solved by physical combat between the accused and the accuser.

The lawyer-detective (*e.g.*, Joshua Clunk) is never quite satisfactory, therefore, because his interest in the truth or in all the innocent is subordinate to his interest in his client, whom he cannot desert, even if he should really be the guilty party, without ceasing to be a lawyer.

Sherlock Holmes

HOLMES is the exceptional individual who is in a state of grace because he is a genius in whom scientific curiosity is raised to the status of a heroic passion. He is erudite but his knowledge is absolutely specialized (*e.g.*, his ignorance of the Copernican system); he is in all matters outside his field as helpless as a child (*e.g.*, his untidiness), and he pays the price for his scientific detachment (his neglect of feeling) by being the victim of melancholia which attacks him whenever he is unoccupied with a case (*e.g.*, his violin playing and cocaine taking).

His motive for being a detective is, positively, a love of the neutral truth (he has no interest in the feelings of the guilty or the innocent), and, negatively, a need to escape from his own feelings of melancholy. His attitude toward people and his technique of observation and deduction are those of the chemist or physicist. If he chooses human beings rather than inanimate matter as his material, it is because investigating the inanimate is unheroically easy since it cannot tell lies, which human beings can and do, so that in dealing with them, observation must be twice as sharp and logic twice as rigorous.

Inspector French

HIS class and culture are the natural ones for a Scotland Yard inspector. (The old Oxonian Inspector is insufferable.) His motive is love of duty. Holmes detects for his own sake and shows the maximum indifference to all feelings except a negative fear of his own. French detects for the sake of the innocent members of society, and is indifferent only to his own feelings and those of the murderer. (He would much rather stay at home with his wife.) He is exceptional only in his exceptional love of duty which makes him take exceptional pains; he does only what all could do as well if they had the same patient industry (his checking of alibis for tiny flaws which careless hurry had missed). He outwits the murderer, partly because the latter is not quite so painstaking as he, and partly because the murderer must act alone, while he has the help of all the innocent people in the world who are doing their duty (*e.g.*, the postmen, raliway clerks, milkmen, etc., who become, accidentally, witnesses to the truth).

Father Brown

LIKE Holmes, an amateur; yet, like French, not an individual genius. His activities as a detective are an incidental part of his activities as a priest who cares for souls. His prime motive is compassion, of which the guilty are in greater need than the innocent, and he investigates murders, not for his own sake, nor even for the sake of the innocent, but for the sake of the murderer who can save his soul if he will confess and repent. He solves his cases, not by approaching them objectively like a scientist or a policeman, but by subjectively imagining himself to be the murderer, a process which is good not only for the murderer but for Father Brown himself because, as he says, "it gives a man his remorse beforehand."

Holmes and French can only help the murderer as teachers, *i.e.*, they can teach him that murder will out and does not pay. More they cannot do since neither is tempted to murder; Holmes is too gifted, French too well trained in the habit of virtue. Father Brown can go further and help the murderer as an example, *i.e.*, as a man who is also tempted to murder, but is able by faith to resist temptation.

The Reader

THE most curious fact about the detective story is that it makes greatest appeal precisely to those classes of people who are most immune to other forms of daydream literature. The typical detective story addict is a doctor or clergyman or scientist or artist, *i.e.*, a fairly successful professional man with intellectual interests and well-read in his own field, who could never stomach the *Saturday Evening Post* or *True Confessions* or movie magazines or comics. If I ask myself why I cannot enjoy stories about strong silent men and lovely girls who make love in a beautiful landscape and come into millions of dollars, I cannot answer that I have no phantasies of being handsome and loved and rich, because of course I have (though my life is, perhaps, sufficiently fortunate to make me less envious in a naïve way than some). No, I can only say that I am too conscious of the absurdity and evil of such wishes to enjoy seeing them reflected in print.

I can, to some degree, resist yielding to these or similar desires which tempt me, but I cannot prevent myself from having them to resist; and it is the fact that I have them which makes me feel guilty, so that instead of dreaming about indulging my desires, I dream about the removal of the guilt which I feel at their existence. This I still do, and must do, because guilt is a subjective feeling where any further step is only a reduplication—feeling guilty about my guilt. I suspect that the typical reader of detective stories is, like myself, a person who suffers from a sense of sin. From the point of view of ethics, desires and acts are good or bad, and I must choose the good and reject the bad, but the *I* which makes this choice is ethically neutral; it only becomes good or bad in its choice. To have a sense of sin means to feel guilty at there being an ethical choice to make, a guilt which, however "good" I may become, remains unchanged. As St. Paul says: "Except I had known the law, I had not known sin."

IT IS sometimes said that detective stories are read by respectable law-abiding citizens in order to gratify in phantasy the violent or murderous wishes they dare not, or are ashamed to, translate into action. This may be true for the reader of thrillers (which I rarely enjoy), but it is quite false for the reader of detective stories. On the contrary, the magical satisfaction the latter provide (which makes them escape literature not works of art) is the illusion of being dissociated from the murderer.

The magic formula is an innocence which is discovered to contain guilt; then a suspicion of being the guilty one; and finally a real innocence from which the guilty other has been expelled, a cure effected, not by me or my neighbors, but by the miraculous intervention of a genius from outside who removes guilt by giving knowledge of guilt. (The detective story subscribes, in fact, to the Socratic daydream: "Sin is ignorance.")

If one thinks of a work of art which deals with murder, *Crime and Punishment* for example, its effect on the reader is to compel an identification with the murderer which he would prefer not to recognize. The identification of phantasy is always an attempt to avoid one's own suffering: the identification of art is a compelled sharing in the suffering of another. Kafka's *The Trial* is another instructive example of the difference between a work of art and the detective story. In the latter it is certain that a crime has been committed and, temporarily, uncertain to whom the guilt should be attached; as soon as this is known, the innocence of everyone else is certain. (Should it turn out that after all no crime has been committed, then all would be innocent.) In *The Trial,* on the other hand, it is the guilt that is certain and the crime that is uncertain; the aim of the hero's investigation is, not to prove his innocence (which would be impossible for he knows he is guilty), but to discover what, if anything, he has done to make himself guilty. K, the hero, is, in fact, a portrait of the kind of person who reads detective stories for escape.

THE phantasy, then, which the detective story addict indulges is the phantasy of being restored to the Garden of Eden, to a state of innocence, where he may know love as love and not as the law. The driving force behind this daydream is the feeling of guilt, the cause of which is unknown to the dreamer. The phantasy of escape is the same, whether one explains the guilt in Christian, Freudian, or any other terms. One's way of trying to face the reality, on the other hand, will, of course, depend very much on one's creed.

Editor's Note

Oedipus Rex: The Tragic Rhythm of Action is part of a chapter from *The Idea of a Theater* (1949) by Francis Fergusson. The chapter was first published in *Accent,* Spring 1948. Reprinted by permission of the author and of the publisher, Princeton University Press. The translations from Sophocles are the author's.

Francis Fergusson was born in Albuquerque, New Mexico, in 1904, and educated at Harvard and Oxford (as a Rhodes scholar). He has been an associate director of the American Laboratory Theatre, drama critic of *The Bookman,* and a member of the Institute for Advanced Study, and has taught drama and literature at the New School for Social Research, Bennington College, Princeton, and Rutgers, where he is now a professor of comparative literature. Fergusson has published a translation of Sophocles' *Electra,* an edition of Joyce's *Exiles,* and two volumes of criticism, *The Idea of a Theater* and *Dante's Drama of the Mind* (1953).

SEVENTEEN

Francis Fergusson

Oedipus Rex:
The Tragic Rhythm of Action

> ". . . quel secondo regno
> dove l'umano spirito si purga."
> —PURGATORIO, CANTO I.

I suppose there can be little doubt that *Oedipus Rex* is a crucial instance of drama, if not *the* play which best exemplifies this art in its essential nature and completeness. It owes its position partly to the fact that Aristotle founded his definitions upon it. But since the time of Aristotle it has been imitated, rewritten and discussed by many different generations, not only of dramatists, but also of moralists, psychologists, historians, and other students of human nature and destiny.

Though the play is thus generally recognized as an archetype, there has been little agreement about its meaning or its form. It seems to beget, in every period, a different interpretation and a different dramaturgy. From the Seventeenth Century until the end of the Eighteenth, a Neoclassic and Rationalist interpretation of *Oedipus,* of Greek Tragedy, and of Aristotle, was generally accepted; and upon this interpretation was based the dramaturgy of Corneille and Racine. Nietzsche, under the inspiration of Wagner's *Tristan und Isolde,* developed a totally different view of it, and thence a different theory of drama. These two views of Greek Tragedy, Racine's and Nietzsche's, still provide indispensable perspectives upon *Oedipus.* They show a great deal about modern principles of dramatic composition; and they show, when compared, how central and how essential Sophocles' drama is.

In our day a conception of *Oedipus* seems to be developing which is neither that of Racine nor that of Nietzsche. This view is based upon the studies which the Cambridge School—Frazer, Cornford, Harrison, Murray—made of the ritual origins of Greek Tragedy. It also owes a great deal to the current interest in myth as a way of ordering human experience. *Oedipus,* we now see, is both myth and ritual. It assumes and employs these two ancient ways of understanding and representing human experience, which are prior to the arts and sciences and philosophies of modern times. To understand it (it now appears) we must endeavor to recapture the habit of significant make-believe, of the direct perception of action, which underlies Sophocles' theatre.

If *Oedipus* is to be understood in this way, then we shall have to revise our ideas of Sophocles' dramaturgy. The notion of Aristotle's theory of drama, and hence of Greek dramaturgy, which still prevails (in spite of such studies as Butcher's of the *Poetics*), is largely colored by Neoclassic taste and rationalistic habits of mind. If we are to take it that Sophocles was imitating action *before* theory, instead of after it, like Racine, then both the elements and the form of his composition appear in a new light.

In the present essay the attempt is made to draw the deductions, for Sophocles' theatre and dramaturgy, which the present view of *Oedipus* implies. We shall find that the various traditional views of this play are not so much wrong as partial.

Oedipus, Myth and Play

When Sophocles came to write his play he had the myth of Oedipus to start with. Laius and Jocasta, King and Queen of Thebes, are told by the oracle that their son will grow up to kill his father and marry his mother. The infant, his feet pierced, is left on Mount Kitharon to die.

But a shepherd finds him and takes care of him; at last gives him to another shepherd, who takes him to Corinth, and there the King and Queen bring him up as their own son. But Oedipus—"Clubfoot"—is plagued in his turn by the oracle; he hears that he is fated to kill his father and marry his mother; and to escape that fate he leaves Corinth never to return. On his journey he meets an old man with his servants; gets into a dispute with him, and kills him and all his followers. He comes to Thebes at the time when the Sphinx is preying upon that City; solves the riddle which the Sphinx propounds, and saves the City. He marries the widowed Queen, Jocasta; has several children by her; rules prosperously for many years. But when Thebes is suffering under a plague and a drought, the oracle reports that the gods are angry because Laius' slayer is unpunished. Oedipus, as King, undertakes to find him; discovers that he is himself the culprit, and that Jocasta is his own mother. He blinds himself and goes into exile. From this time forth he becomes a sort of sacred relic, like the bones of a saint; perilous, but "good medicine" for the community that possesses him. He dies, at last, at Athens, in a grove sacred to the Eumenides, female spirits of fertility and night.

It is obvious even from this sketch that the myth, which covers several generations, has as much narrative material as *Gone with the Wind*. It is the way of myths that they generate whole progenies of elaborations and varying versions. They are so suggestive, seem to say so much, yet so mysteriously, that the mind cannot rest content with any single form, but must add, or interpret, or simplify— reduce to terms which the reason can accept. Mr. William Troy suggests that "what is possibly most in order at the moment is a thorough-going refurbishment of the medieval four-fold method of interpretation, which was first developed, it will be recalled, for just such a purpose—to make at least partially available to the reason that complex of human problems which are embedded, deep and imponderable, in the Myth." [1] It is my thesis that Sophocles, in

[1] "Myth, Method and the Future." By William Troy. *Chimera*, Spring, 1946.

his play, succeeded in preserving the suggestive mystery of the Oedipus *myth*, while presenting it in a wonderfully unified dramatic form; and this drama has all the dimensions which the fourfold method was intended to explore.

Everyone knows that when Sophocles planned the plot of the play itself, he started almost at the end of the story, when the plague descends upon the City of Thebes, which Oedipus and Jocasta had been ruling with great success for a number of years. The action of the play takes less than a day, and consists of Oedipus' quest for Laius' slayer;— his consulting the Oracle of Apollo, his examination of the Prophet Tiresias, and of a series of witnesses, ending with the old Shepherd who gave him to the King and Queen of Corinth. The play ends when Oedipus is unmistakably revealed as himself the culprit.

At this literal level, the play is intelligible as a murder mystery. Oedipus takes the role of District Attorney; and when he at last convicts himself, we have a *coup de théatre*, of unparalleled excitement. But no one who sees or reads the play can rest content with its literal coherence. Questions as to its meaning arise at once: Is Oedipus really guilty, or simply a victim of the gods, of his famous complex, of fate, of original sin? How much did he know, all along? How much did Jocasta know?—The first, and most deeply instinctive effort of the mind, when confronted with this play, is to endeavor to reduce its meanings to some set of rational categories.

The critics of the Age of Reason tried to understand it as a fable of the enlightened moral will, in accordance with the philosophy of that time. Voltaire's version of the play, following Corneille, and his comments upon it, may be taken as typical. He sees it as essentially a struggle between a strong and righteous Oedipus, and the malicious and very human gods, aided and abetted by the corrupt priest Tiresias; he makes it an anti-religious tract, with an unmistakable moral to satisfy the needs of the discursive intellect. In order to make Oedipus sympathetic to his audience, he elides, as much as possible, the incest motif; and he adds an irrelevant love story. He was aware that his version and interpretation were not Sophocles', but with the complacent provinciality of his period he attributes the differences to the darkness of the age in which *Sophocles* lived.

Other attempts to rationalize *Oedipus Rex* are subtler than Voltaire's, and take us farther toward an understanding of the play. Freud's reduction of the play to the concepts of his psychology reveals a great deal, opens up perspectives which we are still exploring. If one reads *Oedipus* in the light of Fustel de Coulanges's *The Ancient City,* one may see it as the expression of the ancient patriarchal religion of the Greeks. And other interpretations of the play, theological, philosophical, historical, are available, none of them wrong, but all partial, all reductions of Sophocles' masterpiece to an alien set of categories. For the peculiar virtue of Sophocles' presentation of the myth is that it preserves the ultimate mystery by focusing upon the tragic human at a level beneath or prior to any rationalization whatever. The plot is so arranged that we see the action as it were illumined from many sides at once.

By starting the play at the end of the story, and showing on stage only the last crucial episode in Oedipus' life, Sophocles reveals the past and present action of the protagonist together; and in each other's light, past and present are at last felt as one. Oedipus' quest for the slayer of Laius becomes a quest for the hidden reality of his own past; and as that slowly comes into focus, like repressed material under psychoanalysis—with sensory and emotional immediacy, yet in the light of acceptance and understanding—his immediate quest also reaches its end; he comes to see himself (the savior of the City) and the guilty one, the plague of Thebes, at once and at one.

This presentation of the myth of Oedipus constitutes, in one sense, an interpretation of it. What Sophocles saw as the essence of Oedipus' nature and destiny, is not what Seneca or Dryden or Cocteau saw; and one may grant that even Sophocles did not exhaust the possibilities of the materials of the myth. But it is my contention that Sophocles' version of the myth does not constitute a "reduction" in the same sense as the rest.

I have said that the action which Sophocles shows is a quest, the quest for Laius' slayer; and that as Oedipus' past is unrolled before us his whole life is seen as a kind of quest for his true nature and destiny. But since the object of this quest is not clear until the end, the seeking action takes many forms, as its object appears in different lights. The object indeed,—the final perception, the "truth,"—looks so different at the end from what it did at the beginning, that Oedipus' action itself may seem not a *quest,* but its opposite, a *flight.* Thus it would be hard to say simply that Oedipus either succeeds or fails. He succeeds; but his success is his undoing. He fails to find what, in one way, he sought, yet from another point of view his search is brilliantly successful. The same ambiguities surround his effort to discover who and what he is. He seems to find that he is nothing; yet thereby finds himself. And what of his relation to the gods? His quest may be regarded as a heroic attempt to escape their decrees, or as an attempt, based upon some deep natural faith, to discover what their wishes are, and what true obedience would be. In one sense Oedipus suffers forces he can neither control nor understand, the puppet of fate; yet at the same time he wills and intelligently intends his every move.

It is my contention that the meaning or spiritual content of the play is not to be sought by trying to resolve such ambiguities as these. The spiritual content of the play is the tragic action which Sophocles directly presents; and this action is in its essence *zweideutig:* triumph and destruction, darkness and enlightenment, mourning and rejoicing, at any moment we care to consider it. But this action has also a shape: a beginning, middle and end, in time . . . It moves, in Mr. Burke's phrase, "from Purpose, to Passion, to Perception." This is the rhythm, or shape, of the action of *Oedipus.* The play as a whole starts with the intelligible purpose of finding Laius' slayer; we suffer the successive facts which destroy that purpose as we had conceived it; from this suffering and uncertainty the final perception comes: we see the slayer in a totally new light. Each scene in the play (smaller figures repeated, with variations, in the movement of the whole) moves also in the Tragic Rhythm, from Purpose to Passion to Perception.

In order to illustrate these points in more detail, it is convenient to examine the scene between Oedipus and Tiresias with the chorus following it. This scene, being early in the play (the big agon) presents, as it were, a preview of the whole action and constitutes a clear and complete example of action in the Tragic Rhythm.

Hero and Scapegoat: The Agon between Oedipus and Tiresias

The scene between Oedipus and Tiresias comes after the opening sections of the play. We have seen the citizens of Thebes beseeching their King to find some way to lift the plague which is on the City. We have had Oedipus' entrance (majestic, but for his tell-tale limp) to reassure them, and we have heard the report which Creon brings from the Delphic Oracle: that the cause of the plague is the unpunished murder of Laius, the former King. Oedipus offers rewards to anyone who will reveal the culprit, and he threatens with dire punishment anyone who conceals or protects him. In the meantime he decides, with the enthusiastic assent of the chorus, to summon Tiresias as the first witness.

Tiresias is that suffering seer whom Sophocles uses in *Antigone* also to reveal a truth which other mortals find it hard and uncomfortable to see. He is physically blind, but Oedipus and chorus alike assume that if anyone can see who the culprit is, it is Tiresias, with his uncanny inner vision of the future. As Tiresias enters, led by a boy, the chorus greets him in these words:

> CHORUS: But the man to convict him is here. Look:
> they are bringing the one human in whom
> the truth is native, the godlike seer.

At this point in the play Oedipus is at the opposite pole of experience from Tiresias; Hero, monarch, helmsman of the State; the solver of the Sphinx's riddle, the triumphant human. He explains his purpose in the following proud clear terms:

OEDIPUS: O Tiresias, you know all things: what may be told, and the unspeakable: things of earth and things of heaven. You understand the City (though you do not see it) in its present mortal illness—from which to save us and protect us, we find, Lord, none but you. For you must know, in case you haven't heard it from the messengers, that Apollo, when we asked him, told us there was one way only with this plague: to discover Laius' slayers, and put them to death or send them into exile. Therefore you must not jealously withhold your omens, whether of birds or other visionary way, but save yourself and the City—save me, save all of us—from the defilement of the dead. In your hand we are. There is no handsomer work for a man, than to bring, with what he has, what help he can.

This speech is the prologue of the scene, and the basis of the agon or struggle which follows. This struggle in effect analyzes Oedipus' purpose; places it in a wider con-scene Oedipus loses his original purpose altogether, and text, reveals it as faulty and dubious. At the end of the suffers a wave of rage and fear, which will have to be rationalized in its turn before he can pull himself together and act again with a clear purpose.

In the first part of the struggle, Oedipus takes the initiative, while Tiresias, on the defensive, tries to avoid replying:

TIRESIAS: Oh, oh. How terrible to know, when nothing can come of knowing! Indeed, I had lost the vision of these things, or I should never have come.

OEDIPUS: What things? . . . In what discouragement have you come to us here!

TIR. : Let me go home. I shall endure this most easily, and so will you, if you do as I say.

OED. : But what you ask is not right. To refuse your word is disloyalty to the City that has fed you.

TIR. : But I see that your demands are exorbitant, and lest I too suffer such a—

OED. : For the sake of the gods, if you know, don't turn away! Speak to us, we are your suppliants here.

TIR. : None of you understands. But I—I never will tell my misery. Or yours.

OED. : What are you saying? You know, but tell us nothing? You intend treachery to us, and death to the City?

TIR. : I intend to grieve neither myself nor you. Why then do you try to know? You will never learn from me.

OED. : Ah, evil old man! You would anger a stone! You will say *nothing*? Stand futile, speechless before us?

TIR. : You curse my temper, but you don't see the one that dwells in you; no, you must blame me.

OED. : And who would *not* lose his temper, if he heard you utter your scorn of the City?

TIR. : It will come. Silent though I be.

OED. : Since it will come, it is your duty to inform me.

TIR. : I shall say no more. Now, if you like, rage to your bitter heart's content.

OED. : Very well: in my "rage" I shall hold back nothing which I now begin to see. I think you planned that deed, even performed it, though not with your own hands. If

you could see, I should say that the work
was yours alone.

In the last speech quoted, Oedipus changes his tack,
specifying his purpose differently; he accuses Tiresias, and
that makes Tiresias attack. In the next part of the fight
the opponents trade blow for blow:

TIR.   : You would? I charge you, abide by the
           decree you uttered: from this day forth,
           speak neither to these present, nor to me,
           unclean as you are, polluter of the earth!
OED.   : You have the impudence to speak out
           words like these! And now how do you
           expect to escape?
TIR.   : I have escaped. The truth strengthens and
           sustains me.
OED.   : Who taught you the truth? Not your
           prophet's art.
TIR.   : You did: you force me against my will
           to speak.
OED.   : Speak what? Speak again, that I may un-
           derstand better.
TIR.   : *Didn't* you understand? Or are you goad-
           ing me?
OED.   : I can't say I really grasp it: speak again.
TIR.   : I say you are the murderer of the man
           whose murderer you seek.
OED.   : You won't be glad to have uttered that
           curse twice.
TIR.   : Must I say more, so you may rage the
           more?
OED.   : As much as you like—all is senseless.
TIR.   : I say you do not know your own
           wretchedness, nor see in what shame you
           live with those you love.
OED.   : Do you think you can say that forever
           with impunity?
TIR.   : If the truth has power.
OED.   : It has, with all but you: helpless is truth

with you: for you are blind, in eye, in
ear, in mind.

TIR. : You are the impotent one: you utter
slanders which every man here will apply
to you.

OED. : You have your being only in the night;
you couldn't hurt me or any man who
sees the sun.

TIR. : No. Your doom is not to fall by me.
Apollo suffices for that, he will bring it
about.

OED. : Are these inventions yours, or Creon's?

TIR. : Your wretchedness is not Creon's, it is
yours.

OED. : O wealth, and power, and skill—which
skill, in emulous life, brings low—what
envy eyes you! If for this kingly power
which the City gave into my hands, un-
sought—if for *this* the faithful Creon, my
friend from the first, has stalked me in
secret, yearning to supplant me! if he
has bribed this juggling wizard, this de-
ceitful beggar, who discerns his profit
only, blind in his own art!

Tell me now, tell me where you have
proved a true diviner? Why, when the
song-singing Sphinx was near, did you
not speak deliverance to the people? Her
riddles were not for any comer to solve,
but for the Mantic Art, and you were apparently instructed neither by birds nor
by any sign from the gods. Yet when I
came, I, Oedipus, all innocent, I stopped
her song. No birds taught me, by my
own wit I found the answer. And it is
I whom you wish to banish, thinking that
you will then stand close to Creon's
throne.

You and your ally will weep, I think,

> for this attempt; and in fact, if you didn't
> seem to be an old man, you would al-
> ready have learned, in pain, of your pre-
> sumption.

In this part the beliefs, the visions, and hence the purposes of the antagonists are directly contrasted. Because both identify themselves so completely with their visions and purposes, the fight descends from the level of dialectic to a level below the rational altogether: it becomes cruelly *ad hominem*. We are made to see the absurd incommensurability of the very *beings* of Oedipus and Tiresias; they shrink from one another as from the uncanny. At the end of the round, it is Oedipus who has received the deeper wound; and his great speech, "O wealth and power," is a far more lyric utterance than the ordered exposition with which he began.

The end of this part of the fight is marked by the intervention of the chorus, which endeavors to recall the antagonists to the most general version of purpose which they supposedly share: the discovery of the truth and the service of the gods:

> CHORUS: To us it appears that this man's words
> were uttered in anger, and yours too,
> Oedipus. No need for that: consider how
> best to discharge the mandate of the god.

The last part of the struggle shows Tiresias presenting his whole vision, and Oedipus, on the defensive, shaken to his depths:

> TIR.   : Although you rule, we have equally the
> right to reply; in that I too have power.
> Indeed, I live to serve, not you, but
> Apollo; and I shall not be enrolled under
> Creon, either. Therefore I say, since you
> have insulted even my blindness, that
> though you have eyesight, you do not see
> what misery you are in, nor where you
> are living, nor with whom. Do you know

whence you came? No, nor that you are
the enemy of your own family, the living
and the dead. The double prayer of
mother and father shall from this land
hound you in horror—who now see
clearly, but then in darkness.

Where then will your cry be bounded?
What part of Kitharon not echo it quickly
back, when you shall come to understand
that marriage, to which you sailed on so
fair a wind, homelessly home? And many
other evils which you do not see will
bring you to yourself at last, your children's equal.

Scorn Creon, therefore, and my words:
you will be struck down more terribly than
any mortal.

OED.   : Can I really hear such things from him?
Are you not gone? To death? To punishment? Not fled from this house?

TIR.   : I should never have come if you hadn't
called me.

OED.   : I didn't know how mad you would sound,
or it would have been a long time before
I asked you here to my house.

TIR.   : This is what I am: foolish, as it seems to
you; but wise, to the parents who gave
you birth.

OED.   : To whom? Wait: *who* gave me birth?

TIR.   : This day shall give you birth, and death.

OED.   : In what dark riddles you always speak.

TIR.   : Aren't you the best diviner of riddles?

OED.   : Very well: mock that gift, which you will
find is mine.

TIR.   : That very gift was your undoing.

OED.   : But if I saved the City, what does it matter?

TIR.   : So be it. I am going. Come, boy, lead
me.

OED.   : Take him away. Your presence impedes
           and trips me; once you are gone, you can
           do no harm.

TIR.   : I shall go when I have done my errand
           without fear of your frowns, for they
           can't hurt me. I tell you, then, that the
           man whom you have long been seeking
           with threats and proclamations, Laius'
           slayer, is here. He is thought to be an
           alien, but will appear a native Theban,
           and this circumstance will not please him.
           Blind, who once could see; destitute, who
           once was rich, leaning on a staff, he will
           make his way through a strange land. He
           will be revealed as brother and father of
           his own children; of the woman who
           bore him, both son and husband; sharer
           of his father's bed; his father's killer.

           Go in and ponder this. If you find me
           wrong, say then that I do not understand
           the prophetic vision.

Oedipus rushes offstage, his clear purpose gone, his
being shaken with fear and anger. Tiresias departs, led by
his boy. The chorus is left to move and chant, suffering
the mixed and ambivalent feelings, the suggestive but
mysterious images, which the Passion in which the agon
eventuated produces in them:

Strophe I : Who is it that the god's voice from the
                Rock of Delphi says
             Accomplished the unspeakable with mur-
                derous hands?
             Time now that windswift
             Stronger than horses
             His feet take flight.
             In panoply of fire and lightning
             Now springs upon him the son of Zeus
             Whom the dread follow,
             The Fates unappeasable.

Anti-
strophe I : New word, like light, from snowy Par-
nassus:
Over all the earth trail the unseen one.
For in rough wood,
In cave or rocks,
Like bull bereft—stampeded, futile
He goes, seeking with futile foot to
Flee the ultimate
Doom, which ever
Lives and flies over him.

Strophe II: In awe now, and soul's disorder, I neither
accept
The augur's wisdom, nor deny: I know
not what to say.
I hover in hope, see neither present nor
future.
Between the House of Laius
And Oedipus, I do not hear, have never
heard, of any feud:
I cannot confirm the public charge
against him, to help
Avenge the dark murder.

Anti-
strophe II: Zeus and Apollo are wise, and all that is
mortal
They know: but whether that human seer
knows more than I
There is no way of telling surely, though
in wisdom
A man may excel.
Ah, never could I, till I see that word
confirmed, consent to blame him!
Before all eyes the winged songstress,
once, assailed him;
Wise showed he in that test, and to the
City, tender: in my heart
I will call him evil never.

The chorus is considered in more detail below. At this point I merely wish to point out that Oedipus and Tiresias show, in their agon, the "Purpose" part of the Tragic Rhythm; that this turns to "passion," and that the chorus presents the Passion and also the new Perception which follows. This new perception is of Oedipus as the *possible* culprit. But his outlines are vague; perhaps the vision itself is illusory, a bad dream. The chorus has not yet reached the end of its quest; that will come only when Oedipus in the flesh before them is unmistakably seen as the guilty one. We have reached merely a provisional resting-place, the end of the first figure in which the Tragic Rhythm is presented. But this figure is a reduced version of the shape of the play as a whole, and the fleeting and unwelcome image of Oedipus as guilty corresponds to the final perception or epiphany, the full-stop, with which the play ends.

Oedipus: Ritual and Play

The Cambridge School of Classical Anthropologists has shown in great detail that the form of Greek Tragedy follows the form of a very ancient ritual, that of the *Enniautos-Daimon,* or seasonal god.[2] This is one of the most influential discoveries of the last few generations, and it gives us new insights into *Oedipus* which I think are not yet completely explored. The clue to Sophocles' dramatizing of the myth of Oedipus is to be found in this ancient ritual, which had a similar form and meaning—that is, it also moved in the "Tragic Rhythm."

Experts in classical anthropology, like experts in other fields, dispute innumerable questions of fact and of interpretation which the layman can only pass over in respectful silence. One of the thornier questions seems to be whether myth or ritual came first. Is the ancient ceremony merely an enactment of the Ur-Myth of the year-god— Attis, or Adonis, or Osiris, or the "Fisher-King"—in any

[2] See especially Jane Ellen Harrison's *Ancient Art and Ritual,* and her *Themis* which contains an "Excursus on the ritual forms preserved in Greek Tragedy" by Professor Gilbert Murray.

case that Hero-King-Father-High-Priest who fights with his
rival, is slain and dismembered, then rises anew with the
Spring season? Or did the innumerable myths of this kind
arise to "explain" a ritual which was perhaps mimed or
danced or sung to celebrate the annual change of season?

For the purpose of understanding the form and meaning of *Oedipus,* it is not necessary to worry about the
answer to this question of historic fact. The figure of
Oedipus himself fulfills all the requirements of the scapegoat, the dismembered king or god-figure. The situation in
which Thebes is presented at the beginning of the play—
in peril of its life; its crops, its herds, its women mysteriously infertile, signs of a mortal disease of the City, and
the disfavor of the gods—is like the withering which
winter brings, and calls in the same way for struggle, dis-
memberment, death and renewal. And this tragic sequence
is the substance of the play. It is enough to know that
myth and ritual are close together in their genesis, two
direct imitations of the perennial experience of the race.

But when one considers *Oedipus* as a ritual one understands it in ways which one cannot when one considers
it merely as a dramatization of a story—even that story.
Harrison has shown that the Festival of Dionysos, based
ultimately upon the yearly vegetation ceremonies, included
rites de passage like that celebrating the assumption of
adulthood—celebrations of the mystery of *individual*
growth and development. At the same time, it was a
prayer for the welfare of the whole City; and this welfare
was understood not only as material prosperity, but also
as the natural order of the family, the ancestors, the
present members, and the generations still to come, and,
by the same token, as obedience to the gods who were
jealous, each in his own province, of this natural and
divinely sanctioned order and proportion.

We must suppose that Sophocles' audience (the whole
population of the City) came early, prepared to spend the
day in the bleachers. At their feet was the semicircular
dancing-ground for the chorus, and the thrones for the
priests, and the altar. Behind that was the raised platform
for the principal actors, backed by the all-purpose, em-

blematic façade, which would presently be taken to represent Oedipus' Palace in Thebes. The actors were not professionals in our sense, but citizens selected for a religious office, and Sophocles himself had trained them and the chorus.

This crowd must have had as much appetite for thrills and diversion as the crowds who assemble in our day for football games and musical comedies, and Sophocles certainly holds the attention with an exciting show. At the same time his audience must have been alert for the fine points of poetry and dramaturgy, for *Oedipus* is being offered in competition with other plays on the same bill. But the element which distinguishes this theatre, giving it its unique directness and depth, is the *ritual expectancy* which Sophocles assumed in his audience. The nearest thing we have to this ritual sense of theatre is, I suppose, to be found at an Easter performance of the *Matthias Passion*. However that may be, Sophocles' audience must have been prepared to consider the playing, the make-believe it was about to see—the choral invocations, with dancing and chanting; the reasoned discourses and the terrible combats of the protagonists; the mourning, the rejoicing, and the contemplation of the final stage-picture or epiphany,—as imitating and celebrating the *mystery* of human nature and destiny. And this mystery was at once that of individual growth and development, and that of the precarious life of the human City.

I have indicated how Sophocles presents the life of the mythic Oedipus in the Tragic Rhythm, the mysterious quest of life. Oedipus is shown seeking his own true being; but at the same time and by the same token, the welfare of the City. When one considers the ritual form of the whole play, it becomes evident that it presents the tragic quest of the whole City for *its* well-being; and that, in this larger action, Oedipus is only the Protagonist, the first and most important champion. This tragic quest is realized by all the characters in their various ways; but in the development of the action as a whole it is the chorus alone that plays a part as important as that of Oedipus—its counterpart, in fact. The chorus holds the balance between Oedipus and his antagonists; marks the progress of their struggles, and restates the main theme, and its new variation, after each agon. The ancient ritual was probably performed by a chorus alone without individual developments and variations, and the chorus in *Oedipus* is still the element that throws most light on the ritual form of the play as a whole.

The chorus consists of twelve or fifteen "Elders of Thebes." This group is not intended to be all of the citizens either of Thebes or of Athens. The play opens with a large delegation of Theban citizens before Oedipus' palace, and the chorus proper does not enter until after the prologue. Nor does the chorus speak directly for the Athenian audience; we are asked throughout to make-believe that the Theatre is the agora of Thebes. It would, I think, be more accurate to say that the chorus *represents* the point of view and the interests of Thebes as a whole, and, by analogy, of the Athenian audience. Their errand before Oedipus' palace is like that of Sophocles' audience in the theatre: they are watching a sacred combat, in the issue of which they have an all-important stake. Thus they represent the audience and the citizens in a particular way —not as a mob formed in response to some momentary feeling, but rather as a highly self-conscious community: something closer to the "conscience of the race" than to the over-heated affectivity of a mob.

According to Aristotle, a Sophoclean chorus is a character that takes an important role in the action of the play, instead of merely making incidental music between the scenes, as in the plays of Euripides. The chorus may be described as a group personality, like an old Parliament. It has its own traditions, habits of thought and feeling, and mode of being. It exists, in a sense, as a living entity; but not with the sharp actuality of an individual. It perceives; but its perception is at once wider and vaguer than that of a single man. It shares, in its way, the seeking action of the play as a whole; but it cannot act in all the modes: it depends upon the chief agonists to invent and try out the detail of policy, just as a rather helpless but critical Parliament depends upon the Prime Minister to act, but in its less specific form of life survives his destruction.

When the chorus enters after the prologue, with its questions, its invocation of the various gods, and its focus upon the hidden and jeopardized welfare of the City—Athens or Thebes—the list of essential *dramatis personae*, as well as the elements needed to celebrate the ritual, are complete, and the main action can begin. It is the function of the chorus to mark the stages of this action, and to perform the *suffering* and *perceiving* part of the Tragic Rhythm. The protagonist and his antagonists develop the "Purpose" with which the tragic sequence begins; the chorus, with its less than individual being, broods over the agons, marks their stages with a word (like that of the chorus leader in the middle of the Tiresias scene), and, with its odes, suffers the results, and the new perception at the end of the fight.

The choral odes are lyrics, but they are not to be understood as the art of words only, for they are intended also to be danced and sung. Though each chorus has its own shape, its beginning, middle and end, it represents also one Passion or Pathos in the changing action of the whole. This Passion, like the other moments in the Tragic Rhythm, is felt at so general, or, rather, so *deep* a level, that it seems to contain both the mob ferocity that Nietzsche felt in it, and, at the other extreme, the patience of prayer. This may be illustrated from the chorus I have quoted at the end of the Tiresias scene.

It begins (close to the savage emotion of the end of the fight) with images suggesting that cruel "Bacchic frenzy" which is supposed to be the common root of Tragedy and of the Old Comedy: "In panoply of fire and lightning/The son of Zeus now springs upon him." In the first antistrophe these images come together more clearly as we relish the chase; and the fleeing culprit, as we imagine him, begins to resemble Oedipus, who is lame, and always associated with the rough wilderness of Kitharon. But in the second strophe, as though appalled by its ambivalent feelings and the imagined possibilities, the chorus sinks back into a more dark and patient posture of suffering, "in awe," "hovering in hope." In the second antistrophe this is developed into something like the orthodox Christian attitude of prayer, based on faith, and assuming the possibility of a hitherto unimaginable truth and answer: "Zeus and Apollo are wise," etc. The whole chorus then ends with a new vision of Oedipus, of the culprit, and of the direction in which the welfare of the City is to be sought. This vision is still colored by the chorus's human love of Oedipus as Hero, for the chorus has still its own purgation to complete, cannot as yet accept completely either the suffering in store for it, nor Oedipus as Scapegoat. But it marks the end of the first complete "Purpose-Passion-Perception" unit, and lays the basis for the new Purpose which will begin the next unit.

The chorus represents an element which is always present in the action of the play, the element of Passion in the deepest, but not, as Nietzsche would have it, in the rawest sense. This "Passion" is felt in the agons as the helpless concern for the common good with which the chorus follows the struggle. When the fighters depart, in fear and anger, and the chorus is left to move and chant, to mull over its sensuous and suggestive images, dreams or mantic inspirations—then "Passion" itself takes the stage, and carries the main action. If one endeavors to think of the play as a whole as the "imitation of an action," then the Tragic Rhythm analyzes human action temporarily, into successive moments or modes, as a crystal analyzes a beam of white light spatially into the colored bands of the spectrum. And the various elements in the play, the parts of the plot, the characters, the forms of discourse from ratiocination to the lyric; the dancing and the singing—all actualize more concretely the appropriate moments in the Tragic Rhythm, the temporal "spectrum of action."

STANLEY EDGAR HYMAN was born in 1919 in Brooklyn, New York. In 1940 he was graduated from Syracuse University. Since that time he has been a staff writer for *The New Yorker* and has contributed articles and reviews to other periodicals. He is the author of *The Armed Vision: A Study in the Methods of Modern Literary Criticism* (1948). He teaches literature and folk literature at Bennington College.

THE TEXT of this book is set on the Linotype in a face called TIMES ROMAN, designed by Stanley Morison for *The Times* (London), and first introduced by that newspaper in 1932. The book was composed, printed, and bound by THE COLONIAL PRESS INC., Clinton, Massachusetts. Paper manufactured by S. D. WARREN COMPANY, Boston, Massachusetts. Cover design by ROBERT FLYNN.

Vintage Books